STUDY GUIDE

Donald R. Babbitt
Lindenwood College

A. Jane Craighead
Concordia University

WITH LOTUS TEMPLATES

Melanie E. Russell
Price Waterhouse

INTRODUCTION TO FINANCIAL ACCOUNTING

First Canadian Edition

Charles T. Horngren
Stanford University

Gary L. Sundem
University of Washington—Seattle

John A. Elliott
Cornell University

Daniel B. Thornton, F.C.A.
Queen's University

Prentice Hall Canada Inc.
Scarborough, Ontario

Canadian Cataloguing in Publication Data

Babbitt, Donald R.
        Study guide with Lotus templates for Introduction
to financial accounting, first Canadian edition

Supplement to: Introduction to financial accounting.
1st Canadian edition.
ISBN 0-13-191776-5

1. Accounting - Problems, exercises, etc.
2. Accounting - Data processing. 3. Lotus 1-2-3
(Computer file). I. Craighead, A. Jane (Audrey, Jane),
1959-   . II. Russell, Melanie E. (Melanie Elizabeth),
1963-   . III. Title. IV. Title: Introduction to financial
accounting. 1st Canadian ed.

HF5635.I772 1995 657 C95-930693-5

Prentice-Hall, Inc., Englewood Cliffs, New Jersey
Prentice-Hall International (UK) Limited, London
Prentice-Hall of Australia, Pty. Limited, Sydney
Prentice-Hall Hispanoamericana, S.A., Mexico City
Prentice-Hall of India Private Limited, New Delhi
Prentice-Hall of Japan, Inc., Tokyo
Simon & Schuster Asia Private Limited, Singapore
Editora Prentice-Hall do Brasil, Ltda., Rio de Janeiro

ISBN 0-13-191776-5

Acquisitions Editor: Patrick Ferrier
Developmental Editor: Dawn du Quesnay
Production Editor: Kelly Dickson
Production Coordinator: Deborah Starks

Original U.S. edition published by Prentice-Hall Inc.
Englewood Cliffs, New Jersey, © 1993

1 2 3 4 5   99 98 97 96 95

Printed and bound in Canada.

Table of Contents

Preface

Welcome to the Study Guide to accompany **Introduction to Financial Accounting, First Canadian Edition by Horngren, Sundem, Elliot and Thornton**. In order for you to realize the maximum benefit from this supplement, it is helpful to have an overview of its features, and the general philosophy underlying its creation.

You will be covering a great deal of material in this course. It is important to understand, however, that most of the chapters can be organized into a few major topics or concepts. This may seem to be an obvious point, but you may have to remind yourself of this as you work through the details. The best strategy for mastering this material is to train yourself to think in terms of the "big picture", and to fill in the details within each topic. Your ability to synthesize the material, and to develop your own framework for it, will depend on how well you are able to prioritize the information that is presented in the text. Very little of the material is difficult in nature, but there is a lot of it, and information overload can cloud the major issues or concepts at hand.

It will be easier to see the "big picture" if you work on developing your understanding of the theoretical side of accounting as you progress through the text. You may be attracted to the quantitative side of accounting because it is easier to practice this aspect of the discipline. But you will find that much of what you do on the quantitative side flows from a few basic theoretical concepts, like the matching principle. As you encounter these concepts, and the conceptual framework, think about them carefully, and why they are important. If you do, you will likely see patterns emerge between chapters, and this will help you organize and integrate the material.

With the explicit objective of helping you prioritize the information in the text, each chapter in the guide begins with a set of notes. Each of the major points or concepts in the chapter appears with the details set out below it. Try to think about the chapter in terms of these major points, and why they are important. Then, once you are comfortable with this, start considering the detail within each topic. This approach helps you see how all the information fits together.

Immediately after the chapter notes, there is a set of practice questions with solutions. The true or false questions test key assumptions or relationships discussed in the chapter. The multiple choice questions give you the opportunity to test your quantitative skills in a single calculation context. Finally, the problems are designed to give you practice in analyzing a situation and selecting the relevant information from a larger data set. In most cases, the problems are indicative of the type of material you could expect to see in an examination. Some of the problem material is advanced in order to prepare you for an examination setting. The problems in chapter five, for example, are comprehensive in nature and test your understanding of the major concepts in the first part of the course. These problems should prove helpful in studying for a mid-term exam.

Finally, at the end of the problems (immediately before the answers and solutions) a reference appears to additional problems that can be found in the LOTUS Templates that accompany this study guide. Many accounting problems can be handled in a spread-sheet format, and these Templates give you an opportunity to practice these skills. The Template problems are problems from the textbook that have been set-up for you to do on a spread-sheet. For more information on using the Templates see the separate instructions immediately following the Preface.

There has been an evolution both in the practice of accounting and in how it is taught during the last ten years. There is an increased emphasis on developing analytical and judgment skills because these are what is required for you to deal with a dynamic business environment. This study guide has been designed to help you achieve a good conceptual perspective, as well as strong technical skills. However, as is always the case, learning is an active process which requires you to work with the concepts and develop you own understanding of them. Good Luck.

A. Jane Craighead
Concordia University

LOTUS Template Instructions

As noted in the Preface, there is a set of LOTUS Templates included with this study guide. The Template problems are problems from the textbook that have been set up in a spread-sheet format for you to practice your accounting and computer skills. The references in each chapter of the study guide give you the specific file name for each problem, so that it will be easy for you to use the Templates. The numbers in the file name usually refer to the textbook problem. For example, file P10-29.wk1 refers to problem 10-29 (i.e. problem 29 in chapter 10 of the text). The other files refer to summary problems, exhibits and examples from select chapters.

The accompanying templates were written with the novice in mind, so don't be afraid to give them a try if you're not a computer expert. The first thing you have to do is access the Lotus program on the computer. Turn on the computer and then select LOTUS from the menu. When you are in LOTUS, you need to tell the computer to read the LOTUS Template disk you received with this book. Let's assume that your hard drive is drive C and your external drive (the one you will put the Template disk in) is drive A. Insert the Template disk in drive A, and type the following:

/	(Slash Key)
F	(for File)
D	(for Directory)

At this time, the current directory will appear as follows:

Enter current directory: C:

The computer is currently reading from drive C. You must switch the directory to A so that you can read a file. To switch the directory, type:

A:

and hit the Enter key. The A drive is now current and the display should read:

Enter current directory: A:

To retrieve a file, hit the following keys:

/	(Slash Key)
F	(File)
R	(Retrieve)
F3	(Function key F3, not the letter F, and number 3)

The list of files will then appear on the screen. These are the same file names that you see referenced in each chapter of the study guide. Move the cursor to the file you want to retrieve (so that it is highlighted) and hit the Enter key. The Template now appears on the screen, and you are ready to begin work.

All of the partially completed Templates are menu driven. To invoke the menu, press the **ALT** key (**CTRL** if you are working in a Windows environment) and **M** simultaneously. At this time, you will see the following choices:

SAVE PRINT EXIT QUIT

SAVE: This option allows you to save your work.

PRINT: This option will print the entire worksheet.

EXIT: This option exits the menu and allows the student to work on the template. Hitting the **ESC** key will achieve the same result.

QUIT: This option clears the screen. If you want to retain your work, be sure to use the SAVE option first, before selecting QUIT.

In order to check your solution, go to the Solutions disk and open up the file that corresponds to your problem.

The following problems are included on the Lotus Templates:

Ch 1
1-26
1-27

Ch 2
Appendix 2 (p. 75)
2-27
2-43
2-44

Ch 4
4-26
4-28
4-29
4-37
4-38

Ch 5
5-37

Ch 6
6-43
6-47

Ch 7
Sum. Prob. 3 (p. 303)
7-23
7-43
7-49

Ch 8
8-25
8-28
8-43
8-44
8-45
8-46

Ch 9
Sum. Prob. 3 (p.407)
9-20
9-26
9-27
9-30

Ch 10
Exh.10-2 (p.439)
10-29
10-30
10-54
10-56
10-58
10-59
10-69

Ch 11
11-42
11-43
11-47
11-48
11-49
11-50
11-61

Ch 12
12-34
12-36

Ch 13
13-25
13-26
13-27
13-28
13-44

Ch 14
14-41

Ch 15
15-28

15-33
15-38
15-39
15-41

Ch 16
16-39

Chapter 1

**Entities and
Balance Sheets**

The purpose of accounting is to provide information in a cost effective, relevant, and reliable manner for decision making purposes. Anyone functioning in a financial decision making role must possess a good understanding of the theories and practices associated with the accounting function. Use the following objectives as an outline for your study of the balance sheet and other topics designed to introduce you to the language of business - accounting.

1. Explain the nature of accounting and its role in decision making.
2. Define and describe a balance sheet and its major elements.
3. Explain the need for generally accepted accounting principles and the basic concepts of entity and reliability.
4. Record transactions on the balance sheet, and analyze their effect on the balance sheet equation.
5. Understand the advantages and disadvantages of the three types of business organizations and how to account for each.
6. Explain the notion of credibility and the function of auditing.
7. Describe public and private accounting and the role of ethics in the accounting profession.

1

Chapter 1

REVIEW OF KEY CONCEPTS

A.   Accounting provides information related to financial activities that may prove useful in a decision making process. Information, such as the financial position of an economic entity and the results of operations, are important measures used in judging the financial success of an organization.

    1.   Financial statements, the outputs of the accounting process, are the result of the accountant's ability to analyze, record, quantify, accumulate, summarize, classify, report, and interpret financial information that impacts an organization.

    2.   Accounting information, by its nature, aids in financial decision making. It may be used to predict future events, confirm or reject past predictions, provide an indication of financial position at any one point in time, or help determine the results of operations for a specific period.

    3.   Accounting, through the financial statements, performs a score keeping function. This is accomplished through the four major statements: the balance sheet, the income statement, the statement of retained earnings, and the statement of cash flows.

        a.   The **balance sheet** provides an indication of a company's financial position at a particular point in time (like a photograph).

        b.   The **income statement** presents the results of operations for a period of time (like a movie).

        c.   The **statement of retained earnings** indicates the amount of previous earnings retained in the business for reinvestment, the profits/losses for the current period (net income), and the distributions of earnings made to the owners during the period (dividends).

        d.   The **statement of cash flows** reports the cash receipts and cash payments of an entity and explains the change in cash during the period.

4. Financial accounting and managerial accounting both use financial data related to a particular entity but their user focus is different. **Financial accounting** reports primarily to *outside* users such as shareholders, the government, and creditors. **Managerial accounting** is concerned primarily with providing information to *inside* users, such as management, for decision making, planning, and control purposes.

In the case of **financial accounting**, because the information is prepared mainly for use by people outside the firm, the nature of the measurement and recording process is very important. Most people who will make use of the information will not have direct access to the preparer for clarification and explanation purposes. Because of this, it is very important that financial statement users understand how events are recorded and summarized, and the nature of the choices made by management in accounting for these events. This is important in much the same way as knowing whether a temperature reading is being measured in fahrenheit or celsius. Our decisions based on this information are very different depending on whether it is 25 degrees fahrenheit or 25 degrees celsius. One of the fundamental objectives of this course is to develop your understanding of *how* information is measured and *why* it is measured in certain ways.

B. The purpose for the balance sheet is to show the financial position of a business at a *particular point in time*. It is designed to show the resources of the firm, classified as assets, and the counterbalancing claims against those assets, in the form of liabilities and owners' equity. The balance sheet answers two basic questions about the organization:

1. What are the organization's assets?

2. How are these assets financed (i.e. through debt or ownership)?

The answers to these questions are found in the balance sheet equation:

Assets = Liabilities + Owners' Equity

1. **Assets** are resources that will provide the organization with *future benefits*. Assets include, but are not limited to, cash, accounts receivable, inventory and capital assets, such as plant and equipment.

2.   **Liabilities** refer to the organization's *obligations*. They may include amounts owed to trade creditors (accounts payable) or bank indebtedness, such as a bank loan or a mortgage.

3.   **Owners' Equity** is the owners' *residual claim* on the assets of the organization after all liabilities have been paid. At the start of a business, owners' equity is measured as the total of the amounts invested by the owners. The balance sheet equation can be rearranged to represent the owners' residual claim as follows:

$$\text{Assets - Liabilities} = \text{Owners' Equity}$$

C.   In order for accounting information to be useable on a wide scale the information presented must be, among other things, **consistent** and **comparable**. Generally Accepted Accounting Principles (GAAP) is the term used to refer to the broad body of concepts and accounting principles applied in Canada.

In addition to encouraging the preparation of consistent and comparable information, GAAP has another related role based on the reporting environment. Managers of an organization have incentives to make the organization's financial picture appear as rosy as possible. This is because there are often contracts and/or informal agreements that depend on firm performance, such as management compensation packages, bank lending agreements, etc.. An efficient way to limit this bias is to set out only certain possibilities that are available to the manager in accounting for transactions. This is one of the main functions of GAAP. We will see as we progress through the text that it is not possible, nor desirable, to eliminate all measurement choices, but GAAP serves to narrow the range of alternatives based on certain measurement criteria, such as objectivity and reliability. Once a defined set of alternatives has been established, the audit function can then be used to verify that management has measured events or transactions within these guidelines and on a consistent basis.

GAAP is built on a few basic concepts; two of these are the **Entity Concept** and the **Reliability Concept**.

1. The distinguishing feature of the **entity concept** is that the affairs of the entity are separate from those of other entities and from the individuals who may manage and/or own the entity. This is necessary so that we can measure and report on the performance and status of the entity. An accounting entity is a **separate unit of accountability**. It may be a company, a division of a company, or even a project, such as a class fundraiser. The balance sheet equation represents a bounded system which is the accounting entity.

2. The **Reliability Concept** is another cornerstone of GAAP. If information is to be useful, it must first be reliable. Reliable information measures the **true economic substance** of a transaction or event. Reliable information must also be **objective or verifiable** so that management is limited in its ability to bias the information. The objectivity/verifiability criteria constrain or limit accounting so that it can only measure events where a monetary value can be clearly established. This suggests that many events which affect the firm, such as the sudden death of its CEO, are not recorded because they can not be measured in an objective manner. (Objectivity can be thought of in terms of the ability of any two people to come to the same decision regarding the value of a transaction given the same information.)

D. **Transactions** are events expressed in monetary terms that affect the financial position of an entity. Transactions are summarized in accounts. **Accounts** are summary records of changes in asset, liability, and owners' equity accounts.

Stop! Before continuing, carefully review each of the individual transactions and the subsequent preparation of the balance sheet presented in the text under the heading, **Balance Sheet Transactions.**

E. When organizing a business there are basically three forms of organization available: a sole proprietorship, a partnership, and a corporation. The choice of form is dependent on variables as diverse as the tax consequences of a particular form of organization, to the desire for continuity of existence of the entity after the death of the founder.

Chapter 1

1. **Sole Proprietorships** are the easiest, and consequently, the cheapest to organize. Business income is taxed at the individual level (i.e. the proprietor). There is no continuity of ownership and a sole proprietor does *not* enjoy limited liability.

2. A **Partnership** is a relationship between two or more persons, or entities, generally structured through a partnership agreement. The agreement defines contributions to, and distribution of, profits and losses, as well as other items of importance to the partnership relationship. Like a sole proprietorship, the partnership does *not* enjoy limited liability, and partnership income is distributed to the individual partners and taxed in their hands.

3. The **Corporation** is a separate *legal* entity and is taxed as such. The owners of a corporation are referred to as shareholders and they enjoy *limited liability*. Some of the other characteristics of a corporation are:

    a. **Continuity of existence** implies that since the corporation is a separate legal entity, it will continue to exist even if ownership changes.

    b. **Transferability** of ownership is a characteristic of corporations, most notably **public corporations**, and is facilitated by the exchange of shares on organized exchanges, such as the Toronto or Montreal Stock Exchange.

4. The owners' equity on the balance sheet of a corporation is generally referred to as **shareholders' equity**, whereas sole proprietorships and partnerships generally refer to owners' equity as **capital.**

> See pages 21-22 of the text for an example of equity presentation under each of the three legal forms of organization.

5. If a corporation has shares without a par value, the entire proceeds of the issue are put into a share capital account. If the firm has par value shares (which still exist in some Canadian companies), **Paid-in capital** is composed of two elements: proceeds at issuance equal to the par value (also known as stated value) of the stock are put into a share

capital account; and paid-in capital in excess of par value is put into a separate account known as **Contributed Surplus**.

F.   Voting shareholders of a corporation elect the board of directors to represent their interests. The board in turn appoints management to carry out the policies established by the board of directors. Two of the most important duties and responsibilities of management include custody of assets and issuance of the financial statements.

G.   Integral to the published financial statements of a publicly held corporation is the **independent auditors report.** This report is prepared by chartered accountants (CA's) (or by certified general accountants in certain provinces) who audit (verify) the accounts of the company to ensure that the company has prepared its financial statements in accordance with GAAP.

H.   Members of the Canadian Institute of Chartered Accountants are bound by a *code of professional conduct*. The presence and importance of the code to the profession helps to build its credibility with the general public and adds to the value of independently audited financial statements.

PRACTICE TEST QUESTIONS AND SOLUTIONS

I   **True or false -** For each of the following statements, enter T or an F in the space provided to indicate whether the statement is true or false.

_____   1.   An accounting entity is always a separate legal entity as well.

_____   2.   Generally accepted accounting principles are all contained in one document known as the Handbook.

_____   3.   A bank loan to the business would increase Owner's Equity on the balance sheet.

Chapter 1

_____ 4. From an accounting point of view a sole proprietorship is a separate entity from the personal activities of the sole proprietor.

_____ 5. One of the advantages a partnership has over a sole proprietorship is the limited liability of the partners.

_____ 6. Paid-in capital in excess of par, the difference between the market price of the outstanding stock when sold and the stated value, is put into the Contributed Surplus account.

_____ 7. Transferring ownership is usually easier for the owners of shares in a corporation than for partners in a partnership.

_____ 8. The major difference between financial and managerial accounting is the ultimate user of the information.

_____ 9. Owners' equity represents a residual interest in the assets of the corporation after all the liabilities have been fulfilled.

_____ 10. When thinking of the balance sheet equation, the assets on the left-side represent the resources of the business, and the liabilities on the right-side represent the manner in which the resources are financed.

_____ 11. Accounting principles become "generally accepted" by regulatory adoption.

_____ 12. Owners' equity on the balance sheet of a partnership can also be called shareholders' equity.

_____ 13. The balance sheet shows all the assets of the business.

_____ 14. GAAP requires all firms to record transactions in exactly the same way.

_____ 15. The purpose of the balance sheet is to show the financial position of a particular company for a specific period of time.

II   **Multiple choice** - For the following multiple choice questions, select the best answer and enter the identifying letter in the space provided.

_____   1.   The balance sheet equation is best expressed as:

    a.   Owners' Equity = Assets - Liabilities
    b.   Assets + Liabilities = Owners' Equity
    c.   Assets = Liabilities - Owners' Equity
    d.   Owners' Equity + Assets = Liabilities

Table 1
Brown Supply Co.
List of Balance Sheet Accounts
12/31/X4

Cash	10	Accounts receivable	60
Accounts payable	30	Plant & Equipment	1,500
Inventory	110	Other liabilities	672
Wages payable	5	Capital stock ($1 par)	500
Notes payable	25	Contributed surplus*	500
Other assets	150	Retained earnings	98

* contains share proceeds in excess of par value only

_____   2.   Using Table 1, what are the total assets for Brown Supply on Dec. 31, 19X4?

    a. $1,098
    b. $1,795
    c. $1,800
    d. $1,830

_____   3.   If during 19X5, 100 new shares of common stock are sold at a market price of $4, what would be the balance in the contributed surplus account in Table 1?

    a. $400
    b. $800
    c. $900
    d. $300

_____ 4. Brown purchased inventory for $50, paying $10 in cash and the balance on account. The effect on the balance sheet accounts in Table 1 would be to:

    a.   Increase total assets $50, increase total liabilities $50.
    b.   Increase accounts receivable $40, increase inventory $50, and decrease cash $10.
    c.   Increase total assets $40, increase accounts payable $40.
    d.   Increase total assets $40, decrease accounts payable $40.

_____ 5. A summary record of changes in an asset, liability, or component of owners' equity is referred to as:

    a.   An entity
    b.   A transaction
    c.   An account
    d.   Paid-in capital

_____ 6. Deedra is trying to decide which form of organization she should adopt for her new business. She is worried about the effects on her children if a customer should be injured in her store and bring suit. Which form of organization should she adopt?

    a.   Corporation
    b.   Partnership
    c.   Sole proprietorship
    d.   Limited partnership

_____ 7. If during 19X2 assets increased $720,000, accounts payable rose 15% to $115,000, and shareholders' equity rose $320,000, what was the change in long-term liabilities?

    a.   Increased $285,000
    b.   Decreased $285,000
    c.   Increased $385,000
    d.   Decreased $385,000

8.   Generally accepted accounting principles (GAAP):

    a.   can be used, or not, by a corporation in the preparation of audited financial statements.

    b.   are the same in Canada and the United States.

    c.   are used to control management bias in the preparation of audited financial statements.

    d.   are very specific and address all known business transactions.

9.   Services provided by a public accounting firm would **not** normally include:

    a.   Managerial accounting

    b.   Auditing

    c.   Management consulting

    d.   Statement compilation

10.   Which of the following would be considered a managerial accounting function?

    a.   Preparation of financial statements to secure a bank loan

    b.   Preparation of quarterly reports for the Ontario Securities Commission

    c.   Preparation of a departmental statement for performance evaluation purposes

    d.   Preparation of corporate income tax returns

Chapter 1

III   Problems

Problem 1:

Based on the following changes in account balances, summarize the underlying transactions. Assume only one transaction per day.

Date	Cash	A/R	Invent	Equip	A/P	LDebt	Equity
9/1	2,000	8,000	10,000	10,000	5,000	10,000	15,000
9/2	12,000	8,000	10,000	10,000	5,000	20,000	15,000
9/3	12,000	8,000	9,000	10,000	4,000	20,000	15,000
0/4	2,000	8,000	13,000	16,000	4,000	20,000	15,000
9/5	8,000	2,000	13,000	16,000	4,000	20,000	15,000
9/6	13,000	2,000	13,000	16,000	4,000	20,000	20,000
9/7	7,000	2,000	13,000	16,000	4,000	14,000	20,000
9/8	4,000	2,000	13,000	16,000	1,000	14,000	20,000

Problem 2:

Alpha Corporation's balance sheet accounts for December 31, 19X7, appear below in random order.

Accounts receivable	$ 60,000	Accounts payable	$ 37,000
Notes payable	130,000	Plant & Equipment	500,000
Inventory	165,000	Land	194,000
Long-term debt	400,000	Capital stock ($10 par)	200,000
Contributed surplus*	177,000	Cash	25,000

* contains share proceeds in excess of par value only

Required:

a.   Prepare the balance sheet in good form as at December 31, 19X7.

b.   Based on the following transactions for 19X8, prepare a balance sheet as at December 31, 19X8:

1. Sold 1,500 additional shares of common stock at a market price of $17.
2. Purchased merchandise inventory for $40,000. Sixty percent of the inventory was purchased on account and the balance for cash.
3. Paid accounts payable totalling $37,000.
4. Purchased new equipment for $50,000 cash.
5. Received payments on account from customers of $55,000.
6. Sold land carried on the books at $110,000 for $110,000.
7. Repaid $45,000 of the notes payable.

Problem 3:

For each of the following scenarios prepare the appropriate owners' equity section of the balance sheet.

a. Ms. Brown, Ms. Moore and Ms. Qualbani formed a partnership to open an accounting practice. Total contributed capital was $650,000 with Brown contributing 50%, Qualbani 30%, and Moore 20%.

b. "Jimbo" Eggert decided to open his own tax preparation service as a sole proprietor. Jimbo contributed his life savings of $125,000 to fund the enterprise.

c. On January 1, 19X1, Jim Blossom incorporated his new business. The board of directors authorized and issued 15,000 shares with a par value of $5. The original issue was purchased for a market price of $23 per share.

For more practice preparing balance sheets, see Lotus Template files P1-26.wk1 and P1-27.wk1.

CHAPTER 1 ANSWERS AND SOLUTIONS

I   True and False

1. False   An accounting entity need *not* be a legal entity (e.g., a class project)
2. False   Part of GAAP is found in the CICA Handbook but it also includes current practices which have not yet been codified.

Chapter 1

3.	False	A bank loan would increase the cash account and increase bank loan or notes payable, a liability.
4.	True	
5.	False	Partnerships and sole proprietorships *do not* enjoy limited liability. In this context only the corporation, as a separate legal entity, enjoys limited liability.
6.	True	
7.	True	
8.	True	
9.	True	
10.	True	
11.	False	Accounting principles become "generally accepted" by agreement. Experience, custom, usage, and practical necessity contribute to the development of a set of principles.
12.	False	Shareholders' equity refers to the equity section of a corporation only.
13.	False	GAAP only recognizes assets which have been acquired through a transaction or exchange where an objective monetary amount can be identified. A firm has many off balance sheet assets, such as well trained employees.
14.	False	GAAP narrows the range of available accounting alternatives for different transactions but it does not eliminate all available choices.
15.	False	The balance sheet represents the financial position of an entity at *a particular point in time*.

II   Multiple choice

1.	A	Assets = Liabilities + Owners' Equity
2.	D	Total assets = cash $10 + inventory $110 + other assets $150 + accounts receivable $60 + plant & equipment $1,500 = $ 1,830
3.	B	Paid-in capital in excess of par is $3/share X 100 shares issued = $ 300. The account has an opening balance of $ 500. When the new issue is included the balance is $ 800.
4.	C	An asset, inventory, is increased by $50 but a corresponding asset, cash, is decreased by $10. The balancing amount is the $40 increase in accounts payable.
5.	C	The question is basically stating the definition of an account.
6.	A	In Deedra's case a corporation would probably be the best choice because of the limited liability nature of the corporate form.

7.   C   Assets = Liabilities + Owners' Equity, therefore,
                720,000 = 15,000 + ? + 320,000.
                (Note: accounts payable only increased $ 15,000 to $ 115,000.)

8.   C   GAAP narrows the range of choice of accounting alternatives available to managers and helps to limit managerial discretion in financial statement preparation.

9.   A   While both financial and managerial accounting draw from the common base of financial data associated with an entity, managerial accounting serves internal decision makers. Financial accounting serves external decision makers.

10.   C   Departmental statements for performance evaluation purposes are typical of the managerial reporting function. Managerial accounting is normally used by internal decision makers for planning, evaluation, and control purposes.

III   Problems

Problem 1:

Sept. 1	Beginning balance for the period.
Sept. 2	Secured a long-term loan for $10,000 in cash.
Sept. 3	Returned $1,000 in inventory to a supplier for credit against my account.
Sept. 4	Used $10,000 in cash to purchase additional inventory of $4,000 and equipment worth $6,000.
Sept. 5	Collected $6,000 from customers that was owed on account.
Sept. 6	Sold additional stock for $5,000.
Sept. 7	Repaid $6,000 of long-term debt.
Sept. 8	Made payments to suppliers (accounts payable) for $ 3,000.

Chapter 1

Problem 2:

a.

Alpha Corporation
Balance Sheet
Dec. 31, 19X7

Assets		Liabilities	
Cash	$ 25,000	Accounts payable	$37,000
Accounts receivable	60,000	Notes payable	130,000
Inventory	165,000	Long-term debt	400,000
Plant & equipment	500,000	Total liabilities	$567,000
Land	194,000		
Total assets	$944,000	Shareholders' equity	
		Capital stock ($10 par)	$200,000
		Cont. Surplus	177,000
		Total equity	$377,000
		Total Liab. & Equity	$944,000

b.

	Cash	A/R	Inventory	Plant & Eq.	Land
Open. bal.	25,000	60,000	165,000	500,000	194,000
1.	25,500				
2.	(16,000)		40,000		
3.	(37,000)				
4.	(50,000)			50,000	
5.	55,000	(55,000)			
6.	110,000				(110,000)
7.	(45,000)				
End. bal.	67,500	5,000	205,000	550,000	84,000

	A/P	Note Pay	LT. Debt	Cap. Stock	Cont.Surp.
Open. bal.	37,000	130,000	400,000	200,000	177,000
1.				15,000	10,500
2.	24,000				
3.	(37,000)				
4.					
5.					
6.					
7.		(45,000)			
End. bal.	24,000	85,000	400,000	215,000	187,500

Alpha Corporation
Balance Sheet
Dec. 31, 19X7

Assets		Liabilities	
Cash	$ 67,500	Accounts payable	$ 24,000
Accounts receivable	5,000	Notes payable	85,000
Inventory	205,000	Long-term debt	400,000
Plant & equipment	550,000	Total liabilities	$509,000
Land	84,000		
Total assets	$911,500	Shareholders' equity	
		Capital Stock ($10 par)	$215,000
		Cont. Surplus	187,500
		Total liabilities and Shareholders' equity	$911,500

17

Chapter 1

Problem 3:

a.   <u>**Owners' equity**</u> - Partnership

Ms. Brown, capital	$325,000
Ms. Qualbani, capital	195,000
Ms. Moore, capital	<u>130,000</u>
Total Partners' Capital	<u>$650,000</u>

b.   <u>**Owner's equity**</u> - Sole proprietor

J. Eggert, capital	<u>$125,000</u>

c.   <u>**Shareholders' equity**</u> - Corporation

Common stock, $5 par value, 15,000 shares authorized and outstanding	$ 75,000
Contributed surplus	<u>270,000</u>
Total paid-in capital	<u>$345,000</u>

Chapter 2

> **Income
> Measurement:
> The Accrual
> Basis**

In the first chapter we discussed the difference between the income statement and the balance sheet. Basically, the income statement measures an organization's performance for a *period of time* and the balance sheet measures the organization's net asset position at a *point in time*. This chapter addresses the fundamental concepts and practices associated with the income statement, as well as introducing the statement of cash flows. Users of financial statement information must understand the concepts associated with performance measurement and the subsequent need for a separate statement to address cash flows. Keep the following objectives in mind and use them as stepping stones to completing your study of this chapter.

1. Explain how revenues and expenses combine to form income for the accounting time period.
2. Compare the accrual basis and cash basis accounting methods and use the ideas of recognition, matching, and cost recovery to record revenues and expenses.
3. Prepare an income statement and show how it relates to a balance sheet.
4. Prepare a statement of cash flows and show how it differs from an income statement.
5. Account for cash dividends and prepare a statement of retained earnings.
6. Identify the major groups that influence generally accepted accounting principles.
7. Compute and explain earnings per share, price earnings ratio, dividend-yield ratio, and dividend-payout ratio. (Appendix 2)

Chapter 2

REVIEW OF KEY CONCEPTS

A.   Income provides a measure of operating performance for a period of time. The employment of assets to produce revenue, and the *matching* of costs incurred in generating the revenue, combine to produce net income.

1.   The **operating cycle** is the time it takes for a company to expend cash for the acquisition of goods and services, sell the goods and services, and collect the corresponding cash associated with the sale.

2.   **Revenue** is the gross *increase* in shareholders' equity due to the increase in net assets received in exchange for goods or services delivered to the customer.

3.   **Expenses** *decrease* shareholders' equity and result from the using-up or expiration of assets during the provision of goods and services to the customer.

4.   **Net Income** is the excess of revenues over expenses and represents a net asset inflow to the firm.

> Exhibits 2-1 and 2-2 on pages 47 and 48 of the text show the effect of revenue-generating activities on the balance sheet equation.

B.   Accountants recognize two basic methods of measuring income; the **accrual basis** and the **cash basis**.

1.   Under the **cash basis** of accounting, **revenue** is recognized when cash is *received*, and **expenses** are recognized when cash is *paid out*.

2.   The **accrual basis** of accounting looks at the economic substance of the transaction.
      a.   **Revenue** is recognized when it is **earned** (i.e. the good has been shipped or the service performed), as long as payment is reasonably assured (i.e. realized or realizable).

b. **Expenses** are recognized on the basis of the **matching principle**. This means that all costs incurred in generating revenue are recognized as expenses in the same accounting period as the revenue.

3. There are basically two types of expenses:
   a. **Product Costs,** which are directly associated with the production of the product, like raw materials or equipment operating expenses (e.g., electricity, depreciation expense, etc.).
   b. **Period Costs**, which are associated with the passage of time, like interest expense or rent expense.

4. **GAAP requires the use of the accrual basis of accounting**. This is partly because the cash basis of accounting is not an *objective* measure of net income. Under the cash basis, the management of an organization can manipulate performance by arranging the inflow (revenues) and outflow (expenses) of cash. The second reason GAAP requires the accrual basis of accounting is because it is a **better measure of performance**.

The accrual basis is a better measure of performance because revenue recognition is based on the **economic substance** of the transaction. If the good has been delivered or the work has been done, and payment is assured, then revenue is recognized. This suggests that a dry cleaner, for example, has earned revenue as soon as the cleaning process has been completed. Revenue recognition does not depend on when the customer pays for the dry cleaning. This also suggests that if a customer leaves a deposit for work to be done, this deposit does not become a revenue until the cleaning is complete, even though the cash has been received.

The accrual basis of accounting is a better measure of performance also because of the **matching principle**. The matching principle requires that only those costs incurred in generating revenue be recognized as expenses in the same accounting period as the revenue. This means that if a company buys 100 units of inventory for cash and sells only 75 units, that the accrual basis of accounting will only recognize the cost of the 75 units as an expense in the current accounting period. The unsold inventory is an asset on the balance sheet. Under the cash basis of accounting, all 100 units would be recognized as an expense because the company paid for 100 units.

5.   **Cost recovery** is the process by which past expenditures for assets are recovered in the period, or periods, in which the assets contribute to the generation of revenue as either a product or period expense. This recovery process is integral to the whole concept of matching expenses with revenues in the period the revenues are recognized. Examples would include expense recognition of a portion of *prepaid rent*, as the business makes use of a rented facility.

> See the example on pages 52 and 53 of the text.

6.   Assets can be thought of as "expenses waiting to happen". This suggests that as assets are used up in revenue-generating activities they expire and become expenses. Supplies inventory becomes supplies expense as it is used up. Prepaid rent becomes an expense as time passes and the right to the use of the property expires. In both cases, the firm has received benefits from these assets as they have contributed to the firm's generation of revenue. The difference between an asset and an expense is a matter of timing. An asset provides benefits in the **future**. Once the benefit has been received by the firm (e.g., it has used supplies inventory or rented property), the asset has expired and it then becomes an expense.

C.   The **income statement** is a report of all revenues and expenses of an entity that correspond to a *particular time period*. The excess of revenues over expenses is **income** or **net income**. Income is associated with a net inflow of assets to the firm and an increase in the shareholders' claim. This increased claim due to profitability is contained in the retained earnings component of shareholders' equity.

D.   It is not enough for a business organization to make a profit (i.e. to have net income). This is because an organization must remain solvent. This means that the organization must be able to meet its debts as they come due. While the accrual basis of accounting is superior to the cash basis in measuring performance, the accrual basis is not a good measure of the availability of cash. Use of the accrual basis of accounting to measure income necessitates that we look at cash flows separately. This is done with the **statement of cash flows**.

The **statement of cash flows** explains the change in cash during an accounting period. All the transactions which affect cash are organized into one of three categories:

1. **Operating activities** involve activities associated with the sale and purchase, or production of, goods or services, as well as collections from customers, payments to suppliers or employees, and payment of operating expenses such as rent, taxes, and interest.

2. **Investing activities** are activities associated with the purchase and sale of long-term assets such as property, plant and equipment, and long-term investments in the shares of other companies.

3. **Financing activities** include the issuance or repayment of long-term debt, the sale and repurchase of equity shares in the business, and the payment of dividends.

> Exhibit 2-4 on page 60 of the text shows how cash transactions affect the statement of cash flows.

E. The balance sheet equation can be expanded to include two components of shareholders' equity; **paid-in capital** and **retained earnings**:

Assets - Liabilities = Paid-in Capital + Retained Earnings

Shareholders' equity represents the owners' or shareholders' claim on the net assets of the firm. The claim arises, in part, from capital contributions made by the shareholders when they buy shares in the firm. This part of equity is called **paid-in capital**. **Retained earnings** represents the shareholders' claim on the past earnings of the company which have been retained by the company for reinvestment purposes. Income is associated with an increase in net assets. The shareholders have a claim to this net asset increase, as well as to the paid-in capital portion of equity. The claim associated with past earnings is kept in a separate component of equity known as retained earnings. Income is added to the opening balance of retained earnings (which would be zero for a new firm) and any dividends that are paid during the year are subtracted in arriving at the ending balance in retained earnings. Losses are associated with a net asset decrease which reduces retained earnings. Changes in retained earnings are detailed in the **statement of retained earnings**.

Chapter 2

1. **Cash dividends** represent distributions of assets to the shareholders and are charged against retained earnings. Cash dividends are a return of capital (i.e. a capital transaction). Cash dividends are **not expenses** of the period and they do **not** appear on the income statement.

2. Dividend transactions normally involve three dates:

    a. The **date of declaration** is the date the board of directors authorizes a dividend to be paid. On this date a *legal liability* to pay the dividend is incurred.

    b. The **date of record** is the ownership cut-off date to be eligible to receive payment of dividends.

    c. The **payment date** is the date cash is distributed to the list of shareholders established on the date of record.

3. A dividend liability is accrued on the balance sheet if the period ends after the date of declaration and before the payment date.

4. Retained earnings is a *cumulative balance* that represents a general claim against the net assets of the entity. There is little relationship between the balance in retained earnings and the cash account since retained earnings may have been "invested" in other assets, such as inventory or plant and equipment, or used to reduce liabilities.

5. The statement of retained earnings details the changes in retained earnings that have occurred during the period. This change is normally due to the addition of profits and the deduction of dividends declared during the period.

F. Generally accepted accounting principles (GAAP) are basic to the structure and practice of accounting in Canada. The principle of a stable monetary unit is the primary means for measuring transactions.

    a. GAAP is set by the Accounting Standards Committee (ASC) of the Canadian Institute of Chartered Accountants (CICA), a private sector, non-profit, professional organization.

b.   The standards are established by the ASC in consultation with business, government and other accounting bodies. The standards are codified as pronouncements and published in the CICA Handbook.

c.   Both the companies acts and securities acts recognize the Handbook as the major source of GAAP and require that financial statements be prepared according to GAAP.

G.   Financial statements, such as the income statement, are created to convey information to the reader concerning a particular entity. Ratio analysis is a popular method of analyzing information found in the statements. Four popular ratios related to the income statement are: earnings per share, price-earnings ratio, dividend-yield ratio, and dividend-payout ratio.

1.   **Earnings per share (EPS)** is probably the most widely used of the ratios and is required to be shown on the face of the income statement. EPS is calculated as follows:

$$\text{EPS} = \frac{\text{Net Income}}{\text{Avg. shares outstanding}}$$

2.   **Price-earnings ratio** measures how much the investing public is willing to pay for prospective earnings. Since the P-E ratio is the ratio of earnings to current market price it may vary considerably depending on the investing public's opinion concerning prospective income.

$$\text{P-E Ratio} = \frac{\text{Market price per share of common stock}}{\text{Earnings per share of common stock}}$$

3.   **Dividend-yield ratio** gives an indication of the return or profitability, in the form of dividends, of a stock relative to its current market price.

$$\text{Dividend-yield ratio} = \frac{\text{Common dividends per share}}{\text{Market price per share}}$$

4.   **Dividend-payout ratio** gives an indication of the percentage of earnings that are distributed to the shareholders in the form of dividends. The dividend-payout ratio gives an indication of the firm's dividend policy or highlights changes in that policy.

$$\text{Dividend-payout ratio} = \frac{\text{Common dividends per share}}{\text{Earnings per share}}$$

PRACTICE TEST QUESTIONS AND SOLUTIONS

I   **True or False -** For each of the following statements, enter a T or an F in the space provided to indicate whether the statement is true or false.

_____   1.   The income statement presents the results of operations at a particular point in time.

_____   2.   For revenue to be recognized it must be either earned or realized.

_____   3.   The accrual basis of accounting is a better measure than the cash basis for relating accomplishments to efforts.

_____   4.   The statement of cash flows is an effort to show how management acquired and used cash during the course of the period.

_____   5.   Dividends are considered an expense of the period and are deducted in the determination of net income.

_____ 6. Cash dividends are distributions of assets that reduce a portion of the ownership claim.

_____ 7. Retained earnings represent a cash reserve available to management in the case of emergency.

_____ 8. The CICA has ultimate authority in Canada for accounting standard setting.

_____ 9. Presentation of earnings per share on the face of the income statement is optional, but desirable.

_____ 10. Sales and sales revenues are synonyms for revenue.

_____ 11. Many governmental units use the cash basis of accounting instead of the accrual basis.

_____ 12. Depreciation expense is an example of the expiration of a portion of an asset's value.

_____ 13. Prepaid expenses are classified as current liabilities that are waiting to expire.

_____ 14. Matching is a basic principle of accrual accounting that dictates recording expenses in the period that the related revenues are recognized.

_____ 15. The accountant's measurement of income is the major means for evaluating a business entity's performance.

II **Multiple Choice** - For the following multiple choice questions, select the best answer and enter the identifying letter in the space provided.

1._____ During 19X1, revenues of $400,000 were generated and expenses of $374,000 were recognized. Retained earnings will:

    a. Decrease $ 26,000
    b. Not be affected
    c. Increase $ 26,000
    d. Decrease $400,000

Chapter 2

2._____   On December 31, 19X3, Henke Cap Sales had retained earnings of
$147,000. During 19X3, the business had income of $68,000 and paid
dividends of $27,200. What was the January 1, **19X3** balance in retained
earnings?

    a. $187,800
    b. $ 79,000
    c. $106,200
    d. $174,200

3._____   On December 31, 19X6 Thurmon Optical sold $10,000 worth of
eyeglasses costing $6,000 to a customer on account. The delivery was
to be made by Thurmon's delivery truck on January 3, 19X7. How
much revenue should Thurmon recognize on December 31?

    a. $10,000
    b. $ 4,000
    c. $ 6,000
    d. $ -0-

4._____   On December 28, 19X3, Concord Ltd. received a prepayment of
$100,000 from a customer for goods to be delivered on January 15,
19X4. Concord will incur $ 78,000 in expenses in providing and
delivering the goods. How much income will be included from this
transaction in the December 31, 19X3 income statement?

    a. $ 100,000
    b. $ 78,000
    c. $ 22,000
    d.   0

5._____   Which of the following is an example of an unexpired cost?

    a.   Rent expense
    b.   Depreciation expense
    c.   Unearned rent revenue
    d.   Prepaid expenses

6._____   Mim's Group had sales of $144,000, cash collections from sales of $123,000, cash payments for expenses totalling $106,000 and recognized expenses of $112,000. Net income would be:

	Cash	Accrual
a.	$11,000	$32,000
b.	$32,000	$17,000
c.	$17,000	$38,000
d.	$17,000	$32,000

7._____   Weinrich Co. had 112,000 shares of common stock outstanding during 19X4. Sales totalled $740,000 and expenses amounted to $484,640. What was Weinrich's earnings per share?

    a. $6.61
    b. $2.28
    c. $4.33
    d. $2.25

8._____   Which of the following would be considered a cash flow from operating activities?

    a.   Purchase of store equipment for cash
    b.   Loan from the bank
    c.   Cash payments to suppliers
    d.   Cash proceeds from the shareholders' initial investment

9._____   Which of the following is true?

    a.   Assets = Liabilities + Paid-in capital - Revenue + Expenses
    b.   Liabilities + Paid-in capital = Revenues - Expenses + Assets
    c.   Liabilities + Paid-in capital + Revenue - Expenses = Assets
    d.   Assets = Liabilities - Paid-in capital + Revenue - Expenses

Chapter 2

10._____ Scheffer Clothing Ltd. purchased inventory on February 1, 19X2 for cash. The merchandise was sold to a major company on March 15, 19X2. Credit terms are thirty days and the customer is expected to pay by the last day of the credit period. What is the length, in days, of the operating cycle?

    a.   60 days
    b.   73 days
    c.   57 days
    d.   28 days

11._____ Jazzy Jeff's Music Store sold merchandise costing $100,000 to customers on account for a sale price of $160,000. What was the effect of this transaction on the following:

	Assets	Retained earnings
a.	Decrease	Increase
b.	Increase	Increase
c.	No effect	Increase

12._____ On March 1, the first day in business for your company, $36,000 in rent was paid to cover the next 36 months. It is now December 31 and you need to recognize rent expense for the period. What is rent expense for the first year?

    a.   -0-
    b. $36,000
    c. $10,000
    d. $ 9,000

III   Problems

Problem 1:

A company is in the television repair business. The owner/manager performs $7,000 of repairs during the month of January. Of this amount, $4,000 has been received in cash and the rest is due in ten days. Collectibility is certain. The company purchased $3,000 of repair supplies for cash at the beginning of the month, and has used $1,800 of the supplies during January. The company has also paid $1,200 cash for a one year insurance policy effective January 1st, and owes $500 rent for the month of January.

Required:
Calculate and compare net income according to the **cash basis** of accounting versus the **accrual basis**.

Problem 2:
The balance sheets and income statements for the Data Co. Ltd. are provided below. Dividends paid during those years are also indicated, but the controller has neglected to include some important figures.

Balance Sheet
As At December 31

Assets

	19X2	19X3	19X4	19X5
Cash	$ 250	$ 500	$?	$ 750
Accounts Receivable	500	250	750	250
Inventory	875	?	250	250
Building and equipment	1500	2250	2000	1000

Liabilities & Shareholder's Equity

	19X2	19X3	19X4	19X5
Accounts Payable	$ 500	$ 250	$ 500	$750
Notes Payable	?	1500	750	250
Common Shares	500	500	500	750
Retained Earnings	250	1000	?	?

Income Statement
For the 12 months ended December 31

	19X2	19X3	19X4	19X5
Sales	$?	$2500	?	3000
Cost of goods sold and other operating expenses	1250	?	1500	?
Net Income	?	?	1000	750
Dividends Paid	$ 0	$ 375	$ 500	$?

Chapter 2

Required:
Provide the figures missing in the statements above, using the assumption that Data Co. Ltd. began operations on January 1, 19X2.

Problem 3:
On December 31, 19X4 the following information was available:

Sales	$ 1,629,600
Rent expense	245,000
Salary expense	380,000
Expired prepaid insurance	25,000
Other expenses	295,000
Market price per share	$ 45.64
Dividend-payout ratio	30%
EPS	$ 3.26

Required:
a.   Calculate the average number of shares outstanding
b.   Calculate the price-earnings ratio
c.   Calculate the common dividends per share
d.   Calculate the dividend yield

Problem 4:
During the month of December 19X4, Osborne Ltd. had the following transactions:
- issued $ 100 of common stock for cash
- purchased $ 50 of inventory for $25 cash and the balance due in thirty days
- sold the inventory on credit for $ 75
- purchased a new piece of equipment for $ 80, the company took out a note payable for $ 60 and paid the balance in cash

Required:
Prepare a statement of cash flows for the month of December.

For additional practice preparing the income statement and statement of retained earnings, see Lotus Template file P2-43.wk1 and P2-44.wk1. For additional practice using ratios see Lotus Template file P2-27.wk1 and PAGE2-52.wk1.

CHAPTER 2 ANSWERS AND SOLUTIONS

I   True and false

1. False The income statement shows the results of operations for a period of time. The balance sheet represents the financial position of an entity on a specific date.
2. False According to the principle of revenue recognition, revenue must be **both** earned and realized, or realizable (i.e. collectibility is reasonably certain), for it to be recognized in the accounting records.
3. True
4. True
5. False Dividends are distributions of assets to the shareholders. Generally these distributions take the form of cash payments to the shareholders and are related to after-tax earnings.
6. True
7. False Retained earnings are past earnings of the firm which have been re-invested in the firm in cash, accounts receivable, inventory, capital assets, etc. or have been used to reduce the firm's liabilities.
8. True
9. False Earnings per share information is required by GAAP to be presented on the face of the income statement. It is the only ratio that is required.
10. True
11. True
12. True
13. False Prepaid expenses are classified as assets on the balance sheet because they represent future benefits arising out of past expenditures. Only when they have expired are they recognized on the income statement as an expense.
14. True
15. True

II Multiple choice

1. C   Just as revenues ($400,000) belong to the shareholders, so too are they responsible for the expenses ($374,000). Retained earnings would increase by the amount of net income which is $ 26,000 ($400,000 - $ 374,000).
2. C
Beg. balance retained earnings	$106,200
add: net income	68,000
less: dividends	(27,200)
End. balance retained earnings	$147,000

Chapter 2

3. D   Since the goods will not be delivered until January 3, 19X7, the revenue has not yet been earned. No revenue will be recognized until delivery on January 3, 19X7.

4. D   Revenue is only recognized when it is earned. The timing of cash collection is irrelevant under accrual accounting.

5. D   Prepaid expenses are unexpired costs recorded on the balance sheet as assets. They are recognized as expenses as they are used up in the generation of revenue. This is the **matching principle**.

6. D

	Cash	Accrual
Sales	$123,000	$144,000
Expenses	106,000	112,000
Income	$ 17,000	$ 32,000

7. B   Sales $740,000
        Expenses   484,640
        Income $255,360
        EPS = $255,360/112,000 shares= **$2.28/sh.**

8. C   Cash payments to suppliers are considered in determining cash flows from operations. Purchase of store equipment, a long-term asset, is classified as an investing activity and both the initial investment and the loan from the bank would be financing activities.

9. C   Assets = Liabilities + Paid-in capital + (Revenue - Expenses)

10. B   The operating cycle is defined as the time period from the expenditure of cash to acquire goods or services (i.e. Feb. 1, 19X2), to the subsequent collection of cash from the sale of the goods or services (estimated as April 15, 19X2).

11. B   Both assets and retained earnings would increase consistent with the balance sheet equation. Specifically, accounts receivable would increase and inventory would decrease (but by a smaller amount), and retained earnings would increase by the difference between the sales value of the transaction and the cost of the merchandise sold.

12. C $36,000 prepaid rent/36 months = $ 1,000 rent expense each month. Rent expense was incurred for 10 months (March 1 to December 31) times $1,000 rent expense/month equals $10,000 total rent expense for the year.

III Problems

Problem 1:
Compare the following calculations of net income:

	Cash Basis	Accrual Basis
Revenue	$ 4,000	$ 7,000
Less expenses:		
Repair supplies	3,000	1,800
Insurance	1,200	100
Rent	- 0 -	500
Net Income	$ (200)	$ 4,600

This example demonstrates that income can be very different depending on the criteria used to recognize revenues and expenses. Under the **cash basis**, revenues are not recognized until they are received in cash - hence revenues are only $ 4,000. On the other hand, expenses are recognized when they are paid, even if they do not relate to the current accounting period which is the month of January. This results in $ 1,200 in insurance expense even though only 1/12 ($ 100) of the policy applies to the month of January. Under the cash basis, no rent expense is recognized in January because cash has not yet been disbursed.

Under the **accrual basis** of measuring income, revenue is recognized on the basis of whether it has been *earned* and whether *collectibility* is reasonably certain. This suggests that revenue is $ 7,000, not just the $ 4,000 that has been received. Expenses are **matched** to revenues which means that only those costs incurred during January in generating revenues are recognized. The company has used $ 1,800 of repair supplies so this is an expense. It has only used one month (not twelve) of insurance coverage, so only $ 100 is recognized as the expense. Finally, the company has had the benefit of one month's rent and this is expense for the company even though it still must be paid.

Problem 2: (all amounts in $)

19X2	Notes Payable 1875	Net Income 250	Sales 1500
19X3	Inventory 250	Expenses 1375	Net Income 1125
19X4	Cash 250	Ret. Earnings 1500	Sales 2500
19X5	Ret. Earnings 500	Expenses 2250	Dividends 1750

Chapter 2

The key to solving for many of the missing amounts is to utilize the balance sheet equation (assets = liabilities + equity) and also to use the relationship between the balance sheet and the income statement, for example:

19X2 retained earnings balance (this is the opening balance for 19X3)	$ 250
+ 19X3 income	?
- 19X3 dividends	(375)
= 19X3 ending retained earnings balance	1,000

solving for net income gives 19X3 income of $ 1,125

Problem 3:

a. EPS = Net income/ Avg. # of shares
Net income = $ 1,629,600- (245,000 + 380,000 +25,000 +295,000) = $684,600
Avg. # of shares = Net income/EPS = $ 684,600/ $3.26 = **210,000 shares**

b. P-E Ratio = Market price/EPS = $ 45.64/ $ 3.26 = **14**

c. Dividend pay-out ratio = Common dividends per share/ EPS
therefore, Common dividends per share　　= Dividend pay-out ratio X EPS
$$= .30 \text{ X } \$ 3.26$$
$$= \$ \underline{.978}$$

d. Dividend yield = Common dividends per share/ Market price = .978/$45.64 = **2%**

Problem 4:

The company has an ending cash balance of $ 55 (0 + 100 - 25 -20 = 55). This represents an increase in cash of $ 55 from the beginning of the month.

Osborne Ltd.
Statement of Cash Flows
For the month ended December 31, 19X4

Cash from operations:	
cash payment to supplier for inventory	$(25)
Investing activities:	
cash payment for acquisition of equipment	(20)
Financing activities:	
issuance of share capital for cash	100
Total increase in cash during the month	$ 55

Chapter 3

The Recording Process: Journals and Ledgers

Many financial statement readers focus entirely on the output of an accounting system; the financial statements. While this is natural, a good understanding of the supporting theories and procedures is needed to be an effective user of the information presented on the face of the statements. This chapter focuses on the concepts associated with double-entry accounting and the rudiments of the accounting cycle. The following learning objectives are presented to help coordinate your study of the material presented and aid your progress toward a better understanding of the accounting function.

1. Explain the double-entry accounting system, the role of ledger accounts, and the meaning of debits and credits.
2. Describe the sequence of steps in recording transactions and explain how transactions are journalized and posted.
3. Analyze transactions for journalizing and posting and explain the relationship of revenue and expenses to shareholders' equity.
4. Prepare journal entries and post them to the ledger.
5. Prepare a trial balance and understand its role relative to the income statement and the balance sheet.
6. Understand the significance of computers in data processing.
7. Explain the meaning of the accounting concepts of going concern, materiality, and cost benefit.

Chapter 3

REVIEW OF KEY CONCEPTS

A. The double-entry system of accounting is considered the foundation of modern business. The **double-entry system** assumes that at least two accounts are affected by each transaction. After a transaction is analyzed, each of the elements of the transaction are grouped by similar characteristics in the **ledger.**

1. The **general ledger** is a record containing the groups of accounts that support the balances presented on the financial statements. Each account provides a summary of activity relating to changes in that particular classification's balance. The **balance** is the difference between the left and right sides of an account.

    a. **Assets** have a *left-side balance* and are increased by additions to the left side. Reductions are made by entries to the right-side.

    b. **Liabilities and shareholders' equity** accounts have *right-side balances* and are increased by entries to that side. Reductions are made by entries to the left-side.

    See the use of t-accounts on page 91 of the text.

2. To denote adjustments to ledger accounts the terms **debit (dr.)** and **credit (cr.)** are commonly used.

    a. **Debit** simply means **left**.
    b. **Credit** simply means **right**.

Normal Balances		
Assets	Debit	
Liabilities		Credit
Shareholders' equity (overall)		Credit
Paid-in capital		Credit
Revenues		Credit
Expenses	Debit	

    See Exhibit 3-3 on page 105 of the text

Prepare an index card for use over the next week or so until you become familiar with the recording convention:

Increase in an **Asset** or an **Expense** = **Debit**
Increase in **Liabilities**, **Equity** or **Revenues** = **Credit**

B. The accounting cycle begins with an analysis of source documents related to entity transactions and ends with the ledger balances being updated and financial statements being prepared.

1. **Source documents** include original evidence of the transaction such as invoices, sales slips, receiving reports, and purchase orders. Contracts and minutes from meetings of the board of directors are additional sources of transaction information.

2. Once a transaction had been analyzed it is recorded in the **general journal** using established account classifications. The general journal is a chronological record of transactions affecting an entity and is often called the "book of original entry". Information concerning a particular individual transaction would be found in the general journal.

---

example: sold $ 100 of merchandise on account
analysis: sales increase - this is a credit
               accounts receivable increase - this is a debit
entry: DR Accounts receivable   100
                 CR Sales   100

---

3. Periodically transactions recorded in the journal are transferred, or **posted**, to the general ledger, updating the account balances.

See Exhibit 3-1 on page 96 of the text

---

4.   After the posting is completed a **trial balance** is prepared. The purpose for the trial balance is to verify the equality of debit and credit dollar balances in the general ledger and to provide a convenient point from which the statements may be prepared. (Note: the trial balance can balance and be incorrect but if it doesn't balance it is **definitely** incorrect)

> See Exhibit 3-6 on page 112 of the text

5.   The final step in the accounting cycle is the preparation of the financial statements from the trial balance.

> **STOP!!** Before proceeding, review the section beginning on page 96 of the textbook entitled **"Analyzing Transactions for the Journal and Ledger"**.

C.   The growth in the use of computers to perform the **data processing** functions of recording, analyzing, storing, and reporting on an entities activities fit well with the functions associated with accounting and the accounting cycle. Think of the steps performed in producing a set of financial statements and at the same time think how a computer may be used to accomplish these functions more quickly.

D.   Just as the concepts associated with accrual accounting are built on the basic principles of matching, revenue recognition, and a stable monetary unit; the principles of materiality, cost/benefit, and going concern are equally important to the development of a cohesive framework of principles and practices.

1.   The **going concern convention** assumes that under normal circumstances an accounting entity has an indefinite life. This convention supports use of the historical or acquisition cost of an asset (e.g., as opposed to liquidation or market value) because this is the true cost incurred in using the asset. The company does not intend to sell the asset (because it will continue to operate as a going-concern) and so market value is not relevant.

2. The **materiality convention** is based on the concept that an item is material if its omission or misstatement would be misleading and cause the reader to reach a different conclusion than would have been reached had the omission or misstatement not occurred.

   a. Materiality is often the basis from which decisions are made whether to capitalize an asset and depreciate it over its expected useful life or expense the amount in the period of acquisition.

   b. Determining whether an item or a procedure is material or not is generally up to the discretion of the accountant. This discretion is guided by generally accepted accounting principles.

3. The **cost-benefit criterion** is a general guideline which suggests the cost of the information should never exceed the benefit it provides to financial statement users. The cost of information includes not only the cost of preparing it but also the costs associated with disclosing information which might harm the company's competitive position. Benefits are associated with the financial statement users making better decisions as a result of having better information. The cost-benefit criterion applies to standard setting.

This chapter is important in developing your understanding of the language of accounting and your ability to complete the functions of the accounting cycle. Review the key objectives and all of the examples and exhibits presented to this point.

PRACTICE TEST QUESTIONS AND SOLUTIONS

I **True and false -** For each of the following statements enter a T or an F in the space provided to indicate whether the statement is true or false.

_____ 1. The terms debit and credit are used in accounting terminology to denote an increase and a decrease.

_____ 2. The normal balance in a liability account is a credit balance.

Chapter 3

_____ 3. When preparing a journal entry it does not matter in which order debits and credits are treated.

_____ 4. The purchase of small hand tools for $100, having an expected useful life of three years, would probably be put in an asset account and depreciated over the three year period.

_____ 5. Revenues are recorded as credits because revenues ultimately increase retained earnings and retained earnings normally has a credit balance.

_____ 6. Accumulated depreciation is an example of a contra-asset account and it has a debit balance.

_____ 7. A compound entry involves more than two accounts but still maintains equality between the dollar values of the debit and credit entries.

_____ 8. The sale of stock by a corporation involves a credit to a shareholders' equity account.

_____ 9. The expiration of a prepaid expense would involve a debit to prepaid expenses.

_____ 10. The trial balance is prepared to assure the accuracy of all entries in the general journal.

_____ 11. Liabilities have a right-side balance and would be increased by a credit entry.

_____ 12. Expenses are increased by a debit entry because retained earnings, a part of shareholders' equity, is reduced by debit entries.

_____ 13. In the accounting cycle transactions are posted to the general ledger after analysis of the source documents.

_____ 14. Paid-in capital normally has a credit balance.

_____ 15. Sales revenue is an asset account and is increased by a debit.

_____ 16. Dividends ultimately decrease retained earnings, therefore, they are recorded as debits.

_____ 17. Inventory returned to a supplier would involve a debit to the inventory account.

_____ 18. Revenue and expense accounts are fundamentally a part of shareholders' equity.

II **Multiple choice** - For each of the following multiple choice questions, select the best answer and enter the identifying letter in the space provided.

_____ 1. The account with a left-side balance is:

a. Accumulated depreciation
b. Retained earnings
c. Prepaid rent
d. Sales revenue

_____ 2. Alpha Corp. purchased inventory on account. The journal entry reflecting this transaction would include a:

a. Credit to Inventory
b. Credit to Accounts payable
c. Debit to Accounts payable
d. Debit to Cash

_____ 3. During 19X2, Simpson Laboratories recognized $150,000 as depreciation expense on lab equipment. The journal entry to record this allocation would be:

a.	Depreciation expense	150,000	
	Equipment		150,000
b.	Accumulated depreciation	150,000	
	Depreciation expense		150,000
c.	Depreciation expense	150,000	
	Accumulated depreciation		150,000
d.	Depreciation expense	150,000	
	Cash		150,000

_____ 4. On January 1 19x2 Cullinen Waste Disposal had a $121,000 credit balance in Accounts payable. During the year purchases on account amounted to $745,000 and payments totalled $767,000. The balance on December 31 19x2 would be:

a. $ 99,000   debit balance
b. $143,000   credit balance
c. $ 99,000   credit balance
d. $143,000   debit balance

_____ 5. Recognition of cost of goods sold would include:

a. Debit Inventory, credit Cost of goods sold
b. Debit Cost of goods sold, credit Inventory expense
c. Credit Cost of goods sold, debit Inventory expense
d. Debit Cost of goods sold, credit Inventory

_____ 6. Sale of merchandise on account for $10,000 would be recorded as:

a. Accounts receivable   10,000
          Sales   10,000
b. Sales   10,000
          Accounts receivable   10,000
c. Sales   10,000
          Cash   10,000
d. Accounts receivable   10,000
          Inventory   10,000

_____ 7. In May 19X4, Black Thumb Landscaping prepaid $1,000 for the rental of a backhoe to be used sometime in June. The journal entry to record the expiration of this prepaid cost in June would include:

a. Debit to Cash
b. Credit to Prepaid rental fees
c. Debit to Prepaid rental fees
d. Credit to backhoe rental expense

8. Expenses and Shareholders' equity have the following normal balances:

	Expenses	Shareholders' equity
a.	Debit	Debit
b.	Debit	Credit
c.	Credit	Credit
d.	Credit	Debit

9. On January 1, 19X1 Brendon Construction purchased a piece of machinery for $125,000. On December 31 depreciation expense of $25,000 was recognized. Current replacement cost for this machine was $128,000 on that date. What was the book value of that asset on January 1 19x2?

a. $125,000
b. $128,000
c. $100,000
d. $ 25,000

10. Which of the following sequence of events is correct relative to the accounting cycle?

a. Post, journalize, trial balance, statements
b. Post, trial balance, journalize
c. Journalize, post, trial balance, statements
d. Journalize, post, trial balance

11. In a journal entry, debit and credit refer to:

a. Right, left
b. Increase, decrease
c. Decrease, increase
d. Left, right

Chapter 3

_____ 12. Archie invested cash totalling $105,000 in his new venture that was organized as a sole proprietorship. The journal entry to record this transaction would include:

a. Credit $105,000 to Capital-Archie
b. Debit $105,000 to Capital-Archie
c. Credit Cash $105,000
d. Credit $105,000 to Shareholders' equity

III   Problems

Problem 1:
Journalize the following transactions for Lambert & Co. Ltd. for the month of January, 19X2:

a. Issued common shares for $ 50,000
b. Signed a bank agreement to borrow $ 100,000 from the local bank
c. The bank deposited the $ 100,000 loan in the company's account
d. Bought a used delivery truck for $ 15,000 cash
e. Paid $ 2,400 for a one year insurance policy effective January 1
f. Billed $ 30,000 worth of fees to clients for services performed
g. Received an advance from a customer for work to be done in February for $4,000
h. Collected $ 25,000 from clients for services previously billed
i. Signed a contract with a new employee which promises to pay the employee $60,000/year in salary
j. Transferred the amount of expired insurance to insurance expense
k. Determined depreciation expense on the delivery truck of $ 250 for the month

Problem 2:
Journalize the following transactions for Preville Lawn Care Ltd. for its first month of operations

a. Issued share capital of $ 200,000
b. Signed a new lease for office space and paid a $ 10,000 damage deposit
c. Bought two new trucks for $ 30,000 cash each
d. Bought office equipment on credit for $ 20,000
e. Billed customers for lawn care of $ 12,000
f. Paid employees $ 5,000 for work done during the month

g.   Paid expenses as follows; gas $ 350, fertilizer spray $ 2,500, repairs $ 100

h.   Hired a new receptionist at a salary of $ 500/week

i.   Determined depreciation expense as $ 500 per truck per month

j.   Paid for advertising of $ 300 to appear in the next month's issue of a local magazine for horticulturalists

k.   Received a nasty phone call from a customer who is threatening to sue the company for damage done to her lawn

l.   Collected $ 10,000 from customers on account, and received a $ 2,000 advance from a customer for landscaping work to be done next month.

Problem 3:

The following balances appeared in the general ledger of Perfect Party Co. Ltd. at the end of November, 19X1. Assume all account balances are normal (e.g., accounts payable normally has a credit balance).

Cash	$ 2,400	Accounts payable	$ 2,000
Accounts receivable	3,900	Bank loan	500
Prepaid rent	1,000	Common stock	4,350
Supplies inventory	350	Retained earnings	800

The following transactions took place during the month of December, 19X1

a.   Collected $ 2,000 from customers on account

b.   Billed customers $ 3,000 for party organization services performed during December

c.   Paid $ 300 for an advertisement placed in the December edition of a local magazine

d.   Paid salaries of $ 2,000

e.   Made payments to suppliers of $ 1,000

f.   Transferred $ 500 of prepaid rent to rent expense

g.   Counted $ 200 of supplies on hand at the end of December; recorded the amount used as an expense

Required:

Journalize the above transactions, post to t-accounts, and prepare an income statement and balance sheet at December 31, 19X1.

Chapter 3

Problem 4:
The balance sheet as at **July 31**, 19X2, for Griffin Enterprises Ltd. appears below.

During **August** 19X2, the following transactions occurred:

Aug. 1   Joe invested an additional $50,000 in the business.

Aug. 1   In anticipation of strong sales, an additional $75,000 in inventory was purchased for $25,000 in cash and the balance to be paid in 30 days.

Aug. 1   Griffin renegotiated his lease and prepaid rent of $36,000 for a 36 month period.

Aug. 3   Made sales totalling $40,000 to a customer on account. The merchandise had an original acquisition cost of $20,000.

Aug. 10   Received customer payments totalling $75,000.

Aug. 15   Paid wages totalling $1,500 for work during the preceding two week period.

Aug. 20   Paid the outstanding balance on the note payable.

Aug. 30   Recognized depreciation expense of $2,000.

Aug. 30   Recognized this month's portion of prepaid rent.

Griffin Enterprises Ltd.
Balance Sheet
As At **July 31**, 19X2

Assets:		Liabilities:	
Cash	$ 40,000	Accounts payable	$ 75,000
Accounts receivable	86,000	Notes payable	65,000
Inventory	154,000	Long-term debt	360,000
Equipment	480,000	Common stock	158,000
Accum. Depreciation	(20,000)	Retained earnings	82,000
Total assets	$740,000	Total liabilities & Equity	$740,000

Required:
1. Journalize the transactions for August
2. Post the transactions to t-accounts (remember to first put in the relevant opening account balances, e.g., cash has an opening balance of $ 40,000 debit from the July balance sheet)
3. Prepare an August 31 trial balance, an income statement, balance sheet and statement of retained earnings

CHAPTER 3 ANSWERS AND SOLUTIONS

I   **True and false**

1.   False   Debit and credit simply mean left and right. Understanding the normal balance of an account determines the increase or decrease in the account.

2.   True

3.   False   The proper form for a journal entry would include the date of the transaction, each ledger account that is affected by debit entries, followed by and offset to the right all accounts in the transaction affected by a credit entry, and finally a short description of the transaction.

4.   False   Immaterial expenditures for assets are normally expensed because the financial statement users' decisions are unaffected by whether immaterial expenditures are treated as an asset or an expense. This is an example of the **materiality convention**. Also, the cost of record-keeping if the expenditure is capitalized outweighs the benefits associated with it. This is an example of the cost-benefit convention.

5.   True

6.   False   Accumulated depreciation is a contra-asset account and, therefore, has a **credit balance**.

7.   True

8.   True

9.   False   Prepaid expenses are carried on the balance sheet as assets. The expiration of the prepaid expense, and subsequent reduction in that account would involve a credit to the prepaid expense account.

10.   False   The purpose for the trial balance is to assure the dollar value balance of the debits and credits and provide a basis from which to prepare the statements. If an incorrect amount is used for both the debits and the credits in a journal entry, the trial balance will balance but it will be incorrect.

11.   True

12.   True

13.   False   After analysis of the source documents an entry is made to the general journal. Posting to the general ledger is the next step **after** journalization.

Chapter 3

14. True
15. False   Sales revenue is an income statement account which ultimately increases equity and, therefore, is increased by credits.
16. True
17. False   Inventory carries a debit balance. A reduction to inventory would therefore involve a credit to the account.
18. True

II   Multiple Choice

1. C   As an asset, the normal balance for prepaid rent is a debit-balance. All of the others listed carry a credit, or right-side balance.

2. B   An increase in inventory is a debit and an increase in accounts payable is a credit. The proper entry for this transaction would be:

      Inventory   xxx
          Accounts payable   xxx

3. C   As you can see by this entry, a portion of the asset value is allocated to the income statement through the debit to depreciation expense. This entry is necessary to match revenues and expenses. The offsetting credit is made to a contra-asset account, accumulated depreciation, reducing the book value of the asset.

4. C   The normal balance for a liability is a credit balance. The corresponding calculation of the ending balance is as follows:

Beg. balance	$121,000
add: credit purchases	745,000
less: payments	(767,000)
End. balance	$ 99,000 credit.

5. D   Cost of goods sold is an expense and has a debit balance. Inventory, an asset, is reduced by a credit entry.

6. A   Since the sale is both earned and realizable (collectible), the entry reflects an increase in an asset account and an increase in a revenue account.

7. B   The proper journal entry would be:

      Equipment expense   1,000
          Prepaid rental fees   1,000

8. B   The answer is self explanatory.

9. C   Book value of the asset is defined as the historical cost of the asset ($125,000) minus the accumulated depreciation ($25,000). Since this is the first period for which depreciation is recorded on this asset the depreciation expense and the accumulated depreciation are the same value.

10. C   The accounting cycle is as follows: Transaction, transaction analysis, journalize, post, prepare trial balance, prepare financial statements.

11. D   Can not emphasis enough, debit means left. Credit means right.

12. A   The proper journal entry is as follows: (Explanation eliminated)

Cash	105,000	
Capital-Archie		105,000

III   Problems

Problem 1:

a. DR Cash   50,000
        CR Common Stock   50,000

b. no entry required as no cash has been received yet (unexecuted contract)

c. DR Cash   100,000
        CR Bank Loan   100,000

d. DR Truck   15,000
        CR Cash   15,000

e. DR Prepaid insurance   2,400
        CR Cash   2,400

f. DR Accounts receivable   30,000
        CR Revenue   30,000

g. DR Cash   4,000
        CR Unearned revenue   4,000

h. DR Cash   25,000
        CR Accounts receivable   25,000

Chapter 3

i.   no entry required (unexecuted contract)

j.   DR Insurance expense (2,400/12 months)   200
            CR Prepaid insurance   200

k.   DR Depreciation expense   250
            CR Accumulated depreciation   250

Problem 2:

a.   DR Cash   200,000
            CR Common Stock   200,000

b.   DR Deposit (an asset)   10,000
            CR Cash   10,000

c.   DR Trucks   60,000
            CR Cash   60,000

d.   DR Office equipment   20,000
            CR Accounts payable   20,000

e.   DR Accounts receivable   12,000
            CR Revenue   12,000

f.   DR Wage expense   5,000
            CR Cash   5,000

g.   DR Gas expense   350
        DR Fertilizer expense   2,500
        DR Repair expense   100
            CR Cash   2,950

h.   no entry (unexecuted contract)

i.   DR Depreciation expense   1,000
            CR Accumulated depreciation   1,000

j.   DR Prepaid advertising   300
            CR Cash   300

k.   no entry at this time (not enough information on the outcome of the suit)

l.   DR Cash   12,000

            CR Accounts receivable   10,000

            CR Unearned revenue or Advance from customer 2,000

Problem 3:
Entries:

a.   DR Cash   2,000

            CR Accounts receivable   2,000

b.   DR Accounts receivable   3,000

            CR Revenue   3,000

c.   DR Advertising expense   300

            CR Cash   300

d.   DR Salaries expense   2,000

            CR Cash   2,000

e.   DR Accounts payable   1,000

            CR Cash   1,000

f.   DR Rent expense   500

            CR Prepaid rent   500

g.   DR Supplies expense ($350-200 left)   150

            CR Supplies inventory   150

t-accounts

Cash			Accounts Receivable		
	2400	300 (c)		3900	2000 (a)
(a) 2000		2000 (d)	(b) 3000		
		1000 (e)			
bal. 1100			bal. 4900		

Prepaid Rent

1000	500 (f)

bal. <u>500</u>

Supplies inventory

350	150 (g)

bal. <u>200</u>

Accounts payable

(e) 1000	2000
	<u>1000</u> bal.

Bank loan

	500 (f)
	<u>500</u> bal.

Common stock

	4350
	<u>4350</u> bal.

Retained earnings

	800
	<u>800</u> bal.

Revenue

	3000 (b)
	<u>3000</u> bal.

Advertising expense

(c) 300	
bal. <u>300</u>	

Salaries expense

(d) 2000	
bal. <u>2000</u>	

Rent expense

(f) 500	
bal. <u>500</u>	

Supplies expense

(g) 150	
bal. <u>150</u>	

financial statements:

Perfect Party Co. Ltd.
Income Statement
For the month of December 19X1

Revenue		3,000
Less expenses:		
Salaries expense	2,000	
Rent expense	500	
Advertising expense	300	
Supplies expense	150	2,950
Net income		$ 50

Perfect Party Co. Ltd.
Balance Sheet
As at December 31, 19X1

Assets:	
Cash	$1,100
Accounts receivable	4,900
Prepaid rent	500
Supplies inventory	200
Total Assets	$6,700
Liabilities:	
Accounts payable	$1,000
Bank loan	500
	1,500
Equity:	
Common stock	$4,350
Retained earnings (800 open .bal. + 50 income)	850
Total Liabilities & Equity	6,700

Chapter 3

Problem 4:

1. Journalize Transactions:

a. Aug. 1	Cash		50,000	
	Common stock			50,000
b. Aug. 1	Inventory		75,000	
	Cash			25,000
	Accounts payable			50,000
c. Aug. 1	Prepaid rent		36,000	
	Cash			36,000
d. Aug. 3	Accounts receivable		40,000	
	Sales revenue			40,000
	Cost of goods sold		20,000	
	Inventory			20,000
e. Aug. 10	Cash		75,000	
	Accounts receivable			75,000
f. Aug. 15	Wage expense		1,500	
	Cash			1,500
g. Aug. 20	Notes payable		65,000	
	Cash			65,000
h. Aug. 30	Depreciation expense		2,000	
	Accumulated depreciation			2,000
i. Aug. 30	Rent expense		1,000	
	Prepaid rent			1,000

2. Post to t-accounts

Accounts payable

bb 40,000	25,000 (b)
(a) 50,000	36,000 (c)
(e) 75,000	1,500 (f)
	65,000 (g)
eb $37,500	

Notes payable

bb 86,000	75,000 (e)
(d) 40,000	
eb $51,000	

Inventory

bb 154,000	20,000 (d)
(b) 75,000	
eb $209,000	

Prepaid Rent

(c) 36,000	1,000 (i)
eb 35,000	

Accumulated depreciation

	20,000 bb
	2,000 (h)
	$22,000 eb

Equipment

bb 480,000	
eb $480,000	

Accounts payable

	75,000 bb
	50,000 (b)
	$125,000 eb

Notes payable

(g) 65,000	65,000 bb
	-0-

Long-term debt	
	360,000 bb
	$360,000

Capital	
	158,000 bb
	50,000 (a)
	$208,000

Retained Earnings	
	82,000 bb

Sales revenue	
	40,000 (d)

Cost of Goods Sold	
(d) 20,000	

Wage expense	
(f) 1,500	

Depreciation expense	
(h) 2,000	

Rent expense	
(i) 1,000	

3. August 31 Trial balance

Griffin Enterprises Ltd.
Trial Balance
August 31, 19X2

Account	dr.	cr.
Cash	$ 37,500	
Accounts receivable	51,000	
Inventory	209,000	
Prepaid rent	35,000	
Equipment	480,000	
Accumulated depreciation		22,000
Accounts Payable		125,000
Notes payable		-0-
Long-term debt		360,000
Common Stock		208,000
Retained earnings*		82,000
Sales revenue		40,000
Costs of goods sold	20,000	
Depreciation expense	2,000	
Wage expense	1,500	
Rent expense	1,000	
	$837,000	$837,000

* note that the opening balance in retained earnings appears on the trial balance. Income information for the current period is only reflected in retained earnings after the closing entries have been made. Closing entries are discussed in chapter 5.

Chapter 3

3. cont'd: financial statements

Griffin Enterprises Ltd.
Income Statement
For the month ended August 31, 19X2

Sales revenue	$	40,000
Less: Cost of goods sold		20,000
Gross profit		20,000
Less expenses:		
Depreciation expense	2,000	
Wage expense	1,500	
Rent expense	1,000	4,500
Net income (assume no taxes)		15,500

Griffin Enterprises Ltd.
Balance Sheet
As At August 31, 19X2

Assets

Current assets:		
Cash		$ 37,500
Accounts receivable		51,000
Inventory		209,000
Prepaid rent		35,000
Total Current Assets		$332,500
Equipment	$480,000	
Less: Acc. depreciation	22,000	458,000
Total Assets		790,500

Liabilities & Equity

Current Liabilities:
Accounts payable $125,000

Non-current Liabilities:
Long-term debt   360,000

Shareholders' Equity
Common stock   208,000
Retained earnings   97,500

Total Liabilities & Equity   790,500

Griffin Enterprises Ltd.
Statement of Retained Earnings
As At August 31, 19X2

Opening balance, July 31, $82,000
19X2

Plus net income for August   15,500

Less dividends   0

Balance, August 31, 19x2   97,500

Chapter 4

Accounting Adjustments and Financial Statement Preparations

The foundation of accrual accounting rests on the concepts of recognizing revenue when it is earned and recording expenses in the period that the product, service, or work is done to support contribution to revenue. This approach dictates understanding the process of adjusting account balances to reflect the recognition of revenues and expenses in the proper period. Chapter 4 focuses on the concepts and practices related to adjusting entries, as well as the different methods of presenting balance sheet and income statement information. Utilize the following objectives as an outline for your study of this material.

1. Explain the meaning of explicit and implicit transactions, and tell why adjustments to the accounts are important.
2. Understand and make adjustments for the expiration of unexpired costs.
3. Understand and make adjustments for the earning of unearned revenues.
4. Understand and make adjustments for the accrual of unrecorded expenses, including accrued wages, interest, and income tax.
5. Understand and make adjustments for the accrual of unrecorded revenues.
6. Give the sequence of final steps in the recording process and describe the relationship between cash flows and adjusting entries.
7. Prepare a classified balance sheet and use the current asset and liability classifications to assess solvency.
8. Prepare single and multiple-step income statements and use ratios based on income statement categories to assess profitability.

REVIEW OF KEY CONCEPTS

A.   This chapter focuses on various types of adjusting entries that companies prepare at year-end. Adjusting entries are a fundamental part of accrual accounting. GAAP requires the use of accrual accounting because it is a better measure of performance than the cash basis. Accrual accounting looks at whether revenues have been earned (and are realized or realizable) and what expenses have been incurred in generating the revenues. Because accrual accounting looks at economic substance, and not the exchange of cash, it is often necessary to adjust the accounts at year-end to reflect implicit transactions. Implicit transactions are events which have taken place but which are unrecorded because there has been no exchange of cash to trigger the recording of an entry. Implicit transactions may be linked to the passage of time (e.g., expiration of prepaid insurance, incurrence of interest expense on a loan, etc.), or the delivery of a good or performance of a service (e.g., delivery of a magazine under a one year prepaid subscription). Adjusting entries can be classified into four categories:

Remember: Adjusting entries always affect **both** balance sheet accounts and income statement accounts.

---

1.   **Adjustments to recognize cost expiration (i.e. assets expiring and becoming expenses)**

   Assets provide the company with future benefits. As the company receives these benefits, the asset is said to expire or to be used up. Prepaid insurance, for example, expires with the passage of time and becomes insurance expense. Depreciation expense, as another example, reflects the benefits received (note the past tense) by the company from a capital asset, such as equipment.

   example one:

entry to establish original asset	*entry to record expiration*
DR **Prepaid Insurance**	DR Insurance expense
CR Cash	CR **Prepaid Insurance**

2.   **Adjustments to reflect earned revenues (i.e. liabilities being satisfied and becoming revenues)**

Companies often receive prepayments from customers for work to be done. Once the company accepts the cash (i.e. an asset), it has an obligation (i.e. a liability- unearned revenue or advance from customer) to perform the work. As goods are delivered or services provided, the company reduces its obligation and earns revenue. An adjusting entry is required to reflect the amount earned.

example two:

entry to establish original liability	*entry to recognize work done*
DR Cash	DR **Unearned revenue**
CR **Unearned revenue**	CR Revenue

3.   **Adjustments to record unrecorded expenses**

These entries are made at the end of the period to recognize expenses that have accrued, or accumulated, over the course of the period, but are unrecorded because they have not been paid. Failure to record these expenses would understate expenses and consequently overstate income for the period.

a.   **Accrued wages** is work that has been done for the company since the last pay date and which must be recorded at year-end to properly match expenses with revenues.

    example three:
    there are 3 work days (at a rate of $ 1,000/day) between the last payroll before year-end and year-end

    year-end accrual 3 X $ 1,000 = $ 3,000
    DR Wage expense   3,000
        CR Wages Payable   3,000

b.   **Accrued interest** is a function of, and accumulates with, the passage of time. Interest represents the cost of having the benefit of an asset, such as the proceeds from a loan, available to contribute to the production of revenue for the period. To be consistent with the matching principle, the cost associated with this benefit, interest, should be matched with revenue and expensed in the period the interest-bearing asset was available, even if the interest payment is not made until a future period.

example four:
the company receives a 12% (annual rate) $ 10,000 bank loan 30 days before year-end and no interest must be paid to the bank for the first six months (note: the bank doesn't require a cash interest payment for the first six months but the company still incurs interest on the loan).

year-end accrual .12 X 1/12 X $ 10,000 = $ 100
DR Interest expense   100
  CR Interest payable   100

c. **Accrued income taxes** represent the recognition of income tax expense associated with the development of income over the course of the period. This tax expense is based on **pretax income**, income before the deduction of income taxes.

example five:
income of $ 100,000 is taxed at 40%

year-end accrual .40 X $ 100,000 = $ 40,000
DR Income tax expense 40,000
  CR Income tax payable 40,000

4. **Adjustments to record or accrue unrecorded revenues**

These entries are made to reflect income earned in the period but not yet recorded in the records. For example, an accountant may perform services for a client during the period but not bill that client until all services have been performed in a future period. Failure to recognize revenue for services performed in the period would understate revenue and net income for the period and overstate revenue and income in the following period when the client is billed.

example six:
10 days before year-end, the company loans $ 200,000 to a senior executive on a temporary basis at 12% interest

year-end accrual .12 X 10/365 days X $ 200,000 = $ 658 (rounded)
DR Interest receivable   658
            CR Interest income   658

See Exhibit 4-1 on page 146 of the text

5.   Understanding the *timing* of cash flows associated with different types of adjusting entries provides a better understanding of the timing of income and expense recognition and the impact on the balance sheet and the income statement.

   a.   Adjusting entries to recognize the expiration of costs (i.e. the expiration of assets) and the realization of unearned revenue (i.e. the fulfillment of an obligation) have a *later* impact on the income statement because the adjustment was made subsequent to the cash flow associated with the initial transactions. This type of transaction would have an initial impact on the balance sheet (see examples one and two above).

   b.   Entries for accrual of unrecorded expenses and the accrual of unrecorded revenues are made before the related cash flow. The income statement is affected *before* the *cash disbursement* is made. (Take a look at examples three, four, five, and six above. You will notice that the year-end accrual affects both the balance sheet and income statement, but the balance sheet effect is a receivable or payable, and not a cash disbursement. This demonstrates a general rule that year-end accruals **never** involve cash.)

B.   The balance sheet provides a picture of the financial position of an entity at a particular point in time. A **classified balance sheet** groups balance sheet accounts into related categories, listing them in order of liquidity. These categories include current assets, current liabilities, long-term assets, long-term liabilities, and shareholders' equity. This is done in an effort to facilitate analysis of the entity's financial position and draw attention to major balance sheet classifications.

1. **Current assets** are assets that are expected to be liquidated, or turned into cash within one year or one operating cycle if the operating cycle is longer than one year. Examples of current assets include: cash, accounts receivable, short-term marketable securities, inventory, and prepaid expenses.

2. **Current liabilities** are obligations of the business which are expected to fall due within one year or one operating cycle of the firm if the operating cycle is greater than one year. Examples include: accounts payable, accrued taxes, accrued wages, and the current portion of long-term obligations.

3. **Working capital** is defined as the excess of current assets over current liabilities.

4. The **current ratio** provides an indication of an entity's ability to meet its obligations as they come due. In other words, how solvent is this company? The level of the ratio of current assets to current liabilities is relevant when compared to other companies in the same industry or when compared to the historical trend of the company's current ratio.

$$\text{Current ratio} = \frac{\text{Current assets}}{\text{Current liabilities}}$$

C. The income statement may be presented in a manner that highlights certain accounts or groups of accounts. The two most widely used formats are the single and multi-step income statements. Choice of format is dependent on the amount of detail required by the intended reader.

1. The **single-step income statement** groups all revenues together and lists all expenses together to produce income for the period. No intermediate subtotals are calculated. This type of statement would probably be appropriate for shareholder reporting.

2.   The **multi-step income statement** is designed to highlight significant income statement relationships. Examples include the relationship between sales, cost of goods sold and gross profit and the grouping of operating expenses to be deducted in the determination of operating income.

    a.   **Gross margin** is the excess of sales revenue over the cost of the inventory sold during the period. From gross profit, operating expenses are deducted to arrive at income from operations before taxes.

    b.   From operating income, nonoperating income is added and nonoperating expenses are subtracted to arrive at pretax income. Taxes are determined based on the pretax income and deducted from pretax income to arrive at net income.

> See Exhibit 4-8 on page 155 of the text for examples of both a single and multi-step income statement

D.   Utilizing income statement information makes it possible to determine potential rates of return to investors through the process of **profitability evaluation**. Three of the most popular indicators of return are the gross profit percentage, the return on sales ratio, and the return on stockholders' equity ratio.

1.   The **gross profit percentage** is useful for pricing strategy decisions, trend analysis for monitoring purposes, and can be used as a basis for estimating ending inventory value.

$$\text{Gross margin percentage} = \frac{\text{Gross profit}}{\text{Sales}}$$

2.   The **return on sales ratio** indicates the relationship between net income and sales revenue. This gives the reader an indication of the return on sales after all expenses for the period have been deducted. This would be compared to other companies in the same industry and to historical trends for the company being examined.

$$\text{Return on sales} = \frac{\text{Net income}}{\text{Sales}}$$

3.   The **return on shareholders' equity ratio** gives the user an indication of the return based on invested capital. Again, this return is useful when compared to other companies in the same industry and useful when compared to historical trends.

$$\text{Return on Shareholders' equity} = \frac{\text{Net income}}{\text{Avg. shareholders' equity}}$$

PRACTICE TEST QUESTIONS AND EXERCISES

I   **True or false** - For each of the following statements, enter a T or an F in the space provided to indicate whether the statement is true or false.

_____   1.   Realization of unearned revenue is an explicit transaction and would not be accomplished through an adjusting entry.

_____   2.   Year-end adjustments are necessary because of accrual accounting.

_____ 3. Cash disbursed for equipment has an initial impact on the balance sheet and a subsequent impact on the income statement after an adjusting entry for depreciation is made.

_____ 4. Failure to make an adjusting entry to recognize unrecorded revenue would overstate net income and understate revenue for the period.

_____ 5. Just as adjusting entries are made to recognize revenues and expenses in accrual accounting, adjusting entries are used for the same reason in the cash basis of accounting.

_____ 6. The current ratio may be used to evaluate the solvency of a particular firm.

_____ 7. Implicit transactions, unlike explicit transactions, cannot be reliably or objectively determined.

_____ 8. On a classified balance sheet, an asset that is expected to provide future benefit beyond the next period would be classified as a current asset.

_____ 9. Income taxes payable is an example of a current liability.

_____ 10. The accrual of interest by an adjusting entry is caused by the passage of time.

_____ 11. Season ticket proceeds would be recognized as revenue in the period that the event is staged.

_____ 12. Adjusting entries sometimes involve a debit or credit to the cash account.

_____ 13. Unexpired costs are assets. Expired costs are expenses.

_____ 14. Preparation of the adjusted trial balance is the final procedure undertaken in the accounting cycle prior to preparation of the financial statements.

_____ 15. Adjusting entries affect either income statement or balance sheet account but rarely both.

Accounting Adjustments and Financial Statement Preparations

II   **Multiple choice -** For the following multiple choice questions, select the best answer and enter the identifying letter in the space provided.

_____ 1.   On September 1, 19X3 your company borrowed $10,000 at 12% from the local bank. The principle and interest is due on February 1, 19x4. The adjusting entry on December 31, 19x3 would include:

    a.   Debit interest payable $1,200
    b.   Debit interest expense $400
    c.   Debit interest receivable $400
    d.   Debit interest expense $1,200

_____ 2.   On December 20, 19X6 the payroll expense account balance totalled $62,960. During the period from December 21 to December 31, 19X6, 125 hours were worked by the employees at a wage rate of $12 per hour. Wages are due to be paid to the employees on January 3, 19X7. What is the balance in the payroll expense account after all adjustments on December 31, 19X6?

    a. $62,960
    b. $ 1,500
    c. $61,460
    d. $64,460

_____ 3.   Van Dillon Express had cost of goods sold totaling $412,000 and a gross profit percentage of 44%. What are Van Dillon's total sales?

    a. $821,210
    b. $936,364
    c. $735,714
    d. $679,080

_____ 4.   During 19X2 sales totalled $612,000, gross margin was $165,540 and operating expenses totalled $109,000. What was the gross profit percentage and return on sales ratio respectively?
    a.   9.2%, 17.8%
    b.   27.0%, 9.2%
    c.   73.0%, 9.2%
    d.   27.0%, 17.8%

Chapter 4

_____ 5. If Stewart Nicholson Advertising had $750,000 in common equity, a target return to investors of 23% and a return on sales ratio of 5% what level of sales must be achieved next year?

   a. $4,125,000
   b. $3,450,000
   c. $3,550,000
   d. Cannot determine with information given

_____ 6. During June of 19X1, the law firm of Howard, Fine, and Howard finished work on a case for Curly Joe. A resolution was due on the case by July 15, 19X1, at which time the firm would bill Curly Joe for $40,000. What adjusting entry would you make at the end of June 19X1 for the interim statements?

   a. None
   b. Accounts receivable   40,000
          Fee revenue   40,000
   c. Cash   40,000
          Fee revenue   40,000
   d. Fee revenue   40,000
          Accounts receivable   40,000

_____ 7. Accountants usually show interest revenue and interest expense on a multi-step income statement,

   a. Above operating income
   b. Below operating income
   c. Below pretax income
   d. Above gross profit

_____ 8. You have applied to Last Chance National Bank for a loan. After reviewing your financial statements, the bank agreed to make the loan if you would agree to restrict your current ratio to not less than 2.5. If your current assets are at $385,000, what is the maximum amount of current debt you may carry on your books?

   a. $712,000
   b. $962,500
   c. $221,000
   d. $154,000

III   Problems

Problem 1:
Perfect Party Rentals Ltd., completed its first year of operations on December 31, 19X1. The company bookkeeper prepared the following draft income statement:

Income Statement

Rental revenue		$102,000
Expenses:		
Salaries and wages	$26,400	
Cleaning expense	10,000	
Repair expense	8,000	
Telephone & Utilities expense	3,000	
Delivery expense	2,000	
Miscellaneous expense (items not listed above)	400	
Total expenses		49,800
Income		$ 52,200

You are asked to review the income statement for possible adjustments. You are also given the following additional information:

1. Wages for the last three days of December amounting to $600 have not been recorded or paid (disregard employee benefits).
2. The telephone bill for December amounting to $200 has not been recorded or paid.
3. Depreciation of $ 20,000, on the tables the company rents out for parties, has not been recorded.
4. Interest on a $20,000, one-year, 12% note payable dated November 1, 19X1, has not been recorded. The 12% interest is payable on the maturity date of the note.
5. Rental revenue includes $2,000 received in advance for rentals to take place during the month of January, 19X2.
6. Cleaning expense includes $1,000, which is the cost of maintenance supplies still on hand (per inventory) at December 31, 19X1. These supplies will be used in 19X2.
7. The income tax rate is 20%. Payment of income tax will be made in 19X2.

Required:
a. Give the adjusting journal entries required at December 31, 19X1.
b. Prepare a correct income statement for 19X1.

Chapter 4

Problem 2:

Earth-Guard Ltd., a distributor of environmentally friendly products, had the following account balances at January 1, 19X3.

Account Title	Debit	Credit
Cash	$ 1,640	
Accounts Receivable	1,940	
Allowance for Doubtful Accounts		$ 94
Prepaid Insurance	95	
Supplies Inventory	105	
Truck	10,700	
Accumulated Depreciation, Truck		3,325
Accounts Payable		970
Interest Payable		210
Note Payable		3,500
Common Stock		3,000
Retained Earnings		3,381
Total	$ 14,480	$14,480

Transactions completed during January are summarized below:

1. Sales revenue from cleaning products of $14,300 was earned during the month; $11,970 of this total was received in cash. The remainder represented transactions on account.
2. Sales revenue from health products amounted to $12,700. Cash received totalled $3,400, and accounts receivable increased by $9,300.
3. Supplies costing $170 were purchased during the month on account.
4. On January 1st, the company paid the interest on the note payable which was outstanding from the previous year.
5. Gas and oil for the delivery truck, paid for in cash, totalled $1,340.
6. The insurance policy on the truck expired January 31, 19X3. During January, the company bought a replacement insurance policy for one year and paid the premium of $ 420 in advance.
7. Telephone expense of $1,120 was paid.
8. Accounts receivable of $6,950 were collected.
9. Salaries and wages totalling $ 16,460 were paid.
10. The President, Ms. Green, purchased a home computer for $2,000 on January 15, 19X3 by writing a cheque on her savings account.

Other Information:

1. A physical count of the supplies showed supplies costing $90 on hand at January 31, 19X3.

74

2.   Interest on the note payable is at the rate of 12% per annum.
3.   The truck was purchased July 1, 1989. It is depreciated on a straight line basis.
      (Hint: it has been used 3.5 years as at January 1, 19X3)
4.   The January 1993 telephone bill for $90 has not been paid or recorded.

Required:
Using the above information do the following
a.   Prepare all the necessary journal entries (including adjusting entries) to record the above transactions and events. For any items not requiring an entry, explain **briefly** why no entry is necessary.
b.   Prepare an income statement for the month ended January 31, 19X3 and a balance sheet as at January 31, 19X3. (You may find it helpful to use t-accounts to summarize the transactions and to determine account balances.)

Problem 3:
National Trucking Ltd., a freight company operating throughout Canada, has the following unadjusted trial balance at June 30, 19X3. The adjusting entries and the financial statements are prepared on a monthly basis.

National Trucking Ltd.
Unadjusted Trial Balance
June 30, 19X3

Cash	$23,600	
Accounts receivable	7,200	
Prepaid rent	9,600	
Prepaid insurance	21,000	
Trucks	1,200,000	
Accumulated depreciation: trucks		$380,000
Notes payable		600,000
Advances from customers		60,000
Common stock		100,000
Retained earnings		130,850
Dividends	7,000	
Freight revenue		130,950
Fuel expense	53,800	
Salaries expense	66,700	
Maintenance expense	12,900	
	$1,401,800	$1,401,800

75

Chapter 4

Other information:

1. The company is a little late in its billing for the month. No entry has been made to record $4,600 of freight revenue earned during June but not yet billed.
2. The prepaid rent was paid on June 1 and is for three months.
3. On April 1, a 12-month insurance policy had been purchased for $25,200.
4. The trucks are being depreciated over a period of 10 years.
5. During June, $38,650 of the advances from customers was earned as the company completed some routes into remote areas of Newfoundland.
6. Salaries earned by employees but not yet recorded or paid amount to $3,300 at June 30.
7. There is accrued interest on notes payable of $5,000 at June 30 which has not yet been recorded.

Required:

a. Based on the above information, prepare the adjusting entries.
b. Prepare an income statement for the month of June and a balance sheet as at the end of June. (Don't forget to take the opening account balances into consideration.)

> For additional practice preparing adjusting entries see Lotus Template files P4-26.wk1, P4-28.wk1 and P4-29.wk1. For practice preparing financial statements see files P4-37.wk1 and P4-38.wk1.

CHAPTER 4 ANSWERS AND SOLUTIONS

I True or False

1. False   Realization of unearned revenue is one of the four categories of adjusting entries and arises because it is not part of the normal day-to-day explicit transactions.
2. True
3. True
4. False   Failure to adjust for unrecorded revenue would understate revenue and as a consequence net income as well.
5. False   Recognition of revenues and expenses is part of the accrual basis of accounting. The cash basis recognizes revenue when cash is received and recognizes expenses when cash is paid. The cash basis only recognizes explicit transactions.

6. True   To be meaningful, ratios have to be compared to a benchmark (e.g., past performance or competitor's performance)

7. False   Recognition of implicit transactions is not triggered by an event, like the exchange of cash, but the "facts" used to determine the amount of the adjustment are objectively determined (e.g. the amount of wage expense to accrue at year-end)

8. False   Current assets are assets that are expected to be liquidated within one year or one operating cycle if the operating cycle is longer than one year.

9. True

10. True

11. True

12. False   Adjusting entries, by definition, never involve cash. This is because adjusting entries deal with implicit transactions which, by definition, either preceed or are preceeded by actual cash flows.

13. True

14. True

15. False   Adjusting entries affect **both** the balance sheet and the income statement.

II   Multiple choice

1. B   Time has passed since September 1, 19x3 triggering the implicit accrual of interest for 4 months. Interest expense is calculated as $10,000 x .12 x 4/12 = $400.

2. D   Payroll expense for the last part of December are expenses of December even if they are not paid until January.

Hours worked	125	Begin. bal. payroll	$62,960
rate per hour	x 12	Dec. addition	1,500
Payroll	$1,500	Adjusted balance	$64,460

3. C   Since Van Dillon's gross profit is 44%, their cost of goods sold percentage is 56% of sales.
.56 (sales) = $ 412,000
sales = $ 412,000/.56 = $ 735,714

4. B   Gross profit/Sales = Gross profit percentage
$ 165,540/$ 612,000 = 27%
Gross profit - expenses = net income
$ 165,540 - $ 109,000 = $ 56,540
Net income/Sales = Return on Sales Ratio
$ 56,540/$ 612,000 = 9.2%

Chapter 4

5.   B   ROE = Net income/Shareholders' equity
            .23 = Net income/ $ 750,000
            Net income = $ 750,000 X .23 = $ 172,500, then,
            Return on sales = Net income/Sales
            .05 = $ 172,500/Sales
            Sales = $ 172,500/.05 = <u>$ 3,450,000</u>

6.   B   The fees have been earned by providing the services and are realizable, therefore, the revenue should be recognized in this period.

7.   B   Interest expense and interest income are generally segregated from operations to highlight both the results from normal operations and the existence and amount of additions and subtractions made to achieve the "bottom line", net profit.

8.   D   Current ratio = Current assets/Current liabilities
            2.5 = $ 385,000/Current liabilities
            Current liabilities = <u>$ 154,000</u>

III   Problems

Problem 1:

a. adjusting journal entries:

1.	DR Wage expense	600	
	CR Wages payable		600
2.	DR Telephone expense	200	
	CR Accounts payable		200
3.	DR Depreciation expense	20,000	
	CR Accumulated depreciation		20,000
4.	DR Interest expense*	400	
	CR Interest payable		400

        *.12 X 2/12 months X $20,000 = $400

5.	DR Rental revenue	2,000	
	CR Unearned rent		2,000
6.	DR Supplies inventory	1,000	
	CR Cleaning expense		1,000
7.	DR Income tax expense* (.2 X 30,000)	6,000	
	CR Income tax payable		6,000

* see income statement for income before taxes of $ 30,000

Perfect Party Rentals Ltd.
Income Statement
For the year ended December 31, 19X1

Rental revenue ($102,000-2,000)		100,000
Expenses:		
Salaries ($26,400+600)	27,000	
Depreciation expense	20,000	
Cleaning expense ($10,000-1000)	9,000	
Repair expense	8,000	
Tel. & Utilities (3,000+200)	3,200	
Delivery expense	2,000	
Misc. expense	400	
Interest expense	400	70,000
Net income before tax		30,000
Less income tax expense (20%)		6,000
Net income		24,000

Problem 2:

1)	DR Cash	11,970	
	DR Accounts Receivable	2,330	
	CR Revenue - cleaning products		14,300
2)	DR Cash	3,400	
	DR Accounts Receivable	9,300	
	CR Revenue - health products		12,700
3)	DR Supplies Inventory	170	
	CR Accounts Payable		170
	or		
	DR Supplies Expense	170	
	CR Accounts Payable		170
4)	DR Interest Payable	210	
	CR Cash		210

5) DR Truck Expense   1,340
    CR Cash   1,340

6) DR Insurance Expense   95
    CR Prepaid Insurance   95

    DR Prepaid Expense   420
    CR Cash   420

7) DR Telephone Expense   1,120
    CR Cash   1,120

8) DR Cash   6,950
    CR Accounts Receivable   6,950

9) DR Salaries and Wage Expense   16,460
    CR Cash   16,460

10) no entry - the assets of the owners' are kept separate from the assets of the business

Adjusting Entries:

1) If the purchase of supplies was recorded as an increase in **inventory**, then the adjusting entry is:

    DR Supplies Expense   185
    CR Supplies Inventory   185

If the purchase was recorded as an **expense**, then the adjusting entry is:

    DR Supplies Expense*   15
    CR Supplies Inventory   15

*there was a balance in the inventory account of $105 at the beginning of the year - this must be reduced to $90 (ending inventory).

2) DR Interest Expense (.12 X 1/12 year X $3,500)   35
    CR Interest payable   35

3) DR Depreciation Expense ([3325 acc. dep./3.5 years] /12 months)   79
    CR Accumulated Depreciation   79

4) DR Telephone Expense   90
    CR Accounts Payable   90

Earth-Guard Ltd.
Balance Sheet
As At January 31, 1993

Current Assets:		
Cash		4,410
Accounts Receivable	6,620	
Less Allowance	(94)	6,526
Supplies Inventory		90
Prepaid Insurance		420
Total Current Assets		11,446
Non-Current Assets:		
Truck	10,700	
Less Acc. Depreciation	(3,404)	7,296
Total Assets		18,742
Current Liabilities:		
Accounts Payable		1,230
Interest Payable		35
Total Current Liabilities		1,265
Note Payable		3,500
Total Liabilities		4,765
Shareholders' Equity		
Common Stock		3,000
Retained Earnings (3,381 + 7,596)		10,977
Total Shareholders' Equity		13,977
Total Liabilities and Equity		18,742

Earth-Guard Ltd.
Income Statement
For the Month Ended January 31, 1993

Revenue (14,300 + 12,700)		$27,000
Less Expenses:		
Salaries and Wage Expense	16,460	
Truck Expense	1,340	
Telephone Expense	1,210	
Depreciation Expense	79	
Insurance Expense	95	
Supplies Expense	185	19,369
Operating Income		7,631
Less Interest Expense		35
Net Income Before Tax		$ 7,596

Problem 3:

General Journal (Adjusting Entries)

19X3	(1)		
June 30	Accounts Receivable	4600	
	Freight Revenue		4600

To record unrecorded freight revenue earned during the month during June.

	(2)		
June 30	Rent Expense	3200	
	Prepaid Rent		3200

Rental expense for the month.

	(3)		
June 30	Insurance Expense	2100	
	Prepaid Insurance		2100

Insurance expense for the month ($25,200/12 months).

(4)

| June 30 | Depreciation Expense: Aircraft | 10000 | |
| | Accumulated Depreciation: Aircraft | | 10000 |

Depreciation expense for the month of June (1,200,000/10 year X 1/12).

(5)

| June 30 | Advances from Customers | 38650 | |
| | Freight Revenue | | 38650 |

Freight revenue collected in advance but earned during June.

(6)

| June 30 | Salaries Expense | 3300 | |
| | Salaries Payable | | 3300 |

Salaries earned but not yet recorded or paid during month.

(7)

| June 30 | Interest Expense | 5000 | |
| | Interest Payable | | 5000 |

Interest expense accrued during the month.

National Trucking Ltd.
Income Statement
For the Month Ended June 30, 19X3

Revenue:	$174,200
Expenses:	
Fuel expense	$53,800
Salaries expense	70,000
Maintenance expense	12,900
Rent expense	3,200
Insurance expense	2,100
Depreciation expense: trucks	10,000
Interest expense	5,000
Total expenses	157,000
Net income	$17,200

National Trucking Ltd.
Statement of Retained Earnings*
For the Month Ended June 30, 19X3

Opening balance, June 1, 19X3	$130,850
Add: Net income	17,200
Subtotal	$148,050
Less: Dividends	7,000
Ending balance, June 30, 19X3	$141,050

* not required

National Trucking Ltd.
Balance Sheet
June 30, 19X3

Assets

Cash		$23,600
Accounts receivable		11,800
Prepaid rent		6,400
Prepaid insurance		18,900
Trucks	1,200,000	
Less: Accumulated depreciation: trucks	390,000	810,000
Total assets		$870,700

Liabilities & Shareholders'Equity

Liabilities:	
Notes payable	$600,000
Advances from Customers	21,350
Salaries payable	3,300
Interest payable	5,000
Total liabilities	$629,650
Shareholders' equity:	
Common stock	$100,000
Retained earnings	141,050
Total liabilities & shareholders' equity	$870,700

Chapter 5

Accounting Cycle:
Recording and
Formal
Presentation

Managers who possess a good understanding of the accounting cycle are in a position to better understand, and effectively utilize the end product of the cycle, the financial statements. Your goal upon completion of this chapter is to possess a better understanding of the cycle, the importance of the statement of cash flows, and the use of special journals to process large numbers of transactions. Use of the following learning objectives as an outline will provide a convenient reference for your analysis of this chapter.

1. Explain the accounting cycle and analyze transactions, including those that relate to the adjustments of the preceding period.
2. Analyze cash transactions used in the statement of cash flows.
3. Prepare closing entries for pertinent accounts.
4. Explain the role of auditors of financial statements.
5. Correct erroneous entries and describe how errors affect accounts.
6. Use T-accounts to aid the discovery of unknown amounts.
7. Use a worksheet to prepare adjustments, financial statements, and closing entries (Appendix 5A).
8. Prepare adjustments when alternative recording methods are used for the related originating transactions (Appendix 5B).
9. Use special journals to process transactions (Appendix 5C).

Chapter 5

REVIEW OF KEY CONCEPTS

A. The **accounting cycle** is the process by which transactions are analyzed, recorded, quantified, summarized, and reported. This process is accomplished within the framework of concepts supporting the accrual basis of accounting and ultimately leads to production of financial statements. The steps in the accounting cycle may be summarized as follows:

1. **Journalize** the transactions. The process of journalization forces analysis of the transaction prior to entry in the "book of original entry", the journal.

2. **Post to the ledger.** Remember, the posting process consolidates transactions that are similar in nature and provides a record of all the changes that have occurred during the period to a particular account.

3. **Trial balance.** The trial balance is composed of the ending balance in all accounts, both permanent and temporary. The trial balance ensures dollar-value equality between accounts having debit balances and accounts with credit balances.

4. **Make adjustments.** Analyze, journalize, and post adjustments and corrections to the records.

5. **Adjusted trial balance.** The adjusted trial balance, again ensures adjustments that were made have dollar-value equality between debits and credits.

6. **Prepare formal statements.** At this point the income statement and the balance sheet are prepared, as well as the statement of changes in shareholders' equity, and the statement of cash flows.

7. **Close all temporary accounts.** All temporary accounts are closed to an income summary account, which is then closed to retained earnings.

8. **Prepare a post-closing trial balance.** This ensures all temporary accounts have been closed to permanent accounts and that permanent accounts have been updated for the following period.

Before you proceed, carefully work through the textbook presentation of a practical exercise in the accounting cycle. Compare your work with the detailed analysis of transactions presented after Exhibit 5-7 on page 182 of the text.

B. Only the board of directors has the authority to declare a dividend. A dividend cannot be paid by the company until it is declared.

1. **Dividends declared** is a temporary shareholders' equity account used by some companies to accumulate dividends during the period. The Dividends Declared account carries a debit balance and reduces Retained Earnings when it is closed at the end of the period.

2. **Dividends payable** is a current liability. Its existence indicates that the books were closed after the declaration of the dividend, but before payment was made.

See page 189 of the text for journal entry examples.

C. The statement of cash flows provides a reconciliation of the change in the cash account from the beginning of the period to the end. It provides answers to the questions; what was the source of our cash during the last period? and what did we spend it on? The statement classifies activities involving cash into three categories:

1. **Operating activities.** Cash flow from operating activities involves the receipt of cash from customers and the disbursement of cash for operating purposes during the period. It is essentially a reconciliation of net income from the accrual basis of accounting to a cash measure of operations.

2. **Investing activities.** What cash flows resulted from the purchase or sale of *long-term assets*? Examples include the acquisition of new plant facilities, and the sale of long-term investments in another company's stock.

3.   **Financing activities**. What cash flows resulted from activities associated with *long-term liabilities* and the sale and/or retirement of common stock? Payment of dividends would be included in financing activities.

> See Exhibit 5-8 on page 190 of the text

D.   Closing the books is the process of transferring balances in **temporary accounts** (income statement accounts and dividends) to Retained Earnings. The closing entries are necessary in order to physically put the amount of income or loss into retained earnings. The closing entries also serve to clear the income statement accounts to zero and prepare these accounts to accumulate information for the next accounting period. This is necessary because the income statement accounts measure performance for a period of time, say 12 months, and not on a cumulative basis over the life of the firm. The closing process is facilitated by the use of an **Income Summary account**.

As a simple example, imagine the following income statement for a service company:

Service revenue	$	320,000
Salary expense		180,000
Net income	$	140,000

the **closing entries** are as follows:

DR Service revenue	320,000	
CR Income summary		320,000
DR Income summary	180,000	
CR Salary expense		180,000
DR Income Summary *	140,000	
CR Retained earnings		140,000

* to clear the net credit balance to retained earnings

The income summary account is a bookkeeping convenience. It is not a real account, in that it never appears in the financial statements. It is only used for the closing process. It is possible to close the books without making use of an income summary account. The closing entry to achieve this is as follows:

DR Service revenue	320,000	
CR Salary expense		180,000
CR Retained earnings		140,000

At this point you should review Exhibit 5-9 on page 192 and the detailed analysis of closing transactions beginning on page 193. Match the transactions with the closing sequence summarized above.

E.   Management is responsible for the company's published financial statements. These statements are used by investors, creditors, the government, etc. to make decisions relative to that particular business. **Audited financial statements** provide an independent opinion as to the "fairness" of the financial statements in conformity with generally accepted accounting principles.

   1.   In Canada, audits are conducted by independent auditors that have been certified by the Canadian Institute of Chartered Accountants (CICA).

   2.   The function of the auditor is to express an opinion on whether the financial statements have been prepared according to GAAP. Auditors make use of standard audit procedures as outlined by the CICA, and they verify transactions on a test basis.

F.   Part of the reason for different steps in the accounting cycle is to detect errors in the process. When **errors** occur they may be either characterized as **counterbalanced** errors or **non-counterbalanced** errors.

   1.   **Counterbalanced errors** are offset by errors in the normal bookkeeping process of the following period. They would misstate income in both periods but would only affect the balance sheet in the period of the original mistake. At the end of the second period, retained earnings and the rest of the balance sheet will be correct (e.g., an unrecorded wage accrual at the end of year 10 would cause year 10 income to be overstated, year 11 income will be understated because the year 10 wages are recorded

incorrectly as an expense in year 11 when they are paid, finally retained earnings at the end of year 11 - after the closing entries - will reflect the proper balance because the income overstatement from year 10 is balanced out by the year 11 understatement).

2. **Non-counterbalanced errors** would not be corrected in the subsequent period. All subsequent balance sheets would be in error until the correction is made (e.g., unrecorded depreciation expense misstates the income statement in the year of the omission, and until the error is corrected, accumulated depreciation on the balance sheet will be understated and retained earnings will be overstated).

> See the examples on page 199 of the text

> Before you continue, review once again the steps in the accounting cycle. Specifically the steps involved in closing the books at the end of the period. Is the function of the Income Summary account clear to you?

G. The **worksheet** is a 10 column tool available to assist in preparation of adjustments to the unadjusted trial balance and ultimately the balance sheet and income statement. The normal procedure for completion of the worksheet is:

1. Prepare the unadjusted trial balance from the account totals in the general ledger.

2. Make adjustments to the appropriate accounts in the adjustments columns. By "keying" these adjustments they may be used in the preparation of the adjusting journal entries.

3. The adjusted trial balance provides the basis for preparation of the income statement and the balance sheet.

4. At this point it is only necessary to carry adjusted account balances over to the appropriate statement.

5.   Development of the income statement figures provides the net income (loss) total used to update retained earnings on the balance sheet.

6.   Income statement and retained earnings balances from the worksheet generally provide the basis for preparation of the closing entries.

H.   A variety of acceptable procedures are available for classifying and processing accounting data during the period. The factor having the greatest impact on a chosen procedure is **cost-benefit**.

1.   The "full amount" approach treats all cash disbursements as expenses only to be adjusted to the correct amount at the end of the period.

e.g., record the prepayment of rent as an expense and at year-end set up the unexpired portion as an asset

original entry   **year-end adjustment**
DR Rent expense   DR Prepaid rent
    CR Cash   CR Rent expense

2.   **Reversing entries** are made at the beginning of the next accounting period. The year-end adjusting entry is reversed (e.g., year-end accrual for interest expense). The reversal creates a non-normal balance in the account (i.e. for an expense account the reversal would create a credit balance) because the reversal is made after the closing entries (i.e. the income statement account has a zero balance prior to the reversal). The rationale is that when the cash payment is made in the new accounting period, the company does not have to worry about allocating the payment between an expense (interest expense for the new period, if any) and a liability (the interest payable set up in the prior year's adjusting entry). In the case of an interest payment, the total amount of the payment is debited to interest expense and the credit created by the reversing entry lowers the expense to the true amount applicable to the current period.

See Exhibit 5-11 on page 210 of the text

Chapter 5

I. **Special Journals** are used to process large numbers of transactions that exhibit similar characteristics. Two special journals discussed in the text are the **sales journal** and the **cash receipts journal.**

   1. The **sales journal** only includes transactions involving *credit sales*. As a result only two accounts, accounts receivable and sales are involved. All credit sales are accumulated in a single column and one entry for the total is made at the end of the period in the appropriate general ledger account.

> See Exhibit 5-12 on page 212 of the text

   2. The **cash receipts journal** records all receipts of cash, no matter the source. A column for cash receipts is maintained, the total of which will become a debit to the cash account at the end of the period. Separate columns are maintained for other accounts that exhibit a larger number of transactions, such as accounts receivable.

> See Exhibit 5-13 on page 214 of the text

PRACTICE TEST QUESTIONS AND EXERCISES

I True or False - For each of the following statements, enter a T or an F in the space provided to indicate whether the statement is true or false.

_____ 1. While the worksheet is useful it cannot be used to determine net income for the period.

_____ 2. The journal entry closing the accounts having debit balances would include a debit to Income Summary.

_____ 3. Dividends Declared is closed to Income Summary which is then closed to Retained Earnings.

_____ 4. Accumulated depreciation is an example of a temporary account.

_____ 5. When using special journals it is not necessary to maintain a general journal.

_____ 6. The purpose of the independent auditor is to verify that all transactions and balances reported on the financial statements are true and correct.

_____ 7. One of the functions of the statement of cash flows is to reconcile the change in the cash account from the beginning to the end of the period.

_____ 8. Dividends Declared normally has a credit balance and represents a reduction in retained earnings and shareholders' equity.

_____ 9. Upon declaration by the board of directors, a dividend becomes a legal liability of the corporation.

_____ 10. An error that is not counterbalanced in the ordinary course of the next period's bookkeeping process would affect all subsequent balance sheets until corrected.

_____ 11. Unearned revenue is an example of a permanent account.

_____ 12. Cash flows from operating activities would include receipts from customers and payments to suppliers.

II Multiple choice - For the following multiple choice questions, select the best answer and enter the identifying letter in the space provided.

_____ 1. To close payroll expense you would:

    a. Debit the Payroll Expense account
    b. Credit the Payroll Expense account
    c. Credit the Income Summary account
    d. Credit Retained Earnings

_____   2.   If a company has revenues of $ 150,000 and expenses of $160,000, the final step in the closing process would be to:

       a.   debit income summary and credit retained earnings for $10,000

       b.   credit income summary for $160,000 and debit expenses for $160,000

       c.   credit income summary and debit retained earnings for $10,000

       d.   credit income summary for $150,000 and debit the revenue account(s) for $150,000

_____   3.   After completion of the post-closing trial balance the following account would have a zero balance.

       a.   Accumulated depreciation

       b.   Sales

       c.   Wages payable

       d.   Retained Earnings

_____   4.   Charlotte forgot to make an adjusting entry recognizing depreciation expense for year 1. The effect of this error would be to:

       a.   Understate net income in year 1.

       b.   Understate retained earnings in year 1.

       c.   Understate retained earnings in year 2.

       d.   Overstate retained earnings in year 2.

_____   5.   The company failed to accrue interest revenue in year 10. The interest was subsequently received in year 11 and recorded as revenue. The effect of this error would be to:

       a.   overstate year 10 income, overstate year 11 income

       b.   overstate year 10 income, understate year 11 income

       c.   understate year 10 income, overstate year 11 income

       d.   understate year 10 income, understate year 11 income

6. The error in question 5 above had the following effect on the **year 10** balance sheet:

   a. interest receivable and retained earnings were overstated
   b. interest receivable was understated and retained earnings were overstated
   c. no effect
   d. interest receivable was understated and retained earnings were understated

7. The error in question 5 had the following effect on the **year 11** balance sheet:

   a. interest revenue was overstated and retained earnings were overstated
   b. cash was overstated and retained earnings were overstated
   c. no effect - the balance sheet at the end of year 11 is correct
   d. interest receivable is understated, cash is overstated, and retained earnings are correct

8. The closing process is used to:

   a. Reset the asset and liability accounts to zero so they will be ready for the new period.
   b. Reset shareholders' equity to zero so it will be ready for the new period.
   c. Undo the effects of an adjusting entry made at the end of the last period.
   d. Reset the revenue and expense meters back to zero so the accounts will be ready for the new period.

9. Mrs. O'Leary had a fire in her barn. Calculate the amount of **total purchases** during 1992 from the following partial records:

accounts payable balance, Jan. 1, 19X2	$ 45,000
accounts payable balance, Dec. 31, 19X2	53,000
cash payments to suppliers during 1992	245,000

   a. $253,000
   b. $245,000
   c. $237,000
   d. $256,000

_____ 10. Cash payments made for interest on a long-term loan would be classified on the statement of cash flows as:

     a.   Investing activity
     b.   Operating activity
     c.   Financing activity
     d.   Recreational activity

_____ 11. The company records a new one year insurance policy as a debit to insurance expense for $ 2,400. Three months later, at year-end, the adjusting entry would be:

     a.   DR Insurance expense   600
                  CR Prepaid insurance   600
     b.   DR Prepaid insurance   600
                  CR Insurance expense   600
     c.   DR Prepaid insurance   1800
                  CR Insurance expense   1800
     d.   DR Prepaid insurance   1600
                  CR Insurance expense   1600

_____ 12. The company accrues wage expense of $ 25,000 at the end of year 10. In January of year 11, the company pays employees $ 160,000. The payment includes an advance to one employee for $ 10,000. Wage expense for January of year 11 is:

     a. $ 150,000
     b. $ 125,000
     c. $ 175,000
     d. $ 135,000

III   Problems

Problem 1:

Hannegan Hardware took the following information from their adjusted trial balance prior to closing on June 30, 19X3;

Sales	$ 512,000
Cost of goods sold	357,000
Rent expense	31,000
Salaries expense	57,000
Depreciation expense	21,000
Rental property revenue	13,000
Dividends declared	7,000
Beg. balance, Retained Earnings, 7/1/**X2**	3,000

Required:

a.   Prepare the proper closing entries for 19X3.

b.   Compute net income for 19X3 utilizing the Income Summary account.

c.   What is the balance in Retained Earnings at 7/1/19**X3**?

Problem 2:

Hart Sporting Goods reported the following cash transactions for 19X4.

Cash receipts from customers	$ 400,000
Cash payments to suppliers	220,000
Cash payments for interest	15,000
Cash purchase of new equipment	125,000
Cash dividends	5,000
Sale of common stock	100,000
Cash payments for other operating expenses	100,000
Beginning cash balance	50,000
Ending cash balance	85,000

Required:

Prepare a statement of cash flows (use textbook Exhibit 5-8 as an example).

Chapter 5

Problem 3:

Construct the adjusting entry required for each of the following independent scenarios: {Hint: based on the information given, calculate the correct balance sheet (asset or liability) and income statement (expense or revenue) amounts, look at the actual account balances and then create the adjusting entry which is necessary to shift the balance from the balance sheet account (e.g., prepaid rent) to the income statement account (rent expense) or vice versa}.

a) It is company practice to debit all cash payments made for wages to the Wage Expense account. During June, the company paid $ 50,000 in wages and accounted for them according to this policy. At the end of June, the controller estimates that the company owes wages of $ 3,000 for work done during June. This amount will be paid with the next regular payroll which is in early July. The controller also notices that the Wages Payable account has a balance of $ 2,000 for wages accrued at the end of May. There have been no entries to this account during the month of June.

b) At the beginning of 19X2, the company had a $ 15,000 balance in the Unearned Rent account. The amount represented rent that had been prepaid by tenants during 19X1. During 19X2, the company collected $ 100,000 in rental payments and credited the entire amount to Rental Revenue. At the end of 19X2, the company calculates that only $ 90,000 of the rental payments received were actually earned during the year, and the remainder represents prepayments for 19X3. There have been no entries to the Unearned Rent account during the year.

c) The December 31st, 19X7, balance sheet of the company showed four months Prepaid Rent of $ 24,000. On May 1, 19X8, the company debited the Rent Expense account for rent of $ 48,000 for the period May 1, 19X8 to April 30, 19X9. Assuming there have been no entries made to the Prepaid Rent account since December 31st, 19X7, prepare the adjusting entry for the twelve months ended December 31, 19X8.

d) The December 31st, 19X3 balance sheet showed Prepaid Insurance of $ 60,000. On June 1, 19X3 the company renewed its insurance for the next twelve months. Prepare the adjusting entry for January 31st, 19X4 assuming the company closes its books on a monthly basis.

Problem 4:

During the year-end audit of the books, the audit junior discovered the following errors and was asked to construct the necessary journal entries to correct the errors. Assume you are the audit junior and this is your job: {Hint: the easiest way to tackle this task is to figure out the correct entry and compare this to the actual entry in order to get the correcting entry.}

(A)   A customer made a payment on account of $ 75,000. It was recorded as:
DR Cash $75,000
     CR Sales revenue $75,000

(B)   The company paid rent which had been accrued at the end of the prior period and recorded it as follows:
DR Rent expense $100,000
     CR Cash $100,000

(C)   The company recorded depreciation on the president's car of $ 10,000:
DR Car expense $ 10,000
     CR Car $ 10,000

(D)   The company collected rental payments in advance from its tenants and recorded it as follows:
DR Cash $200,000
     CR Prepaid rent $200,000

(E)   The company paid $13,000 on account to Better Bodies, an auto repair shop, for repairs performed and accrued during the previous year. The transaction was recorded as
DR Rent expense $13,000
     CR Cash $13,000

Problem 5:

Pots' Flowers Ltd., a floral arrangement and delivery service, started business on January 1, 19X1. The owner/manager, Mr. Pots, who has little experience with accounting, has used the cash basis to record all transactions. You have just completed your first accounting course and you have explained to him that the accrual basis is a better measure of performance because it matches revenues and expenses. It is now December 31st, and you have been asked to help prepare the year-end financial statements based on the following information.

Chapter 5

Cash Received:

From common shares	$25,000	
From customers	136,250	
		$161,250

Cash Paid Out:

Rent	$6,500	
Flower refrigerator	15,000	
Insurance	1,750	
Delivery truck costs	21,250	
Decorating supplies	29,500	
Wages	87,500	
		161,500

Bank overdraft	$ (250)

You ascertain the following additional facts:

1. Mr. Pots has a list of customers who owe a total of $3,000 for flower work done on credit. Most of it is owed by one customer, a large corporation, and Mr. Pots is certain it is all collectible.

2. The company has a five year lease on a downtown shop. On January 1 the company paid a damage deposit equal to one month's rent of $ 500, as well as the first rent payment. Payments are due on the first of the month and Mr. Pots has always paid on time.

3. The company bought a used flower refrigerator on January 1, 19X1. It cost $15,000 and is expected to last five-years, but not to be worth much after this time.

4. The company bought two insurance policies on January 1. One premium covered the delivery truck for a one-year period and cost $400. The second premium provided protection from public liability in case someone injured themselves in the shop and covered the next three years at a total cost of $1,350.

5. The delivery truck costs consist of $18,000 paid to acquire the truck on January 1, plus $3,250 paid during the year for gas, oil, and minor repairs to the truck. Mr. Pots expects to use the truck for four years, after which time he estimates it will be worth about $ 4,000. At this point he thinks he will probably sell the truck and buy a new one.

6. As of December 31, 19X1, the company owed its creditors $3,500 for decorating supplies, like baskets, pots and stuffed animals, purchased and delivered, but not yet paid for. Also, an inventory count at year-end shows there are $1,500 of unused decorating supplies on hand.

7. The $87,500 of wages consists of $35,500 paid to Ms. Daisy, an elderly lady who helps out in the shop on a part-time basis, plus $52,000 paid in salary to Mr. Pots during the year. As of December 31, 19X1, the company owes Ms. Daisy $ 250 for work done between Christmas and New Years while Mr. Pots was away on vacation.

Required:
a. Prepare an income statement, on the accrual basis, for Pots' Flowers Ltd. for the twelve months ended December 31, 19X1.
b. Prepare a December 31, 19X1 balance sheet for Pots' Flowers Ltd also on the accrual basis of accounting.

For additional practice in preparing financial statements see Lotus Template file P5-37.wk1.

CHAPTER 5 ANSWERS AND SOLUTIONS

I True and False

1. False   Completion of the income statement column on the worksheet yields an imbalance that represents net income.

2. True
3. False   Dividends Declared is closed directly to Retained Earnings.
4. False   Accumulated Depreciation is a contra-asset account and as such would be a permanent account.

5. False   Special journals are used to accumulate large numbers of like transactions. The general journal is still used for transactions that do not fall into one of the classifications of special journals, as well as for adjusting and closing entries.

6. False   An audit is conducted to verify that the financial statements are prepared according to GAAP. Verification is done on a test basis.

7. True
8. False   Dividends Declared carries a debit balance and represents a reduction in Retained Earnings (and total shareholders' equity).

Chapter 5

9. True

10. True

11. True   Unearned revenue (a liability) is a balance sheet account and is therefore a permanent account.

12. True

II Multiple Choice

1. B Payroll Expense has a normal debit balance, closing would therefore require a credit to Payroll Expense and a debit to Income Summary.

2. C The final step is to transfer the net amount in Income Summary to Retained Earnings. If the company has a $ 10,000 loss, the debits in Income Summary exceed the credits, and the final entry will credit Income Summary and debit Retained Earnings to reduce it by the amount of the loss.

3. B Sales is the only temporary account listed. All the others are permanent and are never closed.

4. D Forgetting to recognize depreciation would overstate net income and overstate retained earnings in the period of the mistake. Unless the correction is made, retained earnings in year two would continue to be overstated.

5. C This is a counterbalancing error in that income and retained earnings are under in Year 10 and income is over in Year 11 but retained earnings are correct at the end of Year 11 (i.e. at the beginning of Year 12).

6. D If income is under in Year 10 then retained earnings are also under at the end of Year 10 by the same amount.

7. C As stated earlier, the income statements are both incorrect in Year 10 and Year 11, but since one is under and one is over the errors cancel out in retained earnings at the end of Year 11.

8. D Revenue and expenses are considered temporary accounts and would be reset at the end of the period.

9. A Since the ending balance in accounts payable is $8,000 more than the beginning balance, we purchased $8,000 more than we paid for. Add the $8,000 difference to payments to arrive at the purchases of $253,000.

10. B Interest accrued on the loan during the current period is considered an expense of the period and therefore would be included in Operating activity.

11. C   The company has used up 3 months of 12 months coverage, so the insurance expense is (3/12 X $2,400) $ 600. Since the payment was originally set up as an expense, this means that $ 2,400-600 is still an asset and should be set up by debiting the asset and crediting the expense for $1,800 (the unexpired amount).

12. B   The payments of $ 160,000 included a $ 10,000 advance which is an asset. The payments also covered the outstanding liability of $ 25,000 (which was recorded as an expense last year). This means that only $ 125,000 ($160,000-10,000-25,000) is a true expense of the current period.

III Problems

Problem 1:

a. Remember, closing is basically a four step process. Three of the steps involve closing the revenue and expense accounts to Income Summary and Income Summary to Retained Earnings. The fourth step closes any balance in the Dividends Declared account to Retained Earnings.

  1. Close temporary accounts with debit balances to Income Summary.

Income Summary	466,000	
Cost of goods sold		357,000
Rent expense		31,000
Salaries expense		57,000
Depreciation expense		21,000

  2. Close temporary accounts with credit balances to Income Summary.

Sales	512,000	
Rental property revenue	13,000	
Income Summary		525,000

  3. Close Income Summary to Retained Earnings.

Income Summary	59,000	
Retained Earnings		59,000

4. Close Dividends Declared to Retained Earnings.

    Retained Earnings   7,000
            Dividends Declared   7,000

b. The difference between the debit and credit balance in Income summary represents net income for the period. (see a)1 and a)2 above) $59,000 (Note: dividends are not part of net income)

c. Beginning balance Retained Earnings $ 3,000
    add: net income   59,000
    less: dividends   (7,000)
    Ending balance Retained Earnings $55,000

Problem 2:

Hart Sporting Goods
Statement of Cash Flows
Period Ended 12/31/X4

Cash flow from operations:
  Cash receipts from outsiders $ 400,000
  Cash payments to suppliers   (220,000)
  Cash payment for interest   (15,000)
  Cash payments for operating expenses   (100,000)
  Cash flows from operations $ 65,000

Cash flows from investing activities:
  Purchase of new equipment   ($ 125,000)
  Cash flows from investing activities   ($125,000)

Cash flows from financing activities:
  Sale of new common stock $ 100,000
  Cash dividends   (5,000)
  Cash flows from financing activities $ 95,000

Net increase in cash $ 35,000
Beginning Cash balance   50,000
Ending Cash balance $ 85,000

Problem 3:

a) The cash payment of $ 50,000 during the year consisted of $ 2,000 settlement of last year's accrual and $ 48,000 true expense for the period. In addition, at year-end the company owes $ 3,000 for work done but unpaid and unrecorded in the accounts. This makes the company's true expense equal to $ 48,000+$3,000 or $ 51,000.

At year-end, the expense account shows a balance of $ 50,000 and the liability account shows a balance of $ 2,000. The expense should be $ 51,000 and the liability should be $ 3,000. Therefore, the adjusting entry needs to increase both accounts by $ 1,000 as follows:

DR Wage expense   1,000
    CR Wages payable   1,000

b) At year-end the company determines that its liability is $ 10,000 at year-end. This means that its real rent revenue is $ 90,000 + the unearned rent of $ 15,000 which was earned during the year. Therefore, rent revenue is $ 105,000 and unearned rent is $ 10,000. The rent revenue account shows a balance of $ 100,000 and the liability account shows a balance of $ 15,000. This means that the liability is too high by $ 5,000 and revenue is too low by $ 5,000. The adjusting entry is as follows:

DR Unearned rent   5,000
    CR Rent revenue   5,000

c) Rent expense is $ 24,000 for the first four months of the year plus eight months at $ 4,000/month for the last eight months of the year. This gives total rent expense of $ 56,000 (24,000+32,000). Unexpired or prepaid rent at year-end is equal to four months at $ 4,000/month which is $ 16,000. The accounts currently show Prepaid Rent at $ 24,000 and Rent Expense at $ 48,000. The required adjusting entry to reduce Prepaid Rent to $ 16,000 and increase Rent Expense to $ 56,000 is as follows:

DR Rent expense   8,000
    CR Prepaid rent   8,000

d) The insurance policy expires on May 31st, 19X4. This means that the 19X3 year-end prepaid is for 5 months. A prepaid of $60,000/5 months = $ 12,000 per month, so the January month-end entry would be:

DR Insurance expense   12,000
    CR Prepaid insurance   12,000

Chapter 5

Problem 4:

NOTE: the answer to each of the following questions is only the entry referred to as "Correcting entry". The other entries are included for explanatory purposes.

a)   This transaction should have been recorded as:

DR Cash	75,000	
CR Accounts receivable		75,000

Since cash was correctly debited in the original entry, the correcting entry need only credit accounts receivable and debit sales revenue to reverse the error as follows:

Correcting entry:

DR Sales revenue	75,000	
CR Accounts receivable		75,000

b)   This transaction should have been recorded as:

DR Rent payable	100,000	
CR Cash		100,000

Again, cash was correctly treated but rent expense was incorrectly debited instead of the rent payable. The correcting entry is as follows:

Correcting entry:

DR Rent payable	100,000	
CR Rent expense		100,000

c)   This transaction should have been recorded as:

DR Depreciation expense	10,000	
CR Accumulated depreciation		10,000

Neither of these accounts were included in the original entry. In this case the easiest way to correct the error is to reverse the original entry and do the correct one as follows:

Correcting entry:

DR Car	10,000	
DR Depreciation expense	10,000	
CR Car expense		10,000
CR Accumulated depreciation		10,000

d) This transaction should have been recorded as:
DR Cash   200,000
     CR Unearned rent   200,000

Cash was correctly debited but prepaid rent was credited instead of unearned rent. The correcting entry is as follows:

Correcting entry:
DR Prepaid rent (to reverse the error)   200,000
     CR Unearned rent   200,000

e) This transaction should have been recorded as:
DR Accounts payable   13,000
     CR Cash   13,000

Cash was correctly credited but rent expense was debited instead of accounts payable. The correcting entry must reverse the expense and reduce the liability as follows:

Correcting entry:
DR Accounts payable   13,000
     CR Rent expense   13,000

Problem 5

Pots' Flowers Ltd.
Income Statement
For the year ended December 31, 19X1

Sales ($136,250+3,000credit sales)	$	139,250
Less expenses:		
Rent expense ($6500-500deposit)	6,000	
Insurance expense ($400truck ins.+450*public liab.)	850	
Truck expense	3,250	
Refrigerator depreciation expense ($15,000/5yrs)	3,000	
Truck depreciation expense {($18,000-4,000)/4yrs}	3,500	
Decorating supplies expense		
($29,500+3,500unrecorded purch.-1,500end. inv.)	31,500	
Wage expense	87,750	135,850
Net income		3,400

      * 3 year policy for $1,350= $ 450/year

Pots' Flowers Ltd.
Balance Sheet
As at December 31, 19X1

Current assets:
Accounts receivable	3,000
Inventory of decorating supplies	1,500
Prepaid insurance (2/3 X 1,350)	900
Refundable rent deposit	500
	$ 5,900

Non-current assets:
Flower refrigerator	$ 15,000
less acc. depreciation	3,000
	12,000
Truck	18,000
less acc. depreciation	3,500
	$ 14,500

Total Assets	$ 32,400

Current liabilities:
Bank overdraft	250
Wages payable	250
Accounts payable	3,500
	4,000

Shareholders' Equity
Common stock	25,000
Retained earnings	3,400
	28,400

Total Liabilities & Equity	$ 32,400

Chapter 6

**Sales Revenue,
Cash, and
Accounts Receivable**

A thorough understanding of the interrelationships that exist between the elements of the financial statements is important to both managers and practitioners alike. Several of these interrelationships are illustrated through the concepts presented in this chapter. Your ability to assimilate the following objectives will enhance your understanding of these concepts.

1. Determine the proper time to record a particular revenue item on the income statement.
2. Explain how to account for sales returns and allowances, sales discounts, and bank credit card sales.
3. Explain why cash is important and how it is managed.
4. Explain how uncollectible accounts affect the valuation of accounts receivable.
5. Estimate bad debt expense under the allowance method using (a) percentage of sales, (b) percentage of ending accounts receivable, and (c) aging of accounts.
6. Understand techniques for assessing the level of accounts receivable.

Chapter 6

REVIEW OF KEY CONCEPTS

A. When considering recognition of revenue under the accrual basis of accounting, there are several basic concepts to remember:

   1. Revenues must be **earned** - that is goods must be delivered or services provided.

   2. Revenue must be **realized or realizable** - if cash has not already been received, then collectibility must be reasonably assured in order to recognize revenue.

B. Once the question of **timing** has been answered it is necessary to address the **amount** to be recorded. To that end, you should be familiar with several important concepts and types of transactions that ultimately affect the amount of revenue reported.

   1. Since not all transactions involve cash, a measure must exist to help determine what value is attached to a sale transaction. The general rule for valuing a non-cash transaction is to use the fair market value of the consideration given up or received, whichever is most objectively determined. For example, if a used car dealer accepts your 1966 Mustang convertible, having a fair market value of $3,500, for a 1986 Camero the amount recorded as revenue would be $3,500.

   2. Invariably it becomes necessary to make adjustments to revenue transactions in the form of **sales returns and allowances**. This is accomplished through the use of **contra revenue** accounts. Instead of making adjustments directly to the revenue accounts, contra accounts are utilized to provide information for management control and decision making purposes.

      a. **Sales returns and sales allowances** are contra revenue accounts therefore, they normally carry a **debit** balance.

See the example on page 239 of the text

b. **Purchase returns** and **purchase allowances** are contra expense therefore, they normally carry a **credit** balance.

3. Sound business practices usually dictate the need for companies to extend **trade discounts** and **cash discounts** to their customers.

   a. **Trade discounts** are reductions in the gross selling price, or "list price". These **trade discounts** are extended in order to attract new or additional sales volume for the business. For example, if you increase your order to 1,000 units, we will grant you an extra 10% discount from the current selling price.

   b. **Cash Discounts** are offered by a firm in order to speed collection of accounts receivable. By converting the receivable to cash more quickly, the firm reduces the chance of non-collectibility, as well as being in a position to reinvest or utilize the cash in a more timely manner.

4. When dealing with **cash discounts** it is important to understand the meaning of different credit terms and how credit terms impact financial decision making. For example, a cash discount of 2/10, n/30 means that if you pay within 10 days of the invoice date you get a 2% discount, otherwise the invoice amount must be paid within 30 days or you will be charged interest.

5. Another relevant question concerns the cost of forgoing cash discounts. It is important for the manager to be capable of calculating the annualized cost of cash discounts. This provides a basis from which the manager can compare the costs of borrowing money to take advantage of those cash discounts.

$$\text{FORMULA: ANNUALIZED COST OF CASH DISCOUNTS}$$

$$\frac{\$ \text{ discount}}{\text{gross} - \$} \times \frac{365 \text{ days}}{\text{credit} - \text{discount}}$$
$$\frac{}{\text{invoice} \quad \text{discount}} \qquad \frac{}{\text{period} \quad \text{period}}$$

6.   Part of the merchant's cost associated with bank card charges involves the service fees deducted by the bank card companies. The service fees are part of the normal course of business and are properly recorded as **expenses** of the period. Look carefully at the textbook example and you will see that the bank charge deductions have no effect on the amount recorded in the revenue account.

> See the example on page 243 of the text

7.   The presentation of sales discounts, both cash and trade, as well as sales returns and allowances on the face of the income statement is determined by the needs of the reader. As was discussed in Chapter 4 of the text, either the single-step or the multiple-step income statement may be utilized, depending on the degree of detail required.

> Can you explain how and why the various contra revenue accounts discussed in this chapter would be presented on the single-step and multiple-step income statements?

C.   Proper classification and management of cash is important to the organization. As a manager, you should be familiar with what constitutes **cash** and **cash equivalents**, as well as some of the basic concepts relative to cash management.

    1.   An item is considered **cash** if it is freely available for use (e.g., cash usually excludes compensating balances or required minimum balances in cash bank accounts because these are **not** freely available)

    2.   **Cash Equivalents** are those investments that are highly **liquid** and therefore readily convertible to cash. Cash equivalents are held by management when sufficient cash is available to meet expected short term needs.

3.   Cash, when listed as the first element on the balance sheet under current assets, signals management's intention to make those funds available to satisfy current obligations as they arise.

   a.   **Compensating balances** represent restrictions on the use of cash, generally in accordance with loan agreements made between the bank and management. This may be done to secure a loan at a lower rate of interest.

4.   Cash control and management is important to the operations and survival of any business organization. Elements of control include:

   a.   Proper segregation of duties between the custody of cash and the recording of cash transactions.
   b.   Proper controls over authorization for disbursements and subsequent cash disbursement.
   c.   Independent reconciliation of cash balances by someone outside of the receipt/disbursement function.
   d.   Proper security for cash balances held "on hand" for daily cash transactions.

D.   **Accounts receivable** are uncollected credit sales. Companies extend credit in order to increase their sales. Companies must ensure that the profit on the additional sales exceeds the costs of extending credit (i.e. record-keeping costs, bad debts, etc.).

1.   The extension of credit presents problems relating to year-end **valuation** of accounts receivable on the balance sheet.

2.   The extension of credit also presents problems in terms of the **matching principle** because matching requires that the costs of bad debts be matched with revenue in the same accounting period as the credit sales. This requires firms to make an estimate at year-end of the amount of accounts receivable that will not ultimately be collected.

3.   **Uncollectible accounts** are a natural by-product of the credit granting process. Too low a level of **bad debts** relative to your particular industry may indicate lost sales through excessively stringent credit policies. Alternately, too high a level of **bad debts** indicates that management needs to review and adjust their credit policies.

Chapter 6

E.   The accounting profession has two primary methods of accounting for accounts receivable.

1.   The **specific write-off method** writes off bad debts in the period in which they become uncollectible. In many cases this means that the debt is written-off in the period after the sale. This **violates the matching principle** and so the specific write-off method is **not** permitted by GAAP unless bad debts are immaterial in amount or the amount is very stable from year-to-year.

An actual write-off is recorded as follows:
DR Bad debt expense   XXX
    CR Accounts receivable   XXX

2.   When accounts receivable balances are significant and bad debt write-offs are material the **allowance method** of estimating bad debt expense is preferred. The allowance method uses one of three methods to estimate uncollectible accounts at year-end. This approach fulfils the matching principle because it recognizes bad debt expense in the same accounting period as the credit sales. The allowance method is required by GAAP.

a) The accounting features of the allowance method are:

i) a provision for bad debts is set-up at year-end in order to achieve matching and to adjust the accounts receivable valuation to a more realistic amount

entry to set-up the provision:
DR Bad debt expense   XXX
    CR Allowance for uncollectible accounts   XXX

ii) actual write-offs of uncollectible accounts in the following period have no effect on either the balance sheet or the income statement. The write-off merely identifies the particular account that has become uncollectible and records it as follows:

entry for a write-off:
DR Allowance for uncollectible accounts   XXX
    CR Accounts receivable - Jane Craighead   XXX

Imagine the balances in the accounts receivable and the allowance accounts before the write-off are $ 100,000 and $10,000 respectively, and that the actual account written-off was for $ 1,000. Compare the following to see that the entry above has no effect on the net amount on the balance sheet for accounts receivable. Also note that no income statement accounts are involved in the write-off entry.

	Before write-off	**After write-off**
Accounts receivable	$ 100,000	$ 99,000
Allowance	10,000	9,000
Net accounts receivable	$ 90,000	$ 90,000

b) There are two basic approaches to estimating the amount for the provision in 2.a(i) above at year-end:

i) Focus on the *volume of credit sales* as an indicator of potential bad debts by using a **percentage of credit sales**.

This approach ignores the previous balance in the allowance account because it focuses on volume of credit activity and not on balance sheet valuation of accounts receivable.

example: the company uses 3% of credit sales as a provision for uncollectibles
credit sales = $ 100,000
.03 X $ 100,000 = $ 3,000
entry:
DR Bad debt expense   3,000
    CR Allowance for uncollectibles   3,000

ii) Focus on **balance sheet valuation of accounts receivable** and use either a **percentage of ending accounts receivable** or an amount derived from an **aging of accounts**.

Unlike for the percentage of credit sales amount, the amount derived under either of these two estimation methods (percentage of ending accounts receivable or an aging) is the **final desired balance in the allowance for uncollectibles account**. This approach focuses on balance sheet valuation. Study the following example closely and compare it to the one above for the percentage of credit sales method.

example: year-end unadjusted balance in the allowance account is $ 1,000 credit, the company estimates that 2% of ending accounts receivable will not be collectible, ending accounts receivable are $ 200,000.

.03 X $ 200,000 = $ 6,000 (desired ending balance in allowance) previous unadjusted allowance balance is $ 1,000 - therefore the provision only needs to add another $ 5,000 to the allowance account as follows:
entry:
DR Bad debt expense   5,000
     CR Allowance for uncollectibles   5,000

   c.   It is possible for accounts that have been written off as uncollectible to be recovered at a later date. This occurrence is referred to as **bad debt recovery**. Bad debt recovery is a two step process:

       1.   A journal entry is necessary to reinstate the previously written-off bad debt.
           entry:
           DR Accounts receivable   XXX
              CR Allowance for uncollectibles   XXX

       2.   A journal entry is necessary to reflect collection of the account receivable.
           entry:
           DR Cash   XXX
              CR Accounts receivable   XXX

F.   The ability to analyze and control accounts receivable is a critical management function at any firm. You should be familiar with the financial ratios, like accounts receivable turnover and the number of days to collect accounts receivable, that managers use in controlling accounts receivable.

> Accounts receivable turnover = Credit sales/ Average accounts receivable
> Days to collect accounts receivable = 365 days/ Accounts receivable turnover

1. When analyzing accounts receivable ratios it is important to remember that the ratio by itself is not very meaningful. It is necessary to compare it to the ratio for prior years for the same firm, or to relevant industry averages.

2. It is important to remember that as financial statements and financial statement components are interrelated, so too are the ratios. When used in planning, alteration of one ratio may effect other ratios as well.

PRACTICE TEST QUESTIONS AND PROBLEMS

I True or False - For each of the following statements, enter a T or an F in the space provided to indicate whether the statement is true or false.

_____ 1. In order to recognize sales revenue it is only necessary to deliver the goods or services.

_____ 2. The specific write-off method of accounting for uncollectible accounts would normally be used by a company that incurs an immaterial amount of bad debts.

_____ 3. When using the percentage of sales method for estimating bad debt expense, the ending balance in allowance for doubtful accounts is equal to bad debt expense for the period.

_____ 4. When deciding to extend credit, a company will only offer credit when additional earnings on credit sales **are less than** the cost of credit.

_____ 5. When a company utilizes the allowance method of estimating uncollectible, any write-off should be made directly to bad debt expense in the period the write-off occurs.

_____ 6. When processing cash in the organization, it is acceptable for the person making the deposit to record the deposit in the accounting records.

_____ 7. Sales allowances are reductions in the purchase price originally agreed upon.

_____ 8. The recovery of an account previously written-off should be credited against bad debt expense, thus reducing bad debt expense for the period.

_____ 9. Sales returns and allowances are considered contra revenue accounts and carry debit balances.

_____ 10. When using the aging method for estimating bad debt expense, we are interested only in those accounts receivable transactions that relate to this period.

_____ 11. Purchase returns and allowances are considered contra expense accounts and carry a debit balance.

_____ 12. To arrive at net sales, sales returns and allowances are subtracted from gross sales.

_____ 13. By utilizing the formula for calculating days to collect accounts receivable it is possible to derive accounts receivable turnover.

_____ 14. Since cash is generally a small balance relative to other accounts, it requires less management and control than other balance sheet accounts.

II Multiple choice - For the following multiple choice questions, select the best answer and enter the identifying letter in the space provided.

_____ 1. Before month-end adjustments, Dent's Collectibles had the following account balances:

Accounts receivable	$70,000
Allowance for doubtful accounts	$ 850

An aging of accounts receivable indicated that Dent expected not to collect $1,750. What is the net realizable value of Dent's accounts receivable after adjustment?

 a. $69,150
 b. $67,400
 c. $68,250
 d. $69,100

2. Alpha Racers had an average collection period of 20 days, and credit sales of $825,000. What is their average accounts receivable balance?

 a. $41,250
 b. $45,750
 c. $46,000
 d. $45,205

3. DB's Hobby had credit card sales for the month of April totalling $13,500. Upon deposit the bank deducts 3.5% as a credit card service fee. What would be the journal entry to record both the credit card sales and the service fee for the month of April?

 a. Cash   13,500.00
     Sales   13,500.00

 b. Cash   13,027.50
     Sales   13,027.50

 c. Cash   13,027.50
   Bank card service fee 472.50
     Sales   13,500.00

 d. Sales   13,500.00
     Bank card service fee   472.50
     Cash   13,027.50

Chapter 6

_____ 4. Sliced Tee, a golf ball manufacturer, purchased $148,000 in raw material, terms 2/10, n/30. The controller is deciding whether or not to take the discount. What is the annualized cost of that cash discount?

    a.   37.23 %
    b.   36.50 %
    c.   24.82 %
    d.   38.15 %

_____ 5. Jan's Sportswear sold merchandise on August 24th totalling $3,250 to Dean's House of Fashion on open account. Jan's policy is to offer credit terms of 5/15, n/16. What is the journal entry to record the sale on August 24th? Dean always takes the discounts.

a.

Sales	3,250.00	
Accounts receivable		3,250.00

b.

Accounts receivable	3,087.50	
Cash discounts	162.50	
Sales		3,250.00

c.

Accounts receivable	3,250.00	
Sales		3,250.00

d.

Sales	3,250.00	
Accounts receivable		3,087.50
Cash discounts		162.50

_____ 6. Jan's Sportswear sold merchandise on August 24th totalling $3,250 to Dean's House of Fashion on open account. Jan's policy is to offer credit terms of 5/15, n/16. What is the journal entry to record the receipt of Deans check on Sept. 7th. Dean always takes the discounts.

a.	Cash	3,087.50	
	Cash discounts	162.50	
	Accounts receivable		3,250.00
b.	Cash	3,087.50	
	Accounts receivable		3,087.50
c.	Cash	3,087.50	
	Cash discounts	162.50	
	Sales		3,250.00
d.	Cash	3,087.50	
	Sales		3,087.50

_____ 7. King Consultants apply the allowance method using the percentage of accounts receivable approach to estimating bad debt expense. King had an accounts receivable balance of $121,000 and credit sales of $680,000 at December 31, and estimated 2.5% would prove uncollectible. There is currently a temporary debit balance of $600 in the allowance for doubtful accounts. The adjusting entry to bring the allowance account to the appropriate balance is:

a.	Bad debt expense	3,025	
	Allowance for uncollectibles		3,025
b.	Bad debt expense	2,425	
	Allowance for uncollectibles		2,425
c.	Bad debt expense	17,000	
	Allowance for uncollectibles		17,000
d.	Bad debt expense	3,625	
	Allowance for uncollectibles		3,625

Chapter 6

III Problems

Problem 1:

Bishop Ltd., a company that manufactures chess games, had the following **unadjusted** trial balance at its year-end, December 31, 19**X3**:

	Debit	Credit
Accounts receivable	$ 500,000	
Allowance for uncollectibles		$ 1,000
Sales (all on credit)		3,000,000

The company estimates that 3% of the ending accounts receivable balance will not be collectible.

Bishop Ltd. had the following transactions during 19**X4**:
a) $ 14,500 of accounts receivable were written-off
b) There were credit sales of $ 4,000,000
c) $ 3,500,000 of accounts receivable were collected during the year
d) A payment of $ 2,000 was received from a customer whose account had been written-off last year.
e) Based on a percentage of ending accounts receivable, the company estimates that $20,000 of accounts receivable are uncollectible

Required:
1. Prepare the adjusting entry for the provision at the end of 19X3.
2. Prepare all the necessary journal entries to reflect the 19X4 transactions and year-end adjustment for uncollectibles.

Problem 2:

Knight Ltd., a competitor of Bishop Ltd., had credit sales during the year of $2,000,000. The unadjusted trial balance at year-end showed a debit balance of $150,000 in accounts receivable, and a **debit** balance of $1,000 in the Allowance for uncollectible accounts.

Required:
Prepare the necessary adjusting journal entries at year-end to set-up the provision for uncollectibles under each of the following scenarios:
   a.   the company estimates that 3% of year-end accounts receivables are not collectible

b.   the company bases its provision on credit sales and estimates that .5% (one half of one percent) is the appropriate percentage

c.   the company ages its accounts receivables and estimates that $ 3,500 is uncollectible.

Problem 3:

Fire-Ex Ltd., a fire extinguisher manufacturer, had the following information in its accounting records:

Accounts written-off:

during 19X1	$	32,000
during 19X2		39,000

Recoveries of accounts previously written off:

recovered during 19X1	800
recovered during 19X2	1,200

Adjusted balance in the Allowance for Uncollectibles:

19X0	40,000
19X1	47,000
19X2	45,000

Required:
Calculate the amount of bad debt expense for 19X1 and 19X2

For additional practice in preparing an aging of accounts or in analyzing accounts receivable see Lotus Template files P6-43.wk1 and P6-47.wk1.

CHAPTER 6 ANSWERS AND SOLUTIONS

I   True and False

1.   False   Recognition of revenue is a two part process requiring the revenue to be both earned and realized (i.e. collected or collectible).

2.   True

Chapter 6

3.　　　False　The percentage of sales method concerns itself with a specific period of time. The ending balance in the allowance for doubtful accounts is a composite of the balance that existed prior to adjustment <u>plus</u> the estimated bad debt expense that relates to that period.

4.　　　False　A company will only offer credit when the additional earnings are **greater** than the cost of credit.

5.　　　False　Write-offs to the bad debt account would be double counting. The write-off should reduce the allowance account and accounts receivable.

6.　　　False　Basic control of cash dictates separation of the custody of cash from the record-keeping function.

7.　　　True

8.　　　False　Recovery of bad debts is a two part process. **First**, the balance should be restored to accounts receivable and the allowance account (i.e. the write-off is reversed). **Second**, the receipt of cash should be debited to cash and credited to accounts receivable.

9.　　　True

10.　　　False　Aging of accounts receivable involves all balances existing in accounts receivable regardless of time period of origin.

11.　　　False　Purchase returns and allowances are contra expense accounts. However, they carry a **credit** balance.

12.　　　True

13.　　　True

14.　　　False　Cash, because of its obvious physical size and value, requires more control and attention from management.

II Multiple Choice

1. C.　Net realizable value is calculated as Accounts Receivable - Allowance. The ending balance in the Allowance should be $ 70,000 - $ 1,750 = $ 68,250

2. D.　If credit sales are $ 825,000 per year, this is approximately $ 2260 of sales per day ($ 825,000/365 = $ 2,260.27). If accounts are outstanding 20 days, on average, before collection, then accounts receivable would equal: (20 days x $2260.27/day) = $ 45,205.

3. C.　Bank card service fees are an expense of the period, sales are shown at their gross amount.

4. A. Refer to the outline for the formula to calculate the annualized cost of cash discounts. Now it is just a matter of plug-and-chug.

Annualized cost of cash discounts = ($2,960/$ 145,040) x (365/20)

= .0204 x 18.25

= 37.23%

5. C. At the time of the sale it is not known whether the discount will be taken or not. Accounts receivable should be debited for the full amount and sales credited for the full amount of the sale.

6. A. At this point the receivable is being converted to cash and should be discharged at the full amount. Cash discounts are a contra-sales account used to arrive at net sales.

7. D. The important difference in this case is the existence of a temporary debit balance of $600 in the allowance account. Since the percentage of accounts receivable approach dictates adjusting the account balance to 2.5% of accounts receivable ($3,025), we would have to credit the account for $3,625 to get an ending credit balance of $3,025.

III Problems

Problem 1:

1. calculation of **19X3** adjusting entry:

desired balance in allowance = .03 X $ 500,000 =	$ 15,000 credit
unadjusted balance	1,000 credit
amount to be adjusted in adjusting entry	14,000 credit

entry:

DR Bad debt expense	14,000	
CR Allowance for doubtful accounts		14,000

2. **19X4** entries

a)

DR Allowance for uncollectibles	14,500	
CR Accounts receivable		14,500

b)

DR Accounts receivable	4,000,000	
CR Sales		4,000,000

c)

DR Cash	3,500,000	
CR Accounts receivable		3,500,000

Chapter 6

d) DR Accounts receivable   2,000
        CR Allowance for uncollectibles   2,000

    DR Cash   2,000
        CR Accounts receivable   2,000

e) the amount of the entry for the 19X4 adjustment is calculated as follows:

19X3 adjusted balance	$	15,000
write-offs in 19X4		(14,500)
recoveries in 19X4		2,000
19X4 unadjusted balance		2,500
required 19X4 balance		20,000
adjustment		17,500

    entry:
    DR Bad debt expense   17,500
        CR Allowance for uncollectibles   17,500

Problem 2:

a) method: 3% of ending accounts receivable

required allowance = .03 X $ 150,000 =	$	4,500 credit
unadjusted balance		1,000 debit
adjustment	$	5,500 credit

    adjusting entry:
    DR Bad debt expense   5,500
        CR Allowance for uncollectibles   5,500

b) method: .5% of credit sales
This estimation method ignores the existing unadjusted balance in the Allowance.
The bad debt expense is:
    .005 X $ 2,000,000 = $ 10,000

    adjusting entry:
    DR Bad debt expense   10,000
        CR Allowance for uncollectibles   10,000

c) method: aging of accounts

estimated uncollectible accounts based on aging	$	3,500 credit
unadjusted balance		1,000 debit
adjustment	$	4,500 credit

adjusting entry:
DR Bad debt expense   4,500
    CR Allowance for uncollectibles   4,500

Problem 3:

In order to find the bad debt expense in each of 19X1 and 19X2, it is necessary to reconstruct the entries that went through the allowance account during these two years and to then solve for the missing amount (which is the entry for the provision):

Adjusted Allowance balance, year-end 19X0	$	40,000	credit
less 19X1 write-offs*		32,000	debit
plus 19X1 recoveries**		800	credit
unadjusted Allowance balance, year-end 19X1		8,800	credit
adjusted balance, year-end 19X1		47,000	credit
bad debt expense (& provision) for 19X1		**38,200**	
adjusted Allowance balance, year-end 19X1		47,000	credit
less 19X2 write-offs*		39,000	debit
plus 19X2 recoveries**		1,200	credit
unadjusted balance, year-end 19X2		9,200	credit
adjusted balance, year-end 19X2		45,000	credit
bad debt expense (& provision) for 19X2		**35,800**	credit

* entry	** entry
DR Allowance for uncollectibles	DR Accounts receivable
CR Accounts receivable	CR Allowance for uncollectibles

Chapter 7

**Valuing Inventories,
Cost of Goods Sold,
and Gross Profit**

Understanding the theory and techniques associated with inventory valuation is important to financial statement users. The method of inventory valuation used not only affects the value reported on the balance sheet but, because of the interrelated nature of the balance sheet and income statement, affects the reported gross profit and net income as well. It is important to obtain an understanding of the following objectives which focus on the issues and practices associated with inventory valuation, cost of goods sold, and gross profit.

1. Explain the importance of inventory in measuring profitability.
2. Explain and illustrate the differences between perpetual and periodic inventory systems.
3. Identify the items included in the cost of merchandise acquired.
4. Understand the accounting procedures for the periodic and perpetual inventory systems.
5. Explain the four principal inventory valuation methods and their effect on the measurement of assets and net income.
6. Understand the reasons for choosing and using the inventory methods.
7. Explain the meaning and impact of holding gains and inventory profits.
8. Explain why the lower-of-cost-and- market method is used to value inventories.
9. Show the effects of inventory errors on financial statements.
10. Explain the use of the gross profit percentage and inventory turnover measures.

REVIEW OF KEY CONCEPTS

A. Inventory valuation is the key to calculation of cost of goods sold and the subsequent derivation of **gross profit**.

   1.   **Cost of goods sold** relies on inventory valuation for its derivation and is calculated as follows.

> | | Beginning Inventory |
> |---|---|
> | + | Merch. Purchases (net) |
> | = | **Goods available for sale** |
> | - | Ending inventory |
> | = | **Cost of goods sold** |

   2.   **Gross Profit** is a measure of the profitability of sales revenue for a merchandising business. Gross profit is calculated as:

> Sales (net) - Cost of goods sold = **Gross profit**

B. There are two primary methods of maintaining inventory records, perpetual and periodic. Use of either is dependent upon the characteristics of the inventory and the informational needs of management.

   1.   **Perpetual method** is traditionally used with low turnover, high value inventories, such as automobiles or jewelry. Given the affordability of computerized scanning systems, however, we currently see perpetual inventory systems in low value, high turnover environments, such as grocery stores. A perpetual system updates the inventory records continuously for both purchases and cost of sales. An ending book inventory figure can then be compared to counted inventory at year-end.

   2.   **Periodic method** is often characterized by high turnover, low value inventories, such as art or office supplies. A periodic system records and accumulates the cost of purchases during the period. Inventory must be physically counted at year-end to determine the quantity on hand. At this point an adjusting entry is used to transfer the cost of sold inventory out of the asset account to cost of sales on the income statement.

3.   **Physical count** of inventory is required by GAAP on an annual basis but it is also crucial to verifying the accuracy of record-keeping in the perpetual inventory method.

C. When calculating the cost of merchandise purchased it is important to remember **cost** of merchandise includes:

> Invoice price of merchandise
> - Purchase returns and allowances
> + **Freight In**
> = Cost of merchandise (net)

1.   **Freight-In** is an account classification used to accumulate transportation charges incurred by the buyer. Don't Forget! freight-in is added to merchandise purchases in the calculation of the net cost of merchandise.

2.   Both **purchase returns and allowances** and **freight-in** are presented as adjustments to gross purchases on the face of the income statement.

> Before you begin discussing the principle inventory valuation methods, review the detailed example comparing accounting procedures for periodic and perpetual inventory, including the journal entries, presented in the text.

D. The choice of inventory valuation method can have a significant effect on the reported inventory balance, as well as on the amount of cost of goods sold on the income statement. The four primary methods of inventory valuation are: specific identification, FIFO, LIFO, and weighted average. The last three methods are actually **cost flow assumptions**, whereas specific identification identifies the costs associated with each unit of inventory and maintains these costs while tracking the item through the sales system.

Valuing Inventories, Cost of Goods Sold, and Gross Profit

1. **Specific identification** is generally used with unique or easily identifiable, low turnover inventory items, like works of art, estate jewelry,etc..

    a. Cost of goods sold are accumulated as each individual inventory item is identified and sold.

    b. Ending inventory is the summation of the cost identified with each individual item remaining in inventory.

2. **There are three cost-flow assumptions:**

    a. **First-in, First-out (FIFO)** assumes goods are sold in the same order in which they are acquired. This cost flow approximates the order in which certain goods, such as perishable items (e.g., milk, film, etc.), are sold. In a period of rising prices, FIFO yields an ending inventory figure that more closely approximates current replacement cost. However, cost of goods sold relative to current replacement costs, are understated.

    b. **Last-in, First-out (LIFO)** assumes the most recently purchased goods are sold first. This cost flow assumption approximates the flow of goods for hardware items which are stored in a bin or barrel. Most of us would take an item from the top of the barrel, rather than emptying the barrel and taking one from the bottom. In a period of rising prices, LIFO matches current costs with revenues on the income statement, but because "old costs" apply to ending inventory on the balance sheet it is possible for inventory to be materially below current replacement cost. Because LIFO gives a high cost of goods sold, income is lowest under LIFO in a period of rising prices. For related reasons, LIFO is **not** allowed for income tax purposes in Canada, although it is often used, and is acceptable for use, in financial statements prepared according to GAAP.

    c. **Weighted average** costing is used when individual or batch costing is not practical or beneficial, as would occur at a grain elevator, rock quarry or for oil stored in tanks. Weighted average costing represents a balance between FIFO and LIFO in the calculation of cost of goods sold. Weighted average cost per unit is calculated as follows:

Chapter 7

$$\boxed{\text{Weighted Avg. Cost Per Unit} = \text{Cost of Goods Available} / \text{\# of Units Available}}$$

E. A cost flow assumption is not meant to duplicate the physical flow of goods. This is because it is often more expensive to control the actual flow of goods (e.g., installing milk dispensing machines to prevent consumers from taking the fresher milk at the back of the refrigerator instead of the older inventory at the front) and there is no benefit in doing this if the goods are homogeneous in nature. A cost flow assumption provides a cost efficient and verifiable way to allocate costs between the balance sheet (inventory) and the income statement (cost of goods sold). In the case of homogeneous goods, a cost flow assumption may provide a better measure of performance than specific identification because an assumption limits management's ability to manipulate the allocation of inventory costs.

F. Inventory is valued at the **lower-of-cost-and-market**. This means that if the market value of inventory (defined usually as its net realizable value) is below its acquisition cost then the company must recognize a **holding loss**. This is done through an entry which debits a holding loss and credits or reduces inventory. Valuation of inventory is particularly important, as it is for all current assets, because by definition these assets will become cash within one year or one operating cycle. The **conservatism principle** suggests, as a result, that all losses on current assets be recognized as soon as possible even if they are unrealized.

G. As a user of financial statement information, it is important to understand some of the characteristics associated with inventory errors and their effect on reported statement balances.

   1. The effect of an inventory error in one period on net income is generally **offset** in the following period.

   2. If **ending inventory is overstated** (understated), **net income** will be **overstated** (understated).

   3. If **beginning inventory is overstated** (understated), **net income** will be **understated** (overstated). (Note: an error in beginning inventory has the **opposite** effect on net income as an error in ending inventory)

4. Ending inventory in one accounting period becomes beginning inventory in the next accounting period.

H. You will remember that gross profit is an indicator of the profitability of sales in a merchandising business. Gross profit levels and changes in gross profit are important elements in the decision making process.

1. **Gross profit percentage** is useful for industry comparison and trend analysis. It is also used to estimate ending inventory when calculating cost of goods sold for interim reporting purposes.

See the example on page 297 of the text

2. **Inventory turnover** is defined as cost of goods sold divided by average inventory for the period. As a general rule, an inverse relationship exists between gross profit percentage and inventory turnover. When analyzing inventory be aware of industry standards and remember that potential sales gains should offset decreased gross profit levels.

3. **Gross profit tests** are utilized to detect unusual relationships that may warrant closer attention.

PRACTICE TEST QUESTIONS AND EXERCISES

I **True or False** - For each of the following statements, enter a T or F in the space provided to indicate whether the statement is true or false.

_____ 1. To calculate gross profit, cost of goods sold is subtracted from net sales.

_____ 2. The periodic inventory system keeps a continuous record that tracks inventory and cost of goods sold on a day-to-day basis.

_____ 3. By using the perpetual inventory method it is possible to eliminate the need for a physical inventory count, thus saving both time and money.

_____ 4.   Freight-in appears on the purchases section of the income statement as an additional cost of goods acquired during the period.

_____ 5.   F.O.B. shipping point means the buyer bears the cost of shipping.

_____ 6.   Freight-out represents the cost borne by the seller and is shown as "shipping expense", a form of selling expense, thus affecting gross profit.

_____ 7.   GAAP requires the cost flow assumption to reflect the actual flow of goods.

_____ 8.   Once a firm adopts one of the four methods of inventory valuation they are expected to use it consistently over time.

_____ 9.   When applying LIFO for accounting purposes, you should count the most recently acquired inventory as ending inventory, because sound business practices call for the sale of the oldest inventory first.

_____ 10.   In periods of rising prices, holding gains are greater under LIFO than under FIFO.

_____ 11.   Compared to the pure cost method, the lower-of-cost -and-market method reports less net income in the period of decline in market value and more net income in the period of the sale.

_____ 12.   When actual ending inventory is unavailable for monthly and quarterly financial statements, the gross profit percentage is often used to estimate the amount.

_____ 13.   When the physical level of inventory decreases, LIFO charges the cost of the old LIFO layers to cost of goods sold.

_____ 14.   In periods of rising prices, LIFO will more accurately reflect replacement cost in ending inventory reported on the balance sheet.

_____ 15.   When utilizing the perpetual inventory system, all items purchased for resale are debited to a purchases account.

_____ 16.   Undiscovered inventory errors usually affect two reporting periods but the effect of the original error self-corrects in the next accounting period.

II   **Multiple Choice -** For each of the following statements, select the best answer by entering its identifying letter in the space provided.

_____ 1.   Marklin Marble Mfg. during 19X2 had gross purchases of $450,000, ending inventory of $65,000, beginning inventory of $50,000, freight-out of $2,000, purchase returns of $2,000, sales discounts of $2,000 and freight-in of $3,500. Cost of goods sold is:

      a. $434,500
      b. $436,500
      c. $433,000
      d. $432,500

_____ 2.   During periods of rising prices, the inventory method that yields the lowest tax liability would be:

      a.   FIFO
      b.   LIFO
      c.   Weighted average
      d.   FIDO

_____ 3.   Nichole has been assigned the task of computing ending inventory for the monthly financial statements. No physical inventory was taken but she had the following data available: Sales of $500,000, net purchases of $250,000, and beginning inventory of $200,000. The gross profit percentage has historically been 40%. What is ending inventory?

      a. $150,000
      b. $250,000
      c. $300,000
      d. $325,000

Chapter 7

_____ 4.   During the physical inventory count at year end a $50,000 segment of inventory was missed and subsequently not included in the ending inventory balance. The effect of this error on the following would be:

	Net income	Cost of goods sold
a.	understated	understated
b.	overstated	understated
c.	overstated	overstated
d.	understated	overstated

_____ 5.   During 19X2 Brown Manufacturing Co. had sales of $1,250,000, a gross profit percentage of 60%, and an inventory turnover of 3.5x. What is their average inventory balance?

a. $214,286
b. $142,857
c. $357,143
d. $193,787

_____ 6.   If River City Music had cost of goods sold valued at $285,000, beginning inventory of $60,000, and ending inventory of $55,000. What were goods available for sale and purchases respectively?

a. $340,000 , $285,000
b. $280,000 , $340,000
c. $345,000 , $290,000
d. $340,000 , $280,000

_____ 7.   Nicholson Equipment Sales uses a perpetual inventory system with inventory valued by specific identification. On January 15, 19X3, Nicholson sold a press for $125,000 that had been acquired on January 3, 19X3, for $93,750. What would be the journal entry(s) to record the sale of this equipment?

a.   Accounts receivable   125,000
             Sales   125,000

b.   Accounts receivable   125,000
             Sales   125,000
        Cost of goods sold   93,750
             Inventory   93,750

c.   Accounts receivable   125,000
             Sales   125,000
        Purchases   93,750
             Inventory   93,750

d.   Accounts receivable   125,000
             Inventory   125,000

_____ 8.   Bukowski Fashions understated last year's ending inventory by $30,000 and understated this year's ending inventory by $45,000. As a result, its income for this year was:

a.   understated by $15,000
b.   overstated by $15,000
c.   overstated by $45,000
d.   understated by $30,000

_____ 9.   During 19X4, Duck Soup Manufacturing had available the following information concerning inventory in their Rubber Ducky Division:

Beginning inventory (300,000 units) $300,000
Production run #1   (100,000 units) $125,000
Production run #2   (100,000 units) $135,000
Production run #3   (100,000 units) $160,000
Ending inventory   (235,000 units)

Using weighted average costing, the value of Duck Soup's ending inventory should be:

a. $202,100
b. $282,000
c. $376,000
d. $276,000

_____ 10. During the annual audit of Clay Department Store auditors determined $50,000 of obsolete inventory should be removed from the books. Management agrees and has assigned the task to you. What is the correct journal entry needed to accomplish this write-down?

a. Inventory expense   50,000
        Inventory   50,000

b. Obsolete merchandise inventory   50,000
        Loss on merchandise inventory   50,000

c. Loss on inventory write-down   50,000
        Inventory   50,000

d. no entry needed just note disclosure

III Problems

Problem 1:
Davis Photo has the following data available for 19X3:

Beginning inventory, January 1	$ 75,000
Gross purchases	265,000
Purchase returns and allowances	5,000
Cost of goods sold	259,000
Ending inventory, December 31	76,000

Required:
Prepare in journal entry form, a comparison of the periodic and perpetual inventory systems using the data above for gross purchases, returns and allowances, as goods are sold, and at the end of the accounting period.

Problem 2:
Cherie's Handbags is the exclusive distributor for a line of fine, hand finished women's purses. Presented below is information concerning the acquisition and sale of a particular model of shoulder bag. The company uses the perpetual inventory method to account for inventory.

Date	Purchase	Sales (units)	Balance
12/31/x3			(130 units) $1,950
4/4/x4	170 @ $17 = $2,890		
4/28/x4		175	
6/14/x4	150 @ $19 = $2,850		
9/1/x4	95 @ $20 = $1,900		
10/1/x4		200	
10/15/x4	200 @ $23 = 4,600		
11/10/x4		220	
12/31/x4			(150 units) ?

Sales for the period $ 19,900

Required:

a. Prepare a comparative statement of gross profit for the year ended December 31 19X4, using FIFO, LIFO, and Weighted average. Assume the company uses the perpetual inventory method.

b. Repeat part (a) assuming the company uses the periodic inventory method.

c. If your goal is to maximize reported net income which cost-flow assumption would you choose? Why?

Problem 3:
Mark Twain Hobby reported the following balances for 19X7:

Sales	$520,000
Cost of goods sold	338,000
Gross Profit	$182,000
Beginning inventory	$ 73,000
Ending inventory	$ 77,000

Chapter 7

Required:

a. Compute the gross profit percentage and the inventory turnover.

b. Assume Mark Twain Hobby's goal for 19X8 is to increase inventory turnover to 6x. Utilizing the current level of inventory, what would be the new sales and gross profit level? Assume the current gross profit percentage is maintainable.

c. In the following period an inventory turnover of 6x is achieved, but at the cost of a 3 percent decline in the gross profit percentage. What will be the new dollar value of gross profit?

Problem 4:

A tornado destroyed the building and offices housing Jackie's Shoes. While sifting through the rubble Jackie was able to reconstruct the following:

Beginning inventory	$ 120,000
Purchases year-to-date	$ 210,000
Sales year-to-date	$ 545,000
Operating expenses year-to-date	$ 272,000
(excluding cost of goods sold)	

Jackie remembers the bookkeeper telling her they had maintained a gross profit percentage of 60% during the last three years.

Required:

Compute the cost of goods sold and ending inventory based upon this information.

Problem 5

You have been asked by a friend to review the financial records of Alpine Ski Ltd., a ski distributor. Your friend is interested in purchasing the company and wants your opinion on the accuracy of its unaudited financial statements. In your review of the records you discover two inventory errors, as follows:

       a.   the 19X2 ending inventory was understated by $ 25,000

       b.   the 19X4 ending inventory was overstated by $ 18,000

Required:

Calculate the effect of these errors on Alpine Ski Ltd.'s financial statements.

> For additional practice preparing the cost of goods sold section of the income statement see Lotus Template P7-23.wk1 and P7-43.wk1. For practice applying the cost flow assumptions see file P7-49.wk1.

CHAPTER 7 ANSWERS AND SOLUTIONS

I True and False

1. True
2. False The perpetual inventory system keeps a continuous record that tracks inventory on a daily basis, hence the term perpetual.
3. False A physical inventory count is <u>important to both</u> periodic and perpetual systems. If a physical count is not conducted on a periodic basis how do you know your inventory records are correct?
4. True
5. True
6. False The first part of the statement is true. Freight-out is an expense of the period. However, freight-out belongs as a selling expense (i.e. below the gross profit line) in the calculation of <u>net profit</u> not in the calculation of gross profit.
7. False GAAP does not require that the cost flow assumption mimic or reflect the actual flow of goods.
8. True While this statement is true, changing circumstances can dictate a change in valuation methods. The notes to the financial statements would disclose the details of the change including the dollar effect of income in the current and prior year.
9. False Ending inventory is made up of the oldest goods under LIFO.
10. False Holding gains equal the difference between cost and replacement cost. LIFO cost of goods sold is made up of the most recent costs, and therefore, the holding gain in net income is less under LIFO than under FIFO.
11. True
12. True Be careful to remember that the gross profit percentage is used to derive cost of goods sold, from which ending inventory is calculated.
13. True It is possible that inventory is extremely old.
14. False In periods of rising prices LIFO more accurately represents replacement costs in <u>cost of goods sold</u>. Ending inventory would reflect the oldest costs.

Chapter 7

15. False   The periodic inventory system accumulates items purchased for resale in a purchases account that is closed to the income summary account and then to retained earnings.
16. True

II Multiple Choice

1. B   The key to this question is the formula for calculating cost of good sold and remembering freight-out and sales discounts are **not** part of the determination of cost of goods sold.

Beginning Inventory		$ 50,000
+ Purchases (gross)	$ 450,000	
- Purchase returns	$ (2,000)	
+ Freight-in	$ 3,500	451,500
= Goods available for sale		$ 501,500
- Ending inventory		(65,000)
= Cost of goods sold		$ 436,500

2. C   Weighted average because LIFO (which gives the lowest income in a period of rising prices) is not allowed for tax purposes.

3. A   Using the formulas presented in the chapter we are able to estimate cost of goods sold and therefore ending inventory.

   1.   Sales - Cost of goods sold = Gross profit
        $ 500,000 - CGS = .40 x 500,000 = $ 200,000
        CGS = $ 300,000

   2.   Beg. Inv. + Purch. - End Inv. = CGS
        $ 200,000 + 250,000 - EI = $ 300,000
        EI = $ 150,000

4. D   Ending inventory is understated, so cost of goods sold is overstated (because the deduction from cost of goods available for ending inventory is too small). If cost of goods sold are overstated, then net income is understated since cost of goods sold is a deduction from sales.

5. B   Inventory turnover = Cost of good sold / Avg. Inventory
        3.5 x = $ 500,000* / Avg. Inventory
        Avg. Inventory = $ 142,857
        *cost of goods sold= sales-gross profit=1,250,000-.6(1,250,000) = 500,000

6. D   This question involves solving for goods available for sale first, then solving for the remaining unknown, purchases.

Beg. Inv. + Purch. = Goods avail. - End. Inv. = CGS

CGS + End. Inv. = Goods avail.

Goods avail. = $ 285,000 + 55,000 = **$ 340,000**

Beg. Inv. + Purch. = Goods avail.

$ 60,000 + Purch. = $ 340,000

Purch. = $ 280,000

7. B   The key to this question is that we are dealing with a perpetual inventory system. A perpetual system updates cost of goods sold and inventory on an ongoing basis. The journal entry is two-part.

1.   Recognize the revenue with the increase to accounts receivable and increase to sales.

2.   Increase your cost of goods sold and decrease your inventory.

8. A   Last year's ending inventory becomes this year's beginning inventory. If beginning inventory is under by $ 30,000, cost of goods sold is under by $30,000 as well, and **net income is over by $30,000**. If this year's ending inventory is under by $45,000, then cost of goods sold is over by $45,000, and **net income is under by $45,000**. The two errors must then be added together - income is over by $ 30,000 from one error, and under by $45,000 from the other - the net effect is an **understatement of net income of $15,000**.

9. B   Weighted average cost per unit $= \dfrac{\text{Cost of goods available for sale}}{\text{\# of units available for sale}}$

$ 1.20 per unit = $ 720,000 / 600,000 units

End. inventory = (Wgt. avg. cost per unit) X (# of units of end. inv.)

End. inv. = $ 1.20 x 235,000 units

End. inv. = $ 282,000

10. C   Inventory write-downs are expensed in the period that the loss of "future utility" relative to inventory is recognized. The journal entry reflects the loss in the period and subsequently reduces the inventory account to the new, lower level.

Chapter 7

III Problems

Problem 1:

1. **Perpetual Inventory Method**

   1. Gross purchases

DR Inventory	265,000	
CR Accounts payable		265,000

   2. Returns and Allowances

DR Accounts payable	5,000	
CR Inventory		5,000

   3. As goods are sold

DR Cost of goods sold	259,000	
CR Inventory		259,000

   4. End of the period - no entry (book figure for inventory agrees to the physical count)

   Periodic Inventory Method

   1. Gross purchases

DR Purchases	265,000	
CR Accounts payable		265,000

   2. Returns and Allowances

DR Accounts payable	5,000	
CR Purchase returns		5,000

   3. As goods are sold - no entry in the periodic system

   4. End of period

DR Cost of goods sold	335,000	
DR Purchase returns	5,000	
CR Purchases		265,000
CR Inventory (opening inv.)		75,000
DR Inventory (end. inv.)	76,000	
CR Cost of goods sold		76,000

Problem 2:

Cherie's Handbags
Comparative Statement
of Gross Profit
Year ended Dec. 31 19X4

	FIFO	LIFO	W. Avg.
Sales	$ 19,900	$ 19,900	$ 19,900
Cost of goods sold	(10,740)	(11,840)	(11,335)
Gross profit	$ 9,160	$ 8,060	$ 8,565

Cost of goods sold calculations

FIFO	Cost of goods sold	Ending inventory
sale 4/28/X4 (175 units)	130X$15=1,950	
	45X$17=765	125 x $17
sale 10/1/X4 (200 units)	125X$17=2,125	
	75X$19=1,425	75 x$19, 95 x $20
sale 11/10/X4 (220 units)	75X$19=1,425	
	95X$20=1,900	
	50X$23=1,150	150 x $ 23 = $3,450
Total Cost of goods sold	$ 10,740	

LIFO	Cost of goods sold	Ending inventory
sale 4/28/X4 (175 units)	170X$17=2,890	
	5X$15=75	125X$15
sale 10/1/X4 (200 units)	95X$20=1,900	
	105X$19=1,995	45X$19
sale 11/10/X4 (220 units)	200X$23=4,600	
	20X$19=380	**125X$15=1,875**
Total Cost of goods sold	$ 11,840	**25X$19=475**
Total ending inventory (bold #'s only)		**$ 2,350**

Weighted Average

	Cost of goods sold	Weighted avg. cost
sale 4/28/X4 (175 units)	175X$16.13*=2,823	
sale 10/1/X4 (200 units)	200X$18.29**=3,658	
sale 11/10/X4 (220 units)	220X$20.84***=4,585	
Total Cost of goods sold	$ 11,066	150 x $ 20.84 = $3,124
		(difference due to rounding)

*,**,*** see next page

Chapter 7

Weighted average cost = Total cost of goods available/ Total units available
Weighted average cost must be re-calculated ever time a new unit of inventory is purchased. The weighted average costs are calculated as follows:

*first cost calculated after the 4/4/X4 purchase
[(130unitsX$15)+(170unitsX$17)] / 300 units = **$ 16.13**

** second cost calculated after the 2 consecutive (i.e. no sale in between) purchases ending on 9/1/X4
[(125unitsX**$16.13**)+(150unitsX$19)+(95unitsX$20)] / 370 units = **$ 18.29**

*** third cost calculated after the 10/15/X4 purchase
[(170unitsX**$18.29**)+(200unitsX$23)] / 370 units = **$ 20.84**

b. Periodic inventory

	FIFO	LIFO	W. Avg.
Sales	$ 19,900	$ 19,900	$ 19,900
Cost of goods sold	(10,740)	(11,900)	(11,332)
Gross profit	$ 9,160	$ 8,000	$ 8568

In the **periodic inventory method** you must first value **Ending Inventory** and then subtract this amount from **Cost of Goods Available for Sale** to get **Cost of Goods Sold**. This is because, unlike the perpetual system, the periodic system does not keep track of the costs of the units sold, and so the only way to get this amount is indirectly, as the difference between the total value of the goods that were available during the year and what is left (i.e. unsold) at year-end.

It is important to note that the timing of the **sales** of items is ignored with this method as this information is not part of the periodic system. Study the following calculations carefully and be sure that you understand this point.

Cost of goods sold calculations:

FIFO

ending inventory is 150 units - these units are the most recently purchased items of inventory.

ending inventory   150 units X $ 23 = $3,450
cost of goods available = total of beginning inventory and all purchases = $14,190

Cost of goods available	$ 14,190
Less end. inventory	3,450
Cost of goods sold	$ 10,740

Note: Cost of goods sold for the **FIFO** cost flow assumption is **always the same** regardless of whether a periodic or perpetual inventory method is used. This is **not** the case for any other cost flow assumption.

LIFO
ending inventory is 150 units - these units are assumed to be the oldest units

ending inventory	130 units X $15 =	$ 1,950
	20 units X $17 =	$ 340
total		$ 2,290

Cost of goods available	$ 14,190
Less end. inventory	2,290
Cost of goods sold	11,900

Weighted Average
Note: the weighted average cost is only calculated once (at the end of the year) in the periodic inventory method.

Weighted Average Cost = Total Cost of Goods Available/ Total # of Units Available
$$= \$ 14,190/(130+170+150+95+200)$$
$$= \$ 19.05$$

ending inventory = 150 units X $ 19.05 = $ 2,858 (rounded)

Cost of goods available	$ 14,190
Less end. inventory	2,858
Cost of goods sold	$ 11,332

c. In a period of rising prices (such as this one), the FIFO cost flow assumption always gives the highest net income because the oldest (i.e. lower) costs are charged to cost of goods sold.

Problem 3:
a.
$$\text{Gross profit percentage} = \frac{\text{gross profit}}{\text{Sales}}$$

$$35\% = \frac{182,000}{520,000}$$

$$\text{Inventory turnover} \ = \ \frac{\text{cost of goods sold}}{\text{average inventory}}$$

$$4.51 \ = \ \frac{338{,}000}{75{,}000}$$

b. The key to answering this segment is first to find cost of goods sold and then to solve for sales as follows:

$$\text{Inventory turnover} \ = \ \frac{\text{cost of goods sold}}{\text{average inventory}}$$

$$6x \ = \ \frac{\text{cost of goods sold}}{75{,}000}$$

$$\text{Cost of goods sold} \ = \ 75{,}000 \ x \ 6 = \ \underline{\$ \ 450{,}000}$$

$$\text{Sales} \ = \ \frac{\text{cost of goods sold}}{(1 \ - \ \text{gross profit \%})}$$

$$\text{Sales} \ = \ \frac{450{,}000}{.65}$$

Sales   = $ 692,308
Gross profit = $ 242,308

c. By substituting the new gross profit percentage into the formula used to calculate sales (see above) sales and gross profit may be calculated as follows:

$$\text{Sales} \ = \ \frac{450{,}000}{.68}$$

Sales = $ 661,765
Gross profit = $ 211,765

Problem 4:

a. Calculate cost of goods sold using gross profit percentage as follows:

	Beginning inventory	$ 120,000
+	Purchases year-to-date	210,000
=	Goods available for sale	330,000

	Sales Year-to-date	545,000	
x	Cost of goods sold **percentage**		
	(1 - gross profit percentage)	.40	
	Cost of goods sold		218,000
	Ending inventory		$ 112,000

Problem 5:

The key to dealing with inventory errors is to treat each one separately:

In 19X2:

on the income statement

ending inventory is understated by $ 25,000, therefore

cost of goods sold is overstated by $ 25,000, and

net income is understated by $ 25,000

on the balance sheet:

ending inventory is understated by $ 25,000, and

retained earnings are understated by $ 25,000

In 19X3:

on the income statement

beginning inventory is understated by $ 25,000, therefore

cost of goods sold is understated by $ 25,000, and

net income is overstated by $ 25,000

on the balance sheet:

ending inventory is correct, and

retained earnings are correct (the error has been counterbalanced)

In 19X4:

on the income statement

ending inventory is overstated by $ 18,000, therefore

cost of goods sold is understated by $ 18,000, and

net income is overstated by $ 18,000

on the balance sheet
ending inventory is overstated by $ 18,000, and
retained earnings are overstated by $ 18,000

Finally, the effect this all has for your friend in terms of the financial statements - the only relevant error is the most recent one for $ 18,000, because the previous error for $ 25,000 has corrected itself.

Chapter 8

**Internal Control
and Ethics**

Management is responsible for the fair and accurate representation of the firm's financial position and results of operations. Integral to any fair and accurate representation is the need for a system of internal control. Chapter 8 helps to establish a basis for understanding the critical position internal control plays in the establishment of administrative and accounting controls for the business. The following learning objectives will help to highlight key points in the chapter.

1. Describe the elements of internal control.
2. Explain the role of the audit committee.
3. Judge an internal control system using the checklist of internal control.
4. Describe how computers have changed the internal control environment.
5. Explain the basics of controlling cash and inventories.
6. Incorporate ethical judgements into decision making.

Chapter 8

REVIEW OF KEY CONCEPTS

A.   The firm's internal control structure is made up of the policies and procedures established to provide reasonable assurance that the organization's objectives will be met. The structure of this internal control system may be sub-divided into **administrative controls** and **accounting controls**.

1.   **Administrative controls** are established to ensure the organization's policies are being followed by each element of the organization. They are established to promote operational efficiencies as well.

2.   **Accounting Controls** include the methods and procedures established for authorization of transactions, safeguarding of assets, and ensuring the accuracy of financial records.

a.   **Internal accounting controls** provide reasonable assurance concerning:
1.   Authorization of transactions
2.   Recording transactions
3.   Safeguarding assets
4.   Reconciliation of records
5.   Valuation of assets

> Before continuing to the next section, can you identify the two major classifications of internal control and list some of the distinguishing characteristics of each?

3.   The accounting system is integral to the internal control structure because it consists of the methods and records established to identify, record, classify, and report transactions by the firm. The accounting system provides for the accountability of all assets and liabilities relating to the business as well.

B.   The financial statements of the organization are management's responsibility. The managers of companies that have widely-circulated financial statements (e.g., all public companies and some private companies) are required by the Canadian Institute of Chartered Accountants (CICA) to include a **management report** in the annual report which acknowledges management's responsibility for the following:

> 1.   preparing financial statements
> 2.   accounting judgments and estimates
> 3.   ensuring other information in the annual report is consistent with the statements
> 4.   developing internal controls that produce relevant and reliable information

Management is charged with conducting operations according to policies and guidelines established by the board of directors, representatives of the shareholders. The **audit committee,** composed of members of the board of directors (some of whom are outsiders to the firm), is generally responsible for overseeing the company's internal controls, financial statements and general financial affairs. In some cases the company's internal audit department may report directly to the audit committee.

C.   A well defined internal control structure will have characteristics applicable to all areas of accounting activity. This "checklist" includes many of the following characteristics:

1.   **Reliable personnel with clear responsibilities** are crucial to any system. The most effective plan is only as good as the personnel trained to implement and oversee it.

2.   **Separation of duties** is designed to ensure that any one person is not in a position to defraud the company. Separation of duties may be subdivided into the following four parts:

   a.   Separation of operating responsibility from record-keeping responsibility.
   b.   Separation of the custody of assets from the accounting function.
   c.   Separation of the authorization of transactions from the custody of related assets.
   d.   Separation of duties within the accounting function.

3. **Proper authorization** can be either <u>general</u> or <u>specific.</u>

   a. The board of directors is responsible for establishing general authorization guidelines within which management must conduct daily operations.

   b. Specific authorization guidelines establish levels of authority and responsibility for deviations from general guidelines.

4. **Adequate documentation** is a key element of an effective internal control system. Pre-numbered documents, supporting documentation, such as receiving reports and pre-numbered purchase orders all support an atmosphere of effective control.

5. **Proper procedures** such as daily deposit of cash receipts, or a supervisor's initials next to a journal entry writing-off a customer account as uncollectible are examples of defined procedures that support an effective system of internal control.

6. **Physical safeguards** or custody of assets is one of the primary responsibilities of management. This extends beyond security of cash to areas such as proper plant layout to reduce the chances of raw material and inventory theft.

7. **Bonding, vacations, and rotation of duties** not only help to reduce the chances of defalcation, but also improve morale and production as well.

8. **Independent check** refers to an independent party, such as an outside auditor, having the ability to reproduce a transaction according to established policy and obtain the same results. Independent check also applies to reconciliation of company records to related outside third party documents such as bank reconciliations.

9. **Cost-Benefit** considerations are integral to all of the characteristics discussed to this point. If the value of the asset or information provided is overshadowed by the cost of acquiring the information or safeguarding the asset, prudent management dictates adjustments to the internal control structure relative to those areas.

> TEST YOURSELF! After having reviewed the characteristics of internal control, how many of the nine elements presented by the author can you list? Along with the listing can you give a brief description of each?

D. The use of computers in business has greatly increased the ability to process transactions quickly while also utilizing fewer personnel. This consolidation of duties, however, indicates the need for integration of computer controls with the company's other internal controls. Such application controls would include:

1. **Input controls** control the quality of the input. Input validation checks help ensure the quality of input by rejecting invalid entries and requesting corrected input from the entry source.

2. **Processing controls** are built into the system to help compensate for human input errors. Processing controls also include separation of duties so that no single person has both programming and operations capabilities.

3. **Output controls** are implemented to ensure the quality of the output. Output controls also include guidelines for proper authorization and distribution of output information.

4. **General controls** are internal controls that focus on the organization and operation of the data processing activity

E. Cash and inventory, due to the number of transactions involved, are critical areas for strong internal control procedures.

1. The following list represents internal control guidelines for **cash**.

   a. Receipt of cash should be separated from the disbursement of cash.
   b. Cash receipts should be deposited on a daily basis.
   c. All major disbursements should be made by serially numbered checks.
   d. Bank accounts should be reconciled monthly.

Chapter 8

2.   The following list represents application of some of the internal control elements for **inventory**.

      a.   Separation of duties between purchase, receipt, and shipment.

      b.   Adequate documentation concerning purchase, receipt and shipment of inventory must exist.

      c.   Inventory must be stored and accounted for in such a manner that its physical security is ensured.

      d.   Physical verification and reconciliation of inventory should be conducted on a periodic basis.

G.   The cement that holds the internal control structure together is the control environment established and practiced by management. Important to this philosophy and style is the level of ethical standards practiced by management.

1.   While ethical standards cannot be codified, a framework for ethical decision making is helpful.

      a.   Determine the facts.

      b.   Identify the ethical issues.

      c.   Identify major principles, rules, and values.

      d.   Specify the alternatives.

      e.   Assess the possible consequences.

      f.   Make the decision.

F.   Bank statements are an important source of "outside" information concerning transactions involving the cash account. Reconciliation of internal records relative to cash with the bank statement is important to proper internal control.

1.   **Bank reconciliation** involves investigation and reconciliation of differences between the balance per books kept by the company and the balance per statement as reported by the bank. These differences are generally due to:

      a.   Outstanding checks, written and deducted by the company but not yet paid by the bank.

      b.   Deposits in transit, added to the balance by the company but not yet credited by the bank.

c. Miscellaneous additions and deductions by the bank not yet recorded by the company.

d. Errors by the company or the bank, such as a transposition error by the company in recording a check disbursement or an error by the bank in debiting or crediting the wrong customer account..

> See Exhibit 8-6 and 8-7 on pages 352 and 353 of the text

2. **Petty Cash** is small amounts of cash kept in an **imprest petty cash fund.** This avoids the need for check authorization and disbursement for small cash outlays.

a. Petty cash is reconciled and replenished at the end of the period and when the cash balance is sufficiently low.

b. Upon reconciliation and replenishment, all expenditures are expensed to their appropriate accounts using the proper adjusting entries.

> See the example on page 353 of the text

H. The retail method of estimating ending inventory uses the relationship between merchandise recorded at retail and cost to establish a ratio which can be applied to the retail value of ending inventory to convert it to cost. The relationship between cost and retail also allows us to determine an estimate of the cost of shrinkage, an important control consideration.

1. Application of the retail method is as follows:

a. Compute the **goods available for sale** at both retail and cost.

b. Compute the **ratio** of cost to retail value.

c. Count the **ending inventory** at retail value.

d. Multiply the **ending inventory at retail** by the **ratio** developed in b. above to derive **ending inventory at cost**.

Chapter 8

> See the example on page 354 of the text

I.   The key to determining whether an item of inventory should be included in ending inventory depends on the legal **transfer of ownership**. Who has title to the merchandise at the end of the period? The issue of ownership is at the heart of questions concerning **cutoff errors, consignment,** and **goods-in-transit.**

> Can you explain the basics of controlling cash and inventory and relate those basics to the checklist of internal controls?

PRACTICE TEST QUESTIONS AND SOLUTIONS

I   **True or False** - For each of the following statements, enter a T or an F in the space provided to indicate whether the statement is true or false.

_____   1.   The major focus of internal accounting control is detection and prevention of errors. Safeguarding of assets is a separate issue handled outside the internal control structure.

_____   2.   The need for internal control is not confined to preventing theft. Internal control is also concerned with adherence to management policies and procedures.

_____   3.   Two objectives of internal accounting controls, reconciliation, and valuation are aimed at the prevention of errors and irregularities.

_____   4.   The financial statements of the company are the auditor's responsibility.

_____   5.   Due to the competitive nature of business today it is considered good management to consolidate duties. An example of consolidation would be to utilize the same person to prepare the deposit, then immediately record the deposited items to the individual subsidiary accounts.

_____ 6. Once a code of ethics is adopted, the need to adhere to the code must be continually communicated throughout the organization.

_____ 7. When goods are shipped on consignment, title remains with the shipper but the goods are not part of the shipper's inventory because they are being held by the consignee.

_____ 8. The greatest source of errors in computerized systems is the data input.

_____ 9. Due to the inherent accuracy of computers, fewer controls need to be put into place to ensure the accuracy and reliability of computer-processed data.

_____ 10. Absolute accuracy of the financial statements is necessary. Therefore, any control implemented to guarantee that accuracy is warranted.

_____ 11. Reconciliation of the bank statement with the company records is not considered an independent check because it is usually undertaken by personnel within the organization.

_____ 12. The principles of internal control may be used to appraise any specific procedures for cash, purchases, sales, payroll, and the like.

_____ 13. The audit committee is predominantly composed of senior managers of the firm who are also members of the board of directors.

_____ 14. The act of bonding, which involves the purchase of insurance against embezzlement, is a substitute for rotation of duties, vacations, and similar precautions.

_____ 15. By developing detailed, comprehensive internal control systems, employee ethics play a smaller part in the overall internal control structure.

Chapter 8

II   **Multiple Choice** - For the following multiple choice questions, select the best answer and enter the identifying letter in the space provided.

_____   1.   When reviewing administrative controls within the internal control structure, a manager would be most interested in:

      a.   Procedures for the authorization of transactions
      b.   Safeguarding of assets
      c.   Accuracy of the financial statements
      d.   The organizational plan

_____   2.   Boats 'N Stuff uses a perpetual inventory record keeping system for inventory. As a result of the December 31, 19X3 physical inventory a difference of $ 4,500 existed between the perpetual records and the results of the physical count. The entry to adjust ending inventory to reflect the shortage would be:

      a.   Cost of goods sold   4,500
            Inventory shrinkage   4,500

      b.   Inventory shrinkage   4,500
            Inventory   4,500

      c.   Loss on inventory theft   4,500
            Cost of goods sold   4,500

      d.   Cost of goods sold   4,500
            Shrinkage expense   4,500

_____   3.   Which of the following reflects good internal control practices.

      a.   Sales department approval of returns from customers.
      b.   Preparation of the bank reconciliation by personnel in treasurer's department responsible for making daily deposits.
      c.   Release of raw materials to production after receipt of authorized materials requisition.
      d.   Shipment of inventory to long-time customer on open account without credit approval. This customer has made purchases on credit for many years.

_____ 4. Blossom's Clothing Store had a cost to retail ratio of .55 and an ending inventory at retail of $125,000. What was ending inventory at cost?

    a. $ 68,750
    b. $ 56,250
    c. $ 67,850
    d. $ 57,250

_____ 5. All of the following would be duties delegated to the audit committee **except,**

    a.   Review audited financial statements prior to publication.
    b.   Review of line management for promotion.
    c.   Review of corporate management with the independent auditor.
    d.   Review of independent auditor with corporate management.

_____ 6. When preparing a bank reconciliation, which of the following would **not** affect the bank statement balance?

    a.   Deposits in transit
    b.   Outstanding checks
    c.   Service charges
    d.   Deposit error by bank

_____ 7. Which of the following is responsible for the information presented in the financial statements?

    a.   auditors
    b.   management
    c.   accountants
    d.   controller

_____ 8. Leslie received her bank statement which showed a beginning balance of $ 1,000, deposits of $ 4,000, deductions of $3,300, and an ending balance of $ 1,700. From her records she showed $ 600 in checks outstanding at the end of last month that were paid this month. This month's outstanding checks totalled $800. What should her records show for disbursements this month?

    a. $ 3,500
    b. $ 3,100
    c. $ 1,900
    d. $ 4,100

_____ 9. The petty cash fund had a balance of $11 at the end of the period. Receipts for gas totalled $42, postage $29, and cab fares of $17. The entry to replenish the fund would include:

    a.   Debit to cash for $88.
    b.   Debits to various expenses for $88.
    c.   Credit to petty cash fund for $88.
    d.   Credit to postage for $29

_____ 10. Miscellaneous deductions made by the bank each period should be :

    a.   Deducted from the balance per bank.
    b.   Added to the balance per bank.
    c.   Added to the balance per books.
    d.   Deducted from the balance per books.

III   Problems

Problem 1:

In order to reduce the number of checks being written for small balances, it was decided to establish a petty cash fund. On June 1, 19X1 the fund was established with a balance of $220. On June 31 the fund had a balance of $22, with receipts for the following:

Postage	$58
Delivery charges	45
Parking (misc exp.)	43
Flowers (misc.exp.)	52

Required:

a.   Record the journal entry to establish the petty cash fund on June 1, 19X1.

b.   Record the journal entry to replenish the petty cash fund on June 30, 19X1.

Problem 2:

Clark Hardware, utilizing a perpetual inventory system reported the following information:

	RETAIL	COST
Begin. inventory, Jan. 1, 19X4	$ 220,000	$ 154,000
Purchase year-to-date	823,000	459,800
Markups (from initial retail)	10,000	
Markdowns (from initial retail)	30,000	
Allowable shrinkage	3,000	
Physical inventory, May 31, 19X4	168,600	
Sales, year-to-date	$ 850,000	

Required:

a.   Using the retail method, prepare a schedule showing the estimate for ending inventory at both cost and retail.

b.   Determine if excess shrinkage exists and determine the value at both cost and retail.

Problem 3:

Your boss had given you the following information to use in preparing a bank reconciliation.

Balance per books, April 1	$ 3,000
Receipts during April	45,750
Disbursements during April	44,500
Balance per bank statement, April 30	1,849

Chapter 8

Outstanding checks:		Deposits in transit:	
# 1436	$ 486.50	April 29	$ 2,212.00
# 1475	211.00	April 30	1,874.00
# 1476	105.00		
# 1477	82.75		
# 1479	501.25		
# 1480	173.50		

Adjustments made by the bank but not recorded in the company records:

Returned checks	$ 205.00
Service charges	75.00
Automatic Insurance deduction	220.00
Automatic Deposit of invest. proceeds	625.00

Required:

a. Prepare the bank reconciliation in good form.

b. Prepare the journal entry(ies) necessary to adjust the book balance.

Problem 4:

As controller of Biker's Business Ltd., a cycle retailer, you have assembled the following information regarding the company's bank account:

1. The bank statement shows a balance of $ 75,300, considerably more than the company balance of only $ 43,925.

2. The company has received a $ 15,000 loan from the bank but has not yet recorded it in its records.

3. A $ 1,250 certified cheque the company sent in prepayment of an order has not yet been returned with the bank statement.

4. Cheques amounting to $ 21,450, which were outstanding at the end of last month, have still not been returned with the current month's bank statement.

5. The bank collected a note for the company for $ 5,000. The company has not yet recorded receipt of the amount.

6. The bank cashed a cheque for $ 5,500 drawn on the account of Better Bikers Ltd., but took the funds out of Biker's Business Ltd.'s account by mistake.

7. A cheque collected by the company for a payment on account for $ 1,750 was returned with the bank statement and marked NSF (not sufficient funds).

8.   The bookkeeper recorded the deposit of a cheque of $ 5,555, as $ 5,005.
9.   The last bank deposit of the month by the company for $ 3,000 is not on the current month's bank statement.
10.   Bank service charges for the month amounted to $ 375.

Required:
a.   Prepare a bank reconciliation.
b.   Prepare the adjusting entry(ies) required on the company's books to adjust the cash account to the correct month-end balance.

For additional practice preparing bank reconciliations see Lotus Template files P8-25.wk1 and P8-43.wk1. For practice using the retail inventory method see files P8-28.wk1, P8-44.wk1, P8-45.wk1. and P8-46.wk1..

CHAPTER 8 ANSWERS AND SOLUTIONS

I True and False

1. False Internal accounting controls are designed to detect and prevent errors, as well as to safeguard the assets of the firm.
2. True
3. False The general objectives, reconciliation and valuation, are aimed at the **detection** of errors and irregularities.
4. False Financial statements are management's responsibility - auditors only attest to whether they have been prepared according to GAAP.
5. False Good internal control dictates the separation of the custody of assets from accounting for those assets. Deposits should be prepared by one individual and posting to the subsidiary ledger accounts should be done by another individual.
6. True
7. False Transfer of title is key to this question. The important point is who holds title to the goods, not their physical location. Consignment goods are included in the shipper's inventory.
8. True
9. False The use of computers dictates the need for additional controls to be put into place to ensure accuracy and reliability.
10. False All internal controls must pass a cost/benefit test before they are instituted. Will this additional control cost more than it is designed to save?(Watch such words as absolute or always.)

Chapter 8

11. False   The bank statement is an "outside" document. Reconciliation of company records to this "outside" source is considered a good independent check.
12. True
13. False   The audit committee is normally composed of "outside" directors. "Outside" directors are considered to be more independent than directors who are also part of management.
14. False   Bonding is the act of insuring against embezzlement, but it is **not** a substitute for rotation of duties, vacation, and other similar precautions.
15. False   Employee ethics are key to a successful internal control system.

II Multiple Choice

1. D.   The organizational plan refers to administrative controls. Answers a, b, and c all refer to accounting controls.

2. B.   The $4,500 difference between the physical inventory count and the perpetual records is **inventory shrinkage.** This would be charged against either a shrinkage account or cost of goods sold and a corresponding reduction of inventory per perpetual records. (Note: none of the other entries credit inventory)

3. C.   Release of raw materials to production, after receipt of an authorized materials requisition, is a good example of separation of custody of assets from transaction authorization.
    a. is incorrect because of the separation of duties that should exist between the sales function and the sales returns and allowance function.
    b. is incorrect because the bank reconciliation should be done by someone independent of the treasurers office.
    d. is incorrect because shipment should not take place without correct authorization from the billing department, no matter the standing or longevity of the customer.

4. A.   (End. inv. at retail) X (the cost/retail ratio) = (End. inv. at cost)
    $ 125,000 X .55 = $ 68,750

5. B.   Review of line management for promotion would normally be an operational function of management. All of the other answers conform to the audit committee's function of overseeing financial affairs, financial statements, and internal accounting controls.

6. C.   Service charges have already been deducted in arriving at the bank statement balance. Service charges are normally an adjustment to the balance per books.

7. B.   Management is ultimately responsible for the information presented in the financial statements.

8. A. By starting with the $3,300 reported as deductions on the bank statement, subtracting the $600 from last period (which only cleared the bank in this period), and adding the $800 in outstanding checks (which the bank doesn't know about yet) we should reconcile to a disbursements per books of $3,500.

9. B. When the petty cash fund is replenished, all receipts should be classified and expensed in the period. The offsetting credit is to cash for the amount required to replenish the fund.

10. D. Miscellaneous deductions such as service charges, automatic account deductions not previously accounted for, and NSF checks would be a deduction from the balance per books.

III Problems

Problem 1:

a.	Petty cash	220	
	Cash in bank		220
b.	Postage expense	58	
	Delivery Expense	45	
	Misc. expense	95	
	Cash in bank		198

Chapter 8

Problem 2:

	Retail	Cost	Ratio
Begin. inventory, Jan. 1	$ 220,000	$ 154,000	
Purchases year-to-date	823,000	459,800	
Additional retial price changes:			
Markups	10,000		
Markdowns	(30,000)		
Goods available	$ 1,023,000	$ 613,800	.60*
Less sales	(850,000)	(510,000)	
Less allowable shrinkage	(3,000)	(1,800)	
Inventory (books) May 31, 19X4	$ 170,000	$ 102,000	
Inventory (count) May 31, 19X4	168,600	101,160	
Excess shrinkage	$ 1,400	$ 840	

a) Estimated inventory is inventory per books (retail $ 170,000, cost $ 102,000)
b) Excess shrinkage is the difference between the books and the physical count.

Problem 3:

Open. balance per books, April 1	$ 3,000
Plus Receipt	45,750
Minus Disbursements	(44,500)
Balance per books April 30	$ 4,250
Additions:	
Auto. deposit Invest. income	625
Deductions:	
Returned checks	(205)
Service charges	(75)
Automatic insurance payment	(220)
Adjusted April 30 balance	$ 4,375

April 30 bank balance	$ 1,849
Additions:	
Deposits in transit	4,086
Deductions:	
Outstanding checks	(1,560)
April 30 bank balance	$ 4,375

Adjusting journal entry:

Accounts receivable (net)	205	
Service charges	75	
Insurance expense	220	
Cash	125	
Investment income		625

Problem 4:

a. Unadjusted balance per company $ 43,925

   Additions:

bank loan	15,000
note collected by bank	5,000
error (5555-5005)	550

   Deductions:

NSF cheque	(1,750)
Service charge	(375)
Adjusted company balance	$ 62,350

Bank balance	$ 75,300

   Additions:

bank error	5,500
outstanding deposit	3,000

   Deductions:

outstanding cheques	(21,450)
Adjusted bank balance	$ 62,350

b. Adjusting entries (all items appearing on the company reconciliation must be adjusted).

DR Accounts receivable (NSF cheque)	1,750	
DR Service charge	375	
DR Cash	18,425	
CR Bank loan		15,000
CR Note receivable		5,000
CR Accounts receivable (error*)		550

* in order for the accounts receivable sub-ledger to be correct, the error must be credited to the customer's account, therefore, it can not be netted with the NSF cheque.

Chapter 9

Capital Assets and Depreciation

Management invests in capital assets, such as buildings or equipment, in order to generate revenue through the production of goods and services. The matching principle requires that asset cost be allocated over future periods in order to reflect the costs incurred in generating revenue. There are different alternatives available under GAAP for cost allocation. Choices are provided so that it is possible to select a depreciation method that reflects the actual pattern of benefits received from the capital asset. This chapter also outlines the tax implications of investing in capital assets. The following learning objectives highlight the key points in the chapter.

1. Distinguish between tangible and intangible assets, and explain how to charge their costs to income.
2. Describe how to measure the acquisition cost of tangible assets such as land, buildings, and equipment.
3. Compute depreciation for buildings and equipment using various depreciation methods.
4. Describe the differences in reporting depreciation on financial statements and capital cost allowance for income tax purposes.
5. Explain the relationship between depreciation and cash flow.
6. Discuss other factors that affect the computation of depreciation, including changes in estimates and timing of acquisition.
7. Distinguish between expenses and expenditures, and identify expenditures that should be capitalized.
8. Compute gains and losses on disposal of fixed assets.
9. Explain how to account for depletion of natural resources.
10. Describe how to account for various intangible assets.

REVIEW OF KEY CONCEPTS

A.   Management acquires assets with the intent of using them in the production of goods or services for sale to customers. Accrual accounting, specifically the matching principle, dictates allocation of a portion of the acquisition cost of these assets to the period in which they are used to produce revenue. Your focus at this point is on capital assets and their classification as tangible or intangible assets.

    1.   **Capital assets** are assets that will provide the firm with benefits over an extended period of time (e.g., a few to several years). Examples include land, equipment, buildings, patents, trademarks, and mineral resources.

    2.   **Tangible assets** are physical assets such as buildings or equipment, the value of which is **depreciated**, or allocated to expense, over the useful life of the asset.

        a.   The exception is **land**, which is **not depreciated**.

        b.   Natural resources are **depleted** over their useful life.

    3.   **Intangible assets** include non-physical assets such as franchise rights, purchased goodwill, patents, and trademarks. Their cost is **amortized** over the useful life of the intangible asset.

> See Exhibit 9-1 on page 373 of the text

B.   The **acquisition cost** of a capital asset includes all costs reasonably incurred in putting the asset into use. This includes, for example, transportation, installation and testing. The total acquisition cost is **capitalized** which means that it is entered into an asset account where it will be subject to depreciation, depletion or amortization.

    1.   Assets acquired in a **basket purchase**, or lump sum purchase of two or more assets, must be separated and a portion of cost attached to each asset in the purchased group.

        a.   This cost allocation is accomplished by determining the **relative** fair market value of each asset in the group.

b.   A portion of the lump-sum purchase price is then allocated to the asset in the same proportion that the asset's fair market value has to the total fair market value of the group of purchased assets.

> See the example on page 376 of the text

2.   Allocation of basket purchase costs can have a significant effect on reported net income due to the nature of different capital assets and the corresponding applicable methods of depreciation.

C.   In theory, a depreciation method should be chosen to reflect the **pattern of benefits** received by the firm from the capital asset. If an asset is equally productive (i.e. has the same revenue-generating ability) in all years of its life, then it is appropriate to select the **straight-line method** of depreciation which allocates an equal amount of depreciation expense to each accounting period. If, on the other hand, an asset is more productive in the early years of its life (perhaps because it needs more repairs in the latter years), then it is appropriate to select an accelerated depreciation method. In such a method, depreciation expense is higher in the early years and lower in the latter years of the asset's life. Both **double-declining-balance** and **sum-of-the-years-digits** are accelerated depreciation methods.

Depreciation expense is **not** meant to reflect the decline in the market value of the asset. Market price is affected by many external factors (like technological change or changes in supply or demand) that have nothing to do with the asset's revenue-generating ability. In many cases, the market value of a capital asset is irrelevant to the firm because the firm has no intention of selling the asset. In this setting in particular, depreciation expense is used to allocate cost and to match expenses with revenues.

In practice we find that many firms use capital cost allowance (for tax purposes) as their depreciation expense. This is normally done to simplify the accounting in that using the same method for tax and financial statement purposes avoids having to account for deferred income taxes (which are discussed in chapter 14). This practice continues not because accountants overlook the requirements of GAAP, but because the difference between capital cost allowance in a given year and depreciation expense (based on a theoretically correct method of depreciation) is often not materially different.

D.   As noted above, depreciation is the systematic transfer, or allocation, of a portion of the acquisition cost of a capital asset, from the balance sheet to the income statement as expense in the period the asset is used to produce revenue. Several techniques are commonly used to facilitate the transfer of asset cost. The most popular are: straight-line, sum-of-the-years digits, and double-declining-balance.

1.   Common to all methods of depreciation is the need to determine the asset's **depreciable value, useful life,** and **residual value**.

   a.   **Depreciable value** is the difference between total historical cost and the residual value of an asset.

   b   **Residual value** is the estimated value of the asset at the end of its useful life. An asset is normally not depreciated below its residual value.

   c.   **Estimated useful life** is the time period over which an asset is depreciated. This estimate is the result of prediction, experience, etc.

2.   **Straight-line depreciation** spreads the acquisition cost of the asset, *less the residual value*, equally over the asset's useful life.

(Acquisition cost - residual value)/ useful life=depreciation expense

---

   a.   Straight-line depreciation based on a *unit of measure other than useful life* (e.g., units produced or kilometers travelled) may be more appropriate in some instances.

3.   **Double-declining-balance** is an *accelerated* method of depreciation where a greater portion of the asset's value is expensed early in its life, relative to straight-line depreciation.

   a.   Depreciation expense is calculated by multiplying the beginning book value for the period by the double-declining-balance rate.

Chapter 9

b. It is important to remember that the double-declining-balance *ignores residual value*, but that depreciation expense is limited to an amount that will not reduce book value below residual value. This is demonstrated in the following example:

asset cost $ 10,000
double-declining-balance depreciation rate 50%
residual value $ 2,000

Year	opening nbv* X 50%=	dep. expense
1	$10,000 X .50 = $ 5,000	$ 5,000
2	$ 5,000 X .50 = $ 2,500	$ 2,500
3	$ 2,500 X .50 = $ 1,250	$ 500**

*net book value = cost - accumulated depreciation
** in year 3 the calculated depreciation is $ 1,250 but if the company booked this amount the net book value of the asset would be below the residual value of $ 2,000

4. **Sum-of-the-years-digits** is also an *accelerated* method that produces declining depreciation expense over the life of the asset.

a. The fraction uses the sum of the years of useful life as the denominator and the years of remaining life as the numerator.

b. The depreciable base (historical cost - residual value) is multiplied by the fraction developed in 4a. above.

See the example on page 381 of the text

Review Exhibit 9-3 on page 381 of the text to see the effect that the choice of depreciation method has on depreciation expense and on the asset's book value

D. For tax purposes, depreciation is known as **capital cost allowance** (CCA). The government allows a company to claim an amount less than or equal to that calculated according to the tax act. The government has standard classes, with pre-established CCA rates. This rate is applied to the undepreciated capital cost for the asset class. A company may only claim one-half of the allowable CCA on assets acquired during the year.

E. Depreciation is **not** a savings account. It is **not** a method used to recover the cost of an asset. It is a vehicle for the transfer of acquisition cost from the balance sheet to the income statement. Depreciation itself does not generate cash.

The cash effects associated with depreciation actually arise from its counterpart in the tax act (CCA). The higher the amount of CCA claimed by the firm, the lower the company's taxable income. The lower the taxable income, the lower the amount of taxes paid. The cash effect comes solely from the tax implications. Depreciation expense for financial statement purposes is a non-cash expense (i.e. a book allocation) which reduces accounting income but does not affect cash flow at all.

> See Exhibits 9-5 and 9-6 on page 388

F. It is important to remember that residual value and estimated useful life are only **estimates**. When a change in either estimated useful life or residual value is deemed necessary (because better information becomes available), depreciation expense should be revised prospectively. This means that the new/better information is used to revise depreciation for the remainder of the asset's useful life. We **never** go back and change prior years' depreciation. At the time of the change in the estimate, the revision of future depreciation expense involves:

1. calculating the remaining net book value (i.e. the undepreciated cost) of the asset

2. estimating a new salvage value, or if it hasn't changed, using the previous salvage value

3.   calculating the remaining useful life of the asset based on the best information available

4.   calculating revised depreciation expense as the value in #1 minus the value in #2, all divided by the value in #3.

G.   Assets are normally acquired at various points throughout the year. Cost/benefit dictates development of a company rule or policy regarding depreciation in the year of acquisition. Usually, depreciation is calculated on the basis of the nearest full month but other acceptable methods include:

1.   **Half-year convention** which assumes all assets acquired during the year are placed into service at the mid-point of the year. This assumption is reflected by booking half of the yearly depreciation expense.

2.   **Modified half-year convention** assumes all assets acquired during the first half of the period are depreciated for the full period. Assets acquired during the second half of the period *are not depreciated until the following period.*

H.   Expenditures made by the company on a capital asset during its life are either expensed or capitalized.

1.   Expenditures that merely maintain or repair the asset are **expenses** of the period.

2.   Expenditures that enhance that asset's productivity or extend its life are **capitalized** as capital improvements or betterments.

3.   Capital expenditures in 2. are added to the capital cost of the asset. They then become part of the asset's cost and are depreciated or allocated to income over the remainder of the asset's useful life. When an expenditure is capitalized, depreciation expense must be revised. The revision is calculated in the same way as it is in section F above.

4.   The test to determine whether an expenditure should be expensed or capitalized is generally three-fold:

     a.   Is the item purchased intended for repair or maintenance? If so, expense.

     b.   Is the expenditure minor enough that cost-benefit dictates expensing the item?

     c.   Will the expenditure provide future benefits (i.e. add to the future utility of an existing asset or extend its life) to the firm?

I.   **Gains and losses** for accounting purposes are the difference between the (net) book value of an asset (cost - accumulated depreciation) and the proceeds on disposal (i.e. the cash received or the cash-equivalent of the asset(s) given up). Recording gains and losses is a two-step process:

1.   Record depreciation expense up to the time of the disposal.

2.   In one entry, record the proceeds received on disposal of the asset, remove the asset's historical cost and related accumulated depreciation from the books of the company, and recognize the difference between the proceeds and the book value as a gain or loss on disposal.

     example: equipment with historical cost of $ 10,000, accumulated depreciation $ 7,500, cash received on disposal $ 3,500

        entry:

DR Accumulated depreciation	7,500	
DR Cash	3,500	
CR Equipment		10,000
CR Gain on disposal		1,000

3.   Gains and losses are normally reported under "other income/losses" on the income statement.

J.   **Depletion** is the process of allocating the cost of natural resources to the periods in which the resources are used.

Chapter 9

K.   **Intangible assets** are purchased rights or benefits, such as the acquisition of a copyright from an outside source. *Internally developed* intangibles, such as a well trained work force, are not assets which are recognizable under GAAP, even though they are assets of the firm in the non-accounting sense. It is very difficult to establish a value for internally created assets. Expenditures related to internally developed intangibles are usually expensed as incurred. Intangible assets (i.e. externally purchased) are **amortized** over their estimated useful lives. Examples include:

1.   **Copyrights** are the exclusive rights to reproduce and sell books, musical scores, films etc. Copyrights are amortized over the useful life of the asset.

2.   **Trademarks** are distinctive identifications associated with a particular product or service. Purchased trademarks are amortized over their useful life not to exceed forty years.

3.   **Patents** are granted to an inventor by the federal government and give the holder exclusive right to produce or sell the invention for a period of 17 years. Purchased patents are amortized over their expected useful lives.

4.   **Goodwill** is defined as the difference between the purchase price of a company and the market value of the identifiable individual assets net of associated liabilities. Purchased goodwill is amortized over its useful life which is considered to be a maximum of forty years.

L.   **Research and development expenditures** are the costs of planned investigations undertaken with the hope of gaining new scientific or technical knowledge which can be translated into new products or processes. In Canada, the CICA distinguishes research from development; research expenditures are an expense of the period in which they are incurred. Development expenditures apply to the operationalization of previous research into a marketable product or process. If management can show that the company will recover the costs through profits on future sales, they can capitalize the costs and write them off over future revenues.

M.   **A Leasehold** involves the right to use a fixed asset for the period stated in the lease. **Leasehold improvements** would be any improvements made to the property by the tenant. Examples include installation of new carpeting, permanent equipment, and light fixtures. Leasehold improvements are amortized over the term of the lease or the lease term plus one renewal period, if this option exists and the company is likely to exercise it.

N.   **Deferred charges** are like prepaid expenses, but they have longer-term benefits. Companies capitalize these expenditures and generally write them off over three to seven years. Examples include relocation and/or organization costs.

PRACTICE TEST QUESTIONS AND SOLUTIONS

I   **True and false -** For each of the following statements enter a T or an F in the space provided to indicate whether the statement is true or false.

_____   1.   The underlying purpose of tangible assets is to facilitate the production and sale of goods and services to customers.

_____   2.   Most tangible assets, such as buildings, equipment and machinery are depreciated over their useful lives.

_____   3.   The acquisition cost of capital assets is their cash-equivalent purchase price including all costs incurred to put them into use.

_____   4.   A gain on the sale of a capital asset would be defined as the difference between the proceeds received on sale and the historical cost of the asset.

_____   5.   Repairs done to a piece of equipment that extend its useful life for three years would be expensed to repairs and maintenance.

_____   6.   By utilizing the double-declining balance method of depreciation, it is possible to never fully depreciate the asset.

_____ 7. Once a depreciation method has been adopted it must be used for both financial statement and tax reporting purposes.

_____ 8. Demolition costs of old structures on acquired land would be added to the cost of the land.

_____ 9. In a basket-purchase of assets, the practice is to divide the purchase price equally among all of the assets.

_____ 10. Depreciation expense is used to establish a fund for capital asset replacement.

_____ 11. If J & D Tool buys a patent for a new tool, the company will automatically amortize the cost of the patent over the seventeen year period granted by the federal government.

_____ 12. An example of a deferred charge is organization costs.

_____ 13. Because of cost/benefit considerations it is possible to acquire a depreciable asset four months before year-end and still record six months of depreciation.

_____ 14. When the useful life of an asset is deemed to be greater than that originally used to calculate depreciation charges, it is necessary to adjust retained earnings to reflect this new development.

_____ 15. Practical reasons for adopting straight-line depreciation are simplicity, convenience, and the reporting of higher earnings in early years than would be reported under accelerated depreciation.

II   **Multiple Choice** - For the following multiple choice questions, select the best answer and enter the identifying letter in the space provided.

_____   1.   The systematic allocation of organizational costs to expense in the period in which the organizational costs provide benefits is termed:

           a.   Depletion
           b.   Depreciation
           c.   Amortization
           d.   Transference

_____   2.   Gelcote Manufacturing purchased a fibreglass spraying unit for $50,000. Engineers estimated a useful life of 5 years and a residual value of $1,000. Using the sum-of-the-years-digits method of depreciation, expense in year **two** would be:

           a. $ 9,800
           b. $13,067
           c. $ 6,533
           d. $ 3,267

_____   3.   The plant manager made a basket-purchase of three different pieces of equipment for $100,000. Fair market value of each machine was $49,500, $82,500, and $33,000. The cost allocated to each of the three machines would be:

           a. $33,000, 33,000, 33,000
           b. $30,000, 50,000, 20,000
           c. $30,000, 35,000, 35,000
           d. $49,500, 82,500, 33,000

_____   4.   FFS Ltd. acquired a new computer system. The invoice price was $43,000, transportation costs were $2,000, in-transit insurance was $1,500, installation costs were $4,000 and system training amounted to $2,500. How much will FFS capitalize?

           a. $50,500
           b. $51,500
           c. $53,000
           d. $43,000

5. Ace Delivery purchased a new truck for $63,000. The expected useful life was 240,000 kilometers or approximately 5 years with a residual value of $3,000. Using straight-line depreciation based on unit depreciation, calculate the depreciation expense for the first year if Ace drove the truck 50,000 kilometers.

   a. $12,750
   b. $13,125
   c. $12,000
   d. $12,500

6. A depreciable asset, purchased for $100,000, was expected to have a useful life of 5 years and a residual value of $5,000. New estimates at the beginning of the asset's fourth year of usage indicate that the asset will last 4 more years but will have no residual value after this time. Using straight-line depreciation, what is the depreciation expense for year 4?

   a. $13,571
   b. $19,000
   c. $10,000
   d. $10,750

7. Utilizing double-declining-balance depreciation, what is the net book value, at the end of the **2nd year**, of a packaging machine costing $125,000? The machine has a residual value of $10,000 and a useful life of 8 years.

   a. $95,703.00
   b. $70,312.50
   c. $93,750.00
   d. $69,687.50

8. A forklift costing $62,000 was sold for $21,000. At the time of the sale, records showed $40,000 accumulated depreciation for the forklift. Calculate the gain or loss on the sale.

   a. $21,000 loss
   b. $ 1,000 gain
   c. $ 1,000 loss
   d. $19,000 loss

_____ 9. A company acquires a new car for the president during the year for $ 40,000. The car is categorized as a class 10 asset for tax purposes and is subject to CCA at a rate of 35%. It is the only class 10 asset the company owns. The asset has a residual value of $ 10,000. CCA for tax purposes can be claimed up to a maximum of:

  a. $ 14,000
  b. $ 10,500
  c. $ 7,000
  d. $ 5,250

_____ 10. In 1992 Ace Investors purchased Lost Airlines for $100,000,000. The book value of the identifiable assets were $125,000,000 with liabilities of $45,000,000. The difference between the purchase price and net assets is termed:

  a. Goodwill
  b. Gain-on-sale
  c. A good deal
  d. Depletion

III Problems

Problem 1:
Marilyn Leach, controller for Maritime Tours Ltd., acquired a new 4-wheel drive tour vehicle. The vehicle cost $ 22,000, and was expected to last 4 years and have a salvage value of $ 2,000.

Required:
Calculate the annual depreciation and book value of this vehicle utilizing the straight-line, the sum-of-the-years-digits, and 150% declining balance (i.e. 1.5 times the straight-line rate) methods of depreciation.

Problem 2:
Cookies by Karen Co. Ltd. purchased a new deluxe oven for $150,000. The company planned to keep it for approximately five years, after which time it believed it could sell the oven for approximately $30,000.

Chapter 9

Required:

a. Determine depreciation under each of the following methods for the first four years that the oven is in use:
    - (i) Straight-line
    - (ii) Double Declining balance

b. At the start of the fifth year the company sold the oven to a bakery for $60,000. Determine the gain under each of the two depreciation methods.

Problem 3:

On January 1, 1981, Bishop Ltd. purchased a machine for $ 30,000. The engineers estimated the machine would have a 20 year life with a scrap value equal to 10 percent of the machine's original cost. On January 1, 1988, experts were hired to review the estimates of expected life and residual value. Their findings were as follows:

Estimated life (total)   15 years
Estimated Scrap Value $ 6,000

Depreciation has not yet been recorded in 1988. Assume that the straight-line method of depreciation is used.

Required:

a. Calculate the net book value of the machine on January 1, 1988.

b. Calculate the amount of depreciation expense to be recorded on December 31, 1988, and prepare the necessary journal entry.

c. On January 1, 1993, the machine was completely overhauled for $ 5,000, and is now expected to be used by the company until December 31, 1997. It is expected to have a scrap value of $ 2,000 at this time. Prepare the journal entry to record the overhaul on January 1, 1993.

d. Calculate the revised depreciation expense to be recorded at December 31, 1993, and prepare the necessary journal entry.

Problem 4:

World Trade purchased two new machines during 19X3. Machine # 1 was purchased in early January for $ 26,400 cash and installed for another $ 700. It had an estimated useful life of 10 years and an estimated salvage value of $ 2,400. The Company depreciates this type of machine using the double declining balance method.

Machine # 2 was purchased on October 1, 19X3 for $ 35,000 cash. It had an estimated useful life of 10 years and an estimated salvage value of $ 1,500. The Company depreciates this type of machine using the straight line method.

On January 1, 19X5, machine # 1 was sold for $ 22,000 cash, and machine # 2 had a major overhaul costing $ 2,067. The overhaul extended the life of machine #2 by 2 years to a total of 12 years. The expected salvage value for machine #2 of $ 1,500 is unchanged. The Company had a December 31st year-end.

Assume it is company policy to only depreciate assets in the month of acquisition if they are acquired before the fifteenth of the month.

Required:

a.   Prepare the necessary journal entries to record the acquisition of the machines in 19X3.

b.   Prepare the necessary journal entries to record the depreciation of the machines in 19X4.

c.   What is the amount of the gain or loss on the disposal of machine # 1 in 19X5?

d.   Prepare the necessary journal entries to record the overhaul of machine # 2 in 19X5, and the revised depreciation expense for 19X5.

Chapter 9

Problem 5:

During 19X3, Midnight Equipment Company had the following results from operations:

Sales (in cash)	$ 450,000
Cash operating expenses	275,000
Depreciation expense:	
Accelerated depreciation expense	75,000
Straight-line depreciation expense	37,500
Income tax rate	40%

Required:

a.   Utilizing a schedule similar to Exhibit 9-6, determine the cash provided by operations before and after taxes using straight-line and accelerated depreciation.

b.   Explain the schedule

Problem 6:

Mac Dougal Aircraft purchased a laser-cutting machine, used in the production of aircraft, for $700,000 in 19X1. In addition to the price of the machine, Mac Dougal paid insurance during shipment of $5,000, transportation costs of $7,000, installation costs of $20,000 and training costs of $13,000. Unfortunately during installation, a fire caused damage to the machine of $5,000. The machine was expected to last 6 years and have a residual value of $50,000. Mac Dougal uses double-declining-balance depreciation on all machines of this type. At the beginning of year 3 the machine was sold for $450,000.

Required:

a.   Record the journal entry to capitalize the laser-cutter at acquisition.

b.   Determine the gain or loss on the sale of the machine.

c.   Prepare the journal entry to record the sale of the machine and the journal entry needed to remove the machine from the books.

For additional practice with capital assets see Lotus Template files P9-20.wk1, P9-26.wk1, P9-27.wk1, P9-30.wk1 and Page9-60.wk1.

CHAPTER 9 ANSWERS AND SOLUTIONS

I   True and False

1.   True
2.   True
3.   True
4.   False   Gains or losses are based on the difference between the proceeds received on sale of the asset and the book value of the asset. Book value is equal to historical cost minus accumulated depreciation.
5.   False   Extension of the useful life of an asset is a major factor supporting capitalization of an expenditure. If the expenditure is also material in amount (which it usually is if it extends useful life) it is capitalized.
6.   True
7.   False   Different depreciation methods may be used for financial statement reporting and tax purposes.
8.   True   Expenses required to prepare the land for use.
9.   False   In a basket-purchase situation, proper procedure calls for the basket-purchase price to be divided based upon the ratio of each individual asset's fair market value to the total fair market value of all the assets in the group purchase. This allocation is necessary because often the assets acquired are depreciated at different rates or land is part of the purchase and it is not depreciated at all.
10.   False   Depreciation is the systematic process of allocating unexpired asset costs to expense in the period in which the assets are used to produce revenue. Depreciation expense is a non-cash charge and is not a savings account.
11.   False   Like depreciation, amortization of an intangible asset is over its expected useful life.
12.   True
13.   True   This depends on the company's policy for new acquisitions.
14.   False   When it is necessary to adjust the estimated useful life of an asset it is considered a "change in an accounting estimate" and it is adjusted prospectively (i.e. over the future), not retroactively.
15.   True

Chapter 9

II   Multiple Choice

1.   C.   Depletion is associated with natural resources, depreciation with tangible assets, and transference is a distractor.

2.   B.   Formula to calculate denominator in the fraction:

$$\frac{n(n=1)}{2} = \frac{5(5+1)}{2} = 15$$

$$\frac{\text{Yrs. remaining life}}{\text{Sum-of-years-Digits}} \times \text{Depreciable value} = \text{Dep. expense}$$

$$4/15 \quad \times (50{,}000 - 1{,}000) = \$13{,}067$$

3.   B.   Allocation of the basket purchase price is based on the following:

Machine	FMV	Ratio to total FMV
Machine # 1.	$ 49,500	30%
Machine # 2.	$ 82,500	50%
Machine # 3.	$ 33,000	20%
Total	$165,000	100%

Ratio x total basket-purchase price = allocation value

Mach. # 1.   .30 x 100,000 = $30,000
Mach. # 2.   .50 x 100,000 = $50,000
Mach. # 3.   .20 x 100,000 = $20,000

4.   C.   Capitalizable costs include all costs reasonable and necessary to place the asset in position to contribute to the production of revenue. These costs include: acquisition cost, transportation costs, insurance during transit, installation costs and initial training costs.

5.   D.

$$\frac{\text{Historical cost - Residual value}}{\text{Units of service}} = \text{Depreciation per unit}$$

$$\frac{63,000 - 3,000}{240,000} = .25 \text{ per kilometer}$$

50,000 kilometers x .25 = $12,500

6. D. <u>Step 1.</u> Determine book value at the date useful life is adjusted.

($100,000 - 5,000) / 5 yrs. = $19,000
then $19,000 x 3 = $57,000 accumulated depreciation

$100,000 - 57,000 = $<u>43,000 book value.</u>

<u>Step 2.</u> Divide book value (less any salvage or residual value)by the new estimate of useful life.

($43,000 - 0) / 4 yrs. = $<u>10,750</u>

7. B. Straight-line rate: 100/8 = .125
Double-declining balance rate: .125 x 2 = 25%

Yr.	Rate	Beg. Book Value	Depr. Expense	End. Bk. value
1	.25	$125,000	$31,250.00	$93,750.00
2	.25	$ 93,750	$23,437.50	**$70,312.50**

8. C. Proceeds from sale minus book value equals the gain or loss.

$21,000 - (62,000 - 40,000) = $1,000 loss

9. C. In the year of acquisition, only one half of the CCA can be claimed.
.5 x ($40,000 x .35) = $7,000

10. A. Goodwill is the difference between the identifiable net assets and the purchase price of the firm.

Chapter 9

III   Problems

Problem 1:
a. Straight-line

Depreciation expense = (22,000 - 2,000)/ 4 = $5,000 per year

Year	Depreciation expense	Book Value
0		$22,000
1	$5,000	17,000
2	$5,000	12,000
3	$5,000	7,000
4	$5,000	*2,000

* residual value

b. Sum-of-the-Years-digits

$$\frac{4(4+1)}{2} = 10 = \text{Denominator fraction}$$

Yr.	Yrs. Remain. useful life	Fraction	Depr. base	Depr. exp.	Bk.value
0					$22,000
1	4	4/10	$20,000	$ 8,000	14,000
2	3	3/10	20,000	6,000	8,000
3	2	2/10	20,000	4,000	4,000
4	1	1/10	20,000	2,000	2,000

c.   150%-Declining-Balance

Straight-line rate = 100/4 = 25% or .25
Declining-balance rate = .25 x 1.50 =.375

Year	Rate	Beg. Bk. Value	Dep. expense	End. Bk. Value
0	.375			$22,000
1	.375	$22,000	$8,250	13,750
2	.375	13,750	5,156	8,594
3	.375	8,594	3,223	5,371
4	.375	5,371	2,014	3,357

Problem 2:

a) Straight-line depreciation each year:

$$(\$ 150,000 - 30,000)/5 = \$ 24,000 \text{ per year}$$

Double Declining Balance
Rate is equal to twice the straight-line rate of 20%, therefore 40%

Year	Rate	Depreciation expense	Net book value at year-end
1	.40	.40 X 150,000 = 60,000	90,000
2	.40	.40 X 90,000 = 36,000	54,000
3	.40	.40 X 54,000 = 21,600	32,400
4	.40	$ 2,400*	30,000*

* the asset can never be depreciated below salvage value. In this case, this is equal to $ 30,000. In year 4 depreciation expense would be calculated as .40 X 32,400 = 12,960 but the depreciation of 12,960 exceeds the amount allowed. Depreciation expense may not exceed $ 2,400 in year 4.

b) The gain is the difference between the net book value of the asset (cost - accumulated depreciation) and the proceeds on disposal of $ 60,000.

Under straight-line depreciation:
Net Book Value = 150,000 - (4 X $ 24,000/yr) = $ 54,000
Proceeds $ 60,000
Gain on disposal $ 6,000

Under double declining balance:
Net Book Value at the end of year 4
   (the same as the beginning of year 5) = $ 30,000
Proceeds $ 60,000
Gain on disposal $ 30,000

Chapter 9

Problem 3:

a) January 1, 1988:

      original depreciation = [30,000 - .10(30,000)]/20 years = $ 1,350/year

       7 years depreciation X $1,350/year = $ 9,450 acc. dep.

      therefore, net book value = $ 30,000 - 9450 = $ 20,550

b) (20,550 - 6000)/8years remaining life = 1819/year

      DR Depreciation Expense   1819

          CR Accumulated Depreciation   1819

c)   DR Machine   5000

          CR Cash or Accounts Payable   5000

d)   Accumulated depreciation at Jan. 1, 1988   9450

      New depreciation for 1988-92

                5 X 1819   9095

            Total acc. depreciation   18,545

Revised Depreciation - Jan. 1, 1993:

nbv of (30,000-18,545) + overhaul 5000 - salvage 2000 = 14455

$ 14,455/5 years remaining life = 2891

      DR Depreciation Expense   2891

          CR Accumulated Depreciation   2891

Problem 4:

a)   DR Machine # 1   27,100

          CR Cash   27,100

      DR Machine # 2   35,000

          CR Cash   35,000

b)   Machine # 1:

double-declining balance (twice the straight-line rate of 10%) = 20%

acquired during January 19X4:

          depreciation for 19X3 = .20 X $ 27,100 = $ 5,420

          depreciation for 19X4 = .20 X (27,100 - 5,420) = $ 4,336

entry for 19X4:
DR Depreciation expense   4,336
      CR Accumulated depreciation   4,336

Machine # 2:
      straight-line depreciation, 10 years (120 months) and salvage of $ 1,500
          depreciation expense = (35,000 - 1,500)/10 years = $ 3,350/year
          acquired October 1, 19X3 (3 months of usage in 19X3)
          depreciation for 19X3 = 3/12 X 3,350 = $ 838 (rounded)
          depreciation for 19X4 = $ 3,350

entry for 19X4:
DR Depreciation expense   3,350
      CR Accumulated depreciation   3,350

c)   Machine # 1 is sold January 1, 19X5
       NBV = Cost - Accumulated Depreciation
            = 27,100 - (5,420 + 4,336) = $ 17,344
       Proceeds of $ 22,000 - NBV of $ 17,344 = $ 4,656 GAIN

d)   Overhaul of Machine # 2 in 19X5
       DR Machine # 2   2,067
          CR Cash   2,067

Revised depreciation as at January 1, 19X5:
NBV at December 31, 19X4: $ 35,000 - (838 + 3,350) = $ 30,812
Revised Depreciation:
        = [$ 30,812 + 2,067 overhaul - $ 1,500 salvage]/ [129 months*]
        = $ 31,379/129 months remaining useful life
        = $ 243.25 per month

* 144 months (or 12 years) new life - 15 months usage (in 19X3 and 19X4)

19X5 depreciation = 12 months X 243.25/month = $ 2,919
entry for 19X5:
DR Depreciation expense   2,919
      CR Accumulated depreciation   2,919

Chapter 9

Problem 5:

a.

	Before Taxes		After Taxes	
	S/L depr.	Accel. depr.	S/L depr.	Accel. depr.
Sales	$450,000	$450,000	$450,000	$450,000
Less cash exp.	275,000	275,000	275,000	275,000
Pretax cash from ops.	$175,000	$175,000	$175,000	$175,000
Depre. exp.	37,500	75,000	37,500	75,000
Pretax income	$137,500	$100,000	$137,500	$100,000
Tax exp.	0	0	55,000	40,000
Net income	$137,500	$100,000	$82,500	$60,000
Pretax cash from ops.	$175,000	$175,000	$175,000	$175,000
Tax exp.	0	0	55,000	40,000
Cash flow from ops.	$175,000	$175,000	$120,000	$135,000

b.   The first two columns of part a demonstrate that if there are no taxes, different depreciation methods have no cash flow implications. The last two columns demonstrate that the cash flow implications of different depreciation methods when there are taxes is equal to the tax rate times the difference in depreciation, for example:

Tax rate x difference in depreciation   = cash flow effect
.40 x ($75,000 - 37,500)   = $ 15,000*

* the difference between $ 120,000 and $ 135,000

Problem 6:
a. Capitalized Costs:

invoice price	$700,000
insurance	5,000
transportation costs	7,000
installation costs	20,000
repair costs	5,000
training costs	13,000
total capitalizable costs	$750,000

entry:
DR Equipment   750,000
      CR Cash   750,000

b. Depreciation schedule: Double-declining-balance
straight-line rate is 100/6 = 16.67%, therefore the double-declining rate is 33%

Year	Rate	Beg.Bk. Value	Depr. expense	End. Bk. Value
1	.333	$750,000	$249,750	$500,250
2	.333	500,250	166,583	333,667
total - yr. 2			$416,333	

Historical cost	$750,000	Sale Price		$450,000
Accumulated depr.	(416,333)	Book Value		(333,667)
Book Value	$333,667	Gain on Sale		$116,333

c. entry:
DR Cash   450,000
DR Accum.depreciation   416,333
      CR Equipment   750,000
      CR Gain on sale   116,333

Chapter 10

Liabilities and Interest

Liabilities make up a large portion of the right side of the balance sheet equation. The composition of the various forms of liabilities and equity can have a major impact on the composition of assets that constitute the left-hand side of the equation. Careful study of liabilities, their classification, and their impact on decision making is extremely important to anyone interested in effectively incorporating financial statements into their decision making framework. Utilization of the following objectives while studying this chapter will act as a handy reference to help gauge the progress of your efforts.

1. Explain why information about liabilities is important to readers of financial statements.
2. Explain the accounting for current liabilities.
3. Describe the contractual nature of various long-term liabilities.
4. Use present-value techniques in valuing and accounting for long-term liabilities. (Appendix 10A)
5. Value and account for bond issues over their entire life.
6. Explain the nature of pensions and other postretirement benefits.
7. Define contingent liabilities and explain why they are often disclosed in notes rather than in the financial statements.
8. Apply ratio analysis to assess the debt levels of an entity.
9. Describe, value, and account for long-term lease transactions. (Appendix 10B)

REVIEW OF KEY CONCEPTS

A. Liabilities are an entity's obligations to pay cash or provide goods and services. Liabilities may be broken down into two major classifications, short-term liabilities and long-term liabilities. These classifications give the reader an indication of the timing of these obligations.

   1. **Current liabilities** are liabilities which are expected to come due within one year or one operating cycle.

   2. **Long-term liabilities** are those obligations which are expected to come due beyond one year after the balance sheet date or after one operating cycle for those companies with an operating cycle exceeding one year. *Current portions* of long-term debt are expected to be paid during the coming period and are reclassified as current liabilities.

B. Current liabilities take a variety of forms: accounts payable, notes payable, accrued taxes, product warranty liabilities, refundable deposits, unearned revenue, wages payable, and the current portion of long-term debt are all examples of current liabilities.

   1. **Trade accounts payable** represent obligations made for the purchase of goods and services on credit. Examples include payments to suppliers for merchandise, outstanding utility bills, and newspaper advertising obligations.

   2. **Notes Payable** represent short-term obligations to a lender, such as a bank. An example would be the retailer who borrows money 90 days prior to the holiday season to finance additional inventory at Christmas. Expectations are to repay the principle and interest shortly after Christmas.

   3. **Accrued employee compensation** involves payroll balances outstanding at the end of the period. This classification also includes amounts withheld from employees' paychecks and outstanding employer liabilities for income taxes and other deductions at source.

   4. **Income taxes payable** represents the income taxes payable based on taxable income for the period.

5. **Current portion of long-term debt** represents the portion of long-term debt that is due in the next period. This is consistent with management's intention to utilize current assets to liquidate the current portion of long-term debt.

6. **Sales tax** is collected by retailers from customers on behalf of the provincial and federal governments. Accrued sales tax is generally paid either monthly or quarterly depending on the various regulations.

7. **Product warranty liability** results when expenses associated with product warranties are matched against revenue from the sale of related products. Since no actual claims may have occurred yet, a liability is established to offset the expense that is recorded. Subsequent actual claims are used to reduce the product liability balance.

8. **Returnable deposits** are current liabilities to the *holder* of the deposit. There is recognition that the deposit will be returned upon completion or expiration of the events that "triggered" the reason for the deposit. Classification of a deposit as a current liability indicates that it is expected to be repaid during the subsequent period.

9. **Unearned revenue** constitutes collections, in advance, for goods or services not yet delivered or performed. A good example would be season ticket sales made in advance for the Toronto Maple Leafs hockey season. A portion of the liability will be discharged, and revenue will be recognized upon performance of the games on the schedule.

C. Long-term obligations generally arise from the need to finance a portion of the firm's assets, most notably capital assets, with debt. These obligations, which span several periods, are recorded at the present value of the debt obligation based upon the effective (market) interest rate at the time of the transaction. THIS EFFECTIVE RATE IS OFTEN DIFFERENT FROM THE COUPON RATE STATED IN THE AGREEMENT!

1. Two of the most common forms of long-term liabilities are bonds and notes. Long-term lease obligations and pension liabilities are also two areas which have grown in importance over the last several years.
    a. **Notes** are similar to bonds but are issued to a small group of investors in a **private placement.** Notes issued in private placements are not traded among the general public.

b.   **Bonds** are formal obligations sold to large numbers of investors such as the general public. They are characterized by a **trust indenture** which states such things as: the term to maturity, the face value of the obligation, the coupon rate of interest, the frequency of interest payments, and other items of importance such as call provisions and conversion privileges.

2.   The issue price of the bond depends on the relationship between the **stated or coupon interest rate** on the bond and the interest rate demanded by the market (based on the riskiness of the investment). The interest rate demanded by the market is known as the **effective market interest rate**. It is called the effective rate because unless the terms of the bond issue are adjusted (through the issue price) to generate this return, there is no sale of the bond on the market (i.e. there are no interested buyers). The difference between the stated interest rate and the effective market rate causes the bond to sell at a discount (below par or face value) or at a premium (above par or face value).

a.   A bond will sell at **par** if the coupon rate of interest on the bond is *equal* to the effective rate of interest demanded by the market.

b.   A bond will sell at a **discount** if the coupon rate of interest on the bond is *lower* than the effective rate of interest demanded by the market.

c.   A bond will sell at a **premium** if the coupon rate of interest on the bond is *higher* than the effective rate of interest demanded by the market. (In this case there will be too many buyers for the bond because it offers a superior return. This causes the issue price of the bond to be bid up by buyers who are anxious to invest. In an effort to secure their investment, buyers will effectively offer to lend the company more than the face value of the bond but still receive the same interest and repayment terms. This lowers the return to the buyer and also lowers the real cost of the debt to the company to an amount below the coupon rate of interest.)

d.   Remember, there is an **inverse relationship** between the **market price of the bond** and the **effective rate of interest** in the market. As the effective (market) rate rises, bond prices fall, and vice-versa.

Chapter 10

Before continuing, look carefully at Exhibit 10-3 on page 446 of the text. Notice that the <u>bond price</u> is made up of <u>two components</u>, the <u>present value of the interest payments</u> (a cash flow) and the <u>present value of the face value</u> (also a cash flow) of the bond repaid at maturity.

3.   When a bond is issued at a premium or a discount, a difference exists between the cash amount received, based on the current market price, and the face value of the bond, recorded as a long term liability. This difference is either a bond discount or a bond premium.

   a.   **Bond premiums** are normally carried as a contra account in long-term liabilities and are added to the par value of the bond to obtain the bond's book value.

   b.   **Bond discounts** can also be carried as contra accounts but in Canada the preferred presentation is to show the bond discount as a deferred charge on the asset side of the balance sheet. The bond discount is subtracted from the par value of the bond to get its book value.

   c.   The **bond payable is always** (without exception) **carried at par or face value**. This is the present value of the obligation.

4.   Bond premiums or discounts are to be amortized over the life of the bond using the **effective interest method.** This method determines the value for **interest expense** in the following manner:

Beginning book value of the liability	x	effective interest rate at the date of issue	= Interest expense

   Bond discount or premium amortization is then equal to the difference between interest expense (calculated in the box above) and the cash interest payment (or the accrual for the interest payment if year-end does not fall on an interest payment date)

The following example illustrates the calculation of amortization:

Bond issued at a discount:
example: a two-year, $ 10,000 bond paying semi-annual interest at 10% (the coupon rate) is issued to yield an effective return of 12%. The present value calculation gives an issue price of $ 9654

entry at issue:
DR Cash	9,654	
DR Bond discount	346	
CR Bond payable		10,000

after six months, the first cash interest payment is due:
book value of the bond = $ 10,000 - 346 = $ 9,654
interest expense = .06* X $ 9,654 = $ 579
actual cash payment = .05** X $ 10,000 = $ 500
amortization of bond discount = interest expense - interest payment
amortization = $ 579 - $ 500 = $ 79

* the effective interest rate (on a semi-annual basis which means half the annual rate)
** the coupon or stated interest rate (again on a semi-annual basis)

entry to record interest expense:
DR Interest expense	579	
CR Cash		500
CR Bond discount (amortization)		79

after this entry, the book value of the bond is:
$ 10,000 - ($346 - 79 amortization) = $ 9,733

in six month's time interest expense is based on the new book value of $ 9,733 as follows:

interest expense = .06 X $ 9,733 = $ 584
amortization = $ 584 - $ 500 = $ 84
entry in six month's time (assume interest payment date is at year-end):

DR Interest expense	584	
CR Cash		500
CR Bond discount		84

Chapter 10

Notice the following from the example just presented:

a.   When bonds are issued at a **discount**, the interest expense **increases** each period over the life of the bond, and the **interest expense** is always **greater than** the cash interest payment (or accrued payment).

The **opposite** relationship exists for bonds issued at a premium:

b.   When bonds are issued at a **premium**, the interest expense **decreases** each period over the life of the bond, and the **interest expense** is always **less than** the cash interest payment (or accrued payment).

In both cases this is necessary in order to reflect the real cost of the debt in each accounting period which is the effective interest rate demanded by the market at the issuance date.

Carefully study Exhibits 10-4 through 10-8 beginning on page 447 of the text to review the determination of premiums or discounts and the effective interest method of amortizing premiums or discounts.

5.   Bonds may be redeemed by the issuing company through purchases on the open market. Gains or losses are determined by comparing the book value of the obligation to the repurchase price.

example: the bond in the example above is redeemed at the end of the first six months (when it has a net book value of $ 9,733) at a cash value of $ 9,700.

entry:
DR Bond payable	10,000	
CR Cash		9,700
CR Bond discount		267
CR Gain on redemption		33

6.   The sale price of bonds sold between interest dates includes not only the sale price of the bond but any accrued interest to that point. The full amount of the interest payment is then made to the holder at the next premium date.

> See Exhibit 10-10 on page 454 of the text

7.   When dealing with non-interest bearing notes or bonds it is necessary to **impute** an interest rate at issuance. This rate equates the proceeds on issuance with the present value of the loan payments.

> See Exhibit 10-11 on page 456 of the text

D.   There are two kinds of pension plans:
1.   **Defined contribution** - where the employer must contribute a certain amount to the plan each year based on the employees' terms of employment.

2.   **Defined benefit** - where the employer promises to provide some future benefit to the employees.

The employer's liability is clearly defined in the first type of plan. The second type of plan presents an accounting challenge because the cost of providing future benefits is uncertain, and yet we want to include the cost of providing these future benefits in wage expense for the current period. This is because the right to receive future pension is really just another aspect of current compensation. According to the matching principle, it is appropriate to include these costs in the period in which the rights are *earned* by the employee which is the current period.

Under GAAP, Canadian companies must compute and show their liability (estimated) for future benefits on their current balance sheet. It is also desirable in Canada to show both the value of the liability and the value of the pension fund assets (which have been set aside to fund this liability) in the notes to the financial statements.

Chapter 10

E.   **Contingent liabilities** are potential future liabilities arising out of past transactions. Most contingent liabilities are disclosed in the notes to the financial statements and are not accrued on the face of the statements. This is because the liability may be reasonably certain but the amount of the liability can not be reasonably estimated.

F.   Debt ratios and interest coverage ratios give financial statement readers tools to help determine the amount of debt in a company's capital structure. While this level of debt is relative to the industry, it still remains a good indicator of risk. Generally, the higher the level of debt used by a company, the higher the level of risk associated with that company. This in turn leads to potentially higher interest rates for the company in the debt and equity markets.

> See page 461 of the text for the formulas used to calculate: debt-to-equity ratio, long-term-debt-to-total-capital ratio, debt-to-total-asset ratio, and the interest-coverage ratio.

G.   Money has a time value. In other words, because of opportunity cost, a dollar today is worth more than a dollar one year from now. Many financial decisions utilize some form of time-value-of-money concepts. These concepts are generally classified as calculations to determine the future value of a single sum, the present value of a single sum, and the present value of an ordinary annuity.

1.   **Future value** of a single lump sum uses the concept of compound interest, earning interest on interest. This future value can be calculated in one of two ways:

a.   Future value $= S(1 + i)^n$, where S stands for the value today of a single lump sum, i is equal to the interest rate, and n represents the number of periods.

b.   From a future value table (Table 1 in Appendix 10A) - find the factor corresponding to the time period necessary and the relevant interest rate. Multiply that factor by the present value of the single lump sum to arrive at the future value of the single lump sum.

2.   **Present value** of a single lump sum is calculated as the reciprocal of the formula for compounding and represents the value today, in present dollars, of a future amount. Present value may be calculated as follows:

a.   Since the present value formula is the reciprocal of the future value formula it would be calculated as $PV = FV/(1 + i)^n$.

b.   The alternative calculation involves finding the appropriate present value factor in a present value of a single lump sum table (Table 2 in Appendix 10A), then multiplying that factor by the future value amount to arrive at the present value of the future amount. Again, the factor depends on the appropriate time period and interest rate.

3.   **Present value of an ordinary annuity** involves finding the present value of a series of equal payments to be made at regular intervals in the future. The easiest method involves the use of a present value of an ordinary annuity table (Table 3 in Appendix 10A). The factor corresponding to the appropriate interest rate and time period is multiplied by the value for a single payment to arrive at the present value of the future cash flow annuity payments.

H.   **Leases** are contracts granting rights to the use of property in exchange for lease payments. Because of the increased use of leases the CICA has established criteria for two different types of leases: capital leases, and operating leases.

1.   **Operating leases** are a contractual obligation which is cancellable in nature (albeit for a fee). These are accounted for by the lessee (the user of the asset) as ordinary rent expense in the period in which the benefit (the use of the rental property) is received.

2.   **Capital leases** transfer substantially all the risks and benefits of ownership to the lessee. This is treated as an asset purchase on the books of the lessee (the user of the asset). The obligation for payment under the capital lease is also shown on the lessee's books as a liability.

Generally speaking, the asset and liability are valued at the present value of the lease payments. Over the life of the lease, the asset is amortized (usually straight-line) and the lease payments are recorded as interest expense, and as a reduction in the outstanding liability. The CICA considers a lease to be a **capital** lease if the terms of the lease meet **any** of the following conditions:

1. Title transfers to the lessee by the end of the lease term.

2. The lessee has an option to buy the asset at the end of the lease, and at the inception of the lease, the option- price seems to be a bargain.

3. The lease term is at least 75% of the estimated economic life of the property.

4. When the lease term begins, the present value of the minimum lease payments is at least 90% of the property's fair value.

PRACTICE TEST QUESTIONS AND SOLUTIONS

I **True or false** - For each of the following statements, enter a T or an F in the space provided to indicate whether the statement is true or false.

_____ 1. Potential investors in stocks or bonds are interested in the amount of debt a company carries because of the potential risk the debt represents to their investment.

_____ 2. The current portion of long-term debt is separated from the long-term debt and is classified as a current liability.

_____ 3. Interest expense for the period will be higher than the cash amount of interest paid if a bond was sold at a premium.

_____ 4. Cash received for bonds sold between interest periods will include the accrued interest as well as the market price of the bond.

_____ 5. Current liabilities are past obligations expected to be liquidated in the next period through the use of cash or through the delivery of goods or services.

_____ 6. Cash interest payments made to bondholders are determined by multiplying the par or face value of the bond by the effective rate of interest at the date of the transaction.

_____ 7. Pension and lease obligations are long-term liabilities that are recorded at the present value of future payments.

_____ 8. A debenture is a debt security secured by a specific claim against the assets given as collateral.

_____ 9. A bond is sold at par or face value, if the effective interest rate on the date of the transaction is greater than the bond coupon rate.

_____ 10. The book value of a bond sold at a discount will rise over the course of the bonds life and equal par value at the date of maturity.

_____ 11. The concept of compound interest involves earning interest on interest.

_____ 12. Operating leases are recorded on the books as a leased asset at the present value of the minimum lease payments.

_____ 13. For financial statement purposes, product warranties are expensed when the product is returned for repair or replacement.

_____ 14. Bonds issued at a premium will increase the cash interest payment because the market price is now higher.

_____ 15. Pension assets under the control of an independent manager are not shown on the balance sheet but it is desirable to disclose the information in the notes to the statements.

_____ 16. More often than not, contingent liabilities are indefinite in amount and are referenced in the notes to the financial statements.

Chapter 10

_____ 17. A debt-to-equity ratio in excess of 50% is an indicator of high risk and should be avoided at all costs.

II   Multiple Choice - For the following multiple choice questions, select the best answer and enter the identifying letter in the space provided.

_____ 1. In 19X1, Thess Trucking issued $ 100,000 of bonds at par or face value. These bonds carried a coupon rate of 9%. In 19X3, the effective rate of interest was 12%. Based upon this information, in 19X3, Thess Trucking's bonds will sell at:

a.   a premium
b.   par
c.   a discount
d.   Not enough information is given to tell.

_____ 2. Wilkerson Manufacturing issued bonds having a par value of $1,000, a coupon rate of 10% and 15 years to maturity. The bonds paid interest semi-annually. If the current market rate of interest is 8%, what is the most you would be willing to pay for these bonds? (use the present value tables in Appendix 10A of the textbook)

a. $ 743.22
b. $1,000.00
c. $1,172.90
d. $ 974.86

_____ 3. The book value of Bonds Payable on January 1, 19X3, was $1,135,903. The bonds had a face value of $1,000,000 and a coupon rate of 10%. The effective interest rate at the date of the original transaction was 8%. Using the effective interest rate method, calculate the interest expense for the year.

a. $ 90,872
b. $113,590
c. $100,000
d. $ 80,000

4. Long-term liabilities are generally recorded at:

    a. The face value of the obligation.
    b. The present value of all future payments discounted at the coupon rate of interest.
    c. The future value of the bond obligation plus the interest payments.
    d. The present value of all future payments, discounted at the market interest rate in effect at the date of the original transaction.

5. As the effective (market) rate of interest rises above the coupon rate on the bond, the market price of the bond will:

    a. Rise
    b. Fall
    c. Stay the same
    d. Can't determine without knowing the actual price.

6. Using the present value tables in Appendix 10A of the text, determine how much you would have to invest today to have $1,000,000 in 40 years when you retire. The current interest rate is 8%.

    a. $46,000.00
    b. $47,250.00
    c. $38,623.40
    d. $49,123.40

7. Jeff made a heck of a deal on a bond issue! He found a small group of investors to purchase $50,000 worth of bonds for $34,029. There was no coupon rate on the bonds nor were there any interest payments. The $50,000 is due in five years. What is Jeff's imputed rate of interest in this situation?

    a. -0-
    b. 10%
    c.   8%
    d. 12%

_____ 8. Gay Kendrick leased a piece of equipment that her accountant told her qualified as a capital lease. The lease liability at the beginning of the year was $100,000. The effective interest rate at the date of the inception of the lease was 12%. The current interest rate was 11%. Cash lease payments were set at $19,370.50 per year. What is the capital lease liability at the end of year 1?

a. $ 92,629.50
b. $100,000.00
c. $ 91,629.50
d. $ 88,000.00

_____ 9 Bonds that give the holder the option of trading in the bonds for a specific amount of stock are called:

a. Callable bonds
b. Mortgage bonds
c. Zero coupon bonds
d. Convertible bonds

_____ 10 The law firm of Hardy, Wilkerson, and Weiss has a malpractice suit outstanding at the end of the period. Their counsel, Howard, Fine, and Howard feel there is a good chance the suit will be settled against them and the firm might have to pay anywhere from $ 50,000 to $ 500,000 in damages. This is an example of a:

a. Short-term liability
b. Deferred liability
c. Contingent liability
d. Legal liability

III   Problems

Problem 1:

Hoover Manufacturing produces the finest line of widgets in the world. Total sales for 19X7 were $4,500,000. Experience has indicated that .5% of sales will be refunded due to product warranties.

Required:

a.   Prepare the journal entry necessary to record product warranty expense for 19x7.

b.   Assume that during the first month of the next year $5,000 in refunds are given in cash. What is the entry to record this event?

Problem 2:

You are the agent for Patrick Roy of Les Canadiens de Montreal. Ownership has offered Patrick a lump sum payment of either $10,000,000 today, or $15,000,000 payable at the end of three years. The current market rate of interest is 12%, and Roy does not need the money to live on during the next three years. Which deal should he take? (Your commission depends on the right decision.)

Problem 3:

Sue Bishop purchased 10 Ontario Hydro 15 year, $1,000 par value bonds on **April 1**, 19X1. The bonds carried a coupon rate of 10% and paid interest semi-annually on Jan. 1 and July 1. On the date of the purchase the effective interest rate was 12%.

Required:

a.   How much did Sue pay for the bonds?

b.   Assuming Sue's shares were part of a larger bond issue of $ 10,000,000, prepare the entry on Ontario Hydro's books on April 1, 19X1, to record the total bond issue.

c.   Prepare the journal entries on Ontario Hydro's books relating to the bonds on July 1, 19X1, December 31, 19X1 (the company's year-end) and January 1, 19X2.

Chapter 10

Problem 4:

Perfect Paints Ltd. issued $ 100,000 worth of 5 year bonds on April 1, 19X4. The bonds had a coupon rate of 8%, payable semi-annually on April 1 and October 1. The bonds were issued at a premium to yield an effective rate of 6%.

Required:

a. Calculate the issue price of the bonds and prepare a journal entry to record their issuance on April 1, 19X4.

b. Prepare the journal entry to record the October interest payment and premium amortization.

c. Prepare the entry required at year-end (December 31) to accrue the interest and amortization on the bond.

Problem 5:

In order to finance the purchase of new equipment, Eastern Bay Manufacturing issued $10,000,000 in new bonds. The bonds had a par value of $10,000 each, a coupon rate of 8%, and paid interest semiannually. The bonds had a maturity of 10 years and sold for $7,706 each.

Required:

a. Calculate the effective rate of interest at the date of the sale (Hint: you know it is greater than 8%).

b. Prepare the journal entry for the sale of the bonds.

c. What is the book value of bonds payable immediately after the first semiannual interest payment and adjustment to the amortization account?

d. What is the journal entry to retire the bonds at maturity assuming the last interest payment and amortization adjustment have been made?

For additional practice using compound interest calculations see Lotus Template files P10-29.wk1, P10-30.wk1 and PG10-20.wk1. For practice with bonds issued at a discount see P10-54.wk1 and P10-56.wk1. For practice with bonds issued at a premium see P10-58.wk1 and P10-59.wk1. For practice with ratios see P10-69.wk1.

CHAPTER 10 ANSWERS AND SOLUTIONS

I   **True and False**

1.   True
2.   True
3.   False   Bonds are issued at a premium because the effective market rate of interest is less than the stated or coupon rate. This results in the price of the bond being bid up (because there are many lenders). The premium is amortized over the life of the bond to reduce the interest expense to the lower effective interest rate.
4.   True   The lender in a sense buys the unearned interest so that the borrower can make a regular cash payment.
5.   True
6.   False   Cash interest payments are determined by multiplying the coupon or stated rate of interest by the face (par) value of the bond.
7.   True
8.   False   A debenture is secured by a claim against the total assets of the corporation.
9.   False   Bonds sold at face value (par) have a coupon rate equal to the effective rate of interest at the date of the transaction.
10. True
11. True
12. False   Capital leases are recorded as assets, not operating leases.
13. False   To be consistent with the matching principle, estimates of product warranty expense are made and accrued in the period the revenue is realized.
14. False   The coupon rate and the face value of the bond, when established, become part of the bond indenture. They do not change - only the issue price may vary.
15. True
16. True
17. False   The amount of debt carried in a company's financing structure depends on the practices of the industry. The trend of debt the company carries is also important to the decision.

Chapter 10

II   Multiple Choice

1.   C   A discount, because the market currently yields 12%. For Thess bonds to be competitive the price would have to fall to yield the current market rate of 12%.

2.   C   Bond value = present value of int. payments + present value of bond at maturity.

interest pmt. x (pv. factor, table 3, 4% interest, 30 periods) = pv. interest

$50 x (17.2920) = $ 864.60

plus: Principal x (pv. factor, table 2, 4% interest, 30 periods) = pv. principal

$1,000 x (.3083) = $ 308.30

Total bond value = $1172.90

3.   A   Beg. book value x effective interest rate = interest expense

$1,135,903 x .08 = $90,872.00

4.   D   Per the definition in the chapter.

5.   B   Remember, as interest rates rise, bond prices fall. As interest rates fall, bond prices rise.

6.   A   Future value = pv (present value factor, 8%, 40 years, see Table 2)

$ 1,000,000 = x (.0460)

$ 1,000,000 (.0460) = x

$46,000 = x

7.   C $34,029 = 50,000 x (present value factor, table 2)

$$\frac{\$34,029}{50,000} = \text{(present value factor, table 2)}$$

= .6806 (row 5, table 2)

imputed rate = 8%

8.   A   interest expense = effective rate x beginning book value

$12,000 = .12 x $100,000

$100,000 - 12,000 - 19,370.50 = **$92,629.50**

9.   D   Convertible bonds may be converted to another security, generally common stock, at the discretion of the shareholder. This is done in accordance with the parameters established in the trust indenture.

10.   C   Contingent liabilities are potential liabilities dependent on a future event arising out of a past transaction. Contingent liabilities are disclosed in the notes to the financial statements. No entry is made to record the liability unless the amount can be reasonably determined.

III   Problems

Problem 1:

An estimate of the potential returns associated with the sales must be made in the period of the sales.

a.   Warranty expense (4,500,000 x .005)   22,500
         Liability for warranties   22,500

b.   When the refund is made the warranty liability account is reduced.

     Liability for warranties   5,000
         Cash   5,000

Problem 2:

This problem may be solved two ways: as a present value problem or a future value problem.

<u>Future value:</u>

Future value = present value x (FV factor, table 1, 12%, 3 yrs.)
      x = $10,000,000 x (1.4049)
      x = <u>$14,049,000</u>

According to this calculation, if Roy invests the $10,000,000 at 12%, the best he could do is to earn $14,049,000. This is less than the $15,000.000, so he should take the $15,000,000 and run!

<u>Present value:</u>

Present value = future value x (PV factor, table 2, 12%, 3yrs.)
       x = $15,000,000 x (.7118)
       x = <u>$10,677,000</u>

This confirms our previous calculation. In order for Roy to have $15,000,000 available in three years, he would have to invest $10,677,000 today at 12%. This is obviously an amount greater than the $10,000,000 that was offered. He should definitely take the $15,000,000 and run!

Chapter 10

Problem 3:

Since Sue bought her bonds between interest periods she will pay *both* the market price of the bond and the accrued interest since the last payment.

Bond:(per $ 1,000 bond)
Bond value = semiannual int. pmt x (PV factor, **6%***, 30 periods, table 3)
$\quad$ + $\quad$ principal x (PV factor, **6%***, 30 periods, table 2)

* note the use of the effective rate of interest (one-half of the annual rate of 12%) and the actual cash flows to get the present value issue price
Bond value = $50 (13.7648) + $1,000 (.1741)

$\quad$ $862.34 = $688.24 + $174.10

Interest:(per bond)
Accrued interest = principal x % period outstd. x coupon rate
$\quad\quad$ $25 = $1,000 x 3/6** x (.10 x 1/2***)
** adjustment for 3 months of interest (one-half of a six month period)
*** adjustment because interest is calculated semi-annually

Total:

Mkt. value of bond	$862.34	
Accrued interest	25.00	
a. Total price paid	$887.34 x 10 bonds purch. = $8873.40	

b.

DR Cash	8,873,400	
DR Bond discount	**1,376,600	
$\quad$ CR Bond payable		10,000,000
$\quad$ CR Interest expense		250,000

** 1000 face value - 862.34 market value = $ 137.66 premium per $ 1,000 bond issued. The total discount on the entire premium is $ 137.66 X 10,000 = $ 1,376,600

Ontario Hydro issued 10,000 bonds with a face value of $ 1,000 for a total of $10,000,000. To get the proceeds for the entire issue, multiply the proceeds calculated in part a. by 10,000.

c. $\quad$ **July 1, 19X1**

interest expense = .06($ 8,623,400) =		$517,404
interest payment		500,000
amortization		$ 17,404

entry:

DR Interest expense   517,404

     CR Cash   500,000

     CR Bond discount   17,404

December 31, 19X1 (the accrual is for 6 months)

interest expense = .06 ($8,623,400 + 17,404)   518,448

interest payment accrual   <u>500,000</u>

amortization   <u>$ 18,448</u>

entry:

DR Interest expense   518,448

     CR Bond discount   18,448

     CR Interest payable   500,000

January 1, 19X2 interest payment:

DR Interest payable   500,000

     CR Cash   500,000

Problem 4:

a. <u>Bond:</u>

Bond value = semiannual int. pmt x (PV factor, **3%***, 10 periods, table 3)

       +   principal x (PV factor, **3%***, 10 periods, table 2)

* note the use of the effective rate of interest (one-half of the annual rate of 6%) and the actual cash flows to get the present value issue price

semi-annual interest payments = .04 x $ 100,000 = $ 4,000

Bond value = $4,000 (8.5302) + $100,000 (.7441)

    $108,530.80 = 34,120.80 + 74,410

      $862.34 = $688.24 + $174.10

entry:

DR Cash   108,531

     CR Bond payable   100,000

     CR Bond premium   8,531

b.   October 1 interest payment and entry:

        interest expense = .03 (100,000 + 8,531) = 3,256

        interest payment   <u>4,000</u>

        amortization   <u>$ 744</u>

entry:

DR Interest expense   3256

DR Bond premium   744

           CR Cash   4000

c.   December 31st accrual for 3 months:

interest expense = .03 (100,000 + {8531-744}) x 1/2* =$1617

interest accrual (1/2 of a regular 6 month period)   2,000

amortization   383

entry:

DR Interest expense   1617

DR Bond premium   383

           CR Interest payable   2000

Problem 5:

a.   To find the effective rate of interest you must calculate the yield to maturity on the bond.

(per bond)

$7,706,000 = 400 x (unknown PV annuity factor, 20 periods)

                  + 10,000 x (unknown PV factor, 20 periods)

$7,706,000 = 400 (pv annuity at x) + 10,000 (pv at x)

Using trial-and-error, let (x) equal the factor at a 6% semiannual rate of interest.

$7,706 = 400 (11.4699) + 10,000 (.3118)

$7,706 = 4,588 + 3,118

With a semiannual interest rate of 6% the annual effective interest rate is 12%.

b.   Cash (1,000 x 7,706)   7,706,000

        Discount on Bonds Payable   2,294,000

              Bonds Payable   10,000,000

c.   Interest expense = Effective semiannual rate x beginning book value

Beginning book value	Eff. rate	Int. exp.	Cash int. pmt.	Amortize bond disc.	Ending book value
$7,706,000	.06	$462,360	$400,000	$62,360	$7,768,360

d.   Bonds Payable   10,000,000
                Cash   10,000,000

Chapter 11

```
┌─────────────────────────────┐
│                             │
│   Statement of              │
│   Cash Flows                │
│                             │
│                             │
└─────────────────────────────┘
```

While many users of financial statement information are interested in the results of operations, as reflected in the income statement, the ability to generate sufficient cash to satisfy maturing obligations may mean the difference between survival and closing the doors to the business. In recognition of the difference between net income and cash flows from operations, the CICA requires companies to include a Statement of Cash Flows (also known as a Statement of Changes in Financial Position) as part of the set of audited financial statements. The following objectives will act as a guide for your study of this interesting and informative statement.

1. Explain the ideas behind the statement of cash flows.
2. Classify activities affecting cash as operating, investing, or financing activities.
3. Prepare a statement of cash flows using the direct method.
4. Calculate cash flows from operations using the indirect method.
5. Explain how depreciation relates to cash flow provided by operating activities.
6. Describe several reconciling items between net income and cash provided by operating activities.
7. Explain the treatment of gains and losses from capital asset sales and debt extinguishments in the statement of cash flows (Appendix 11A).
8. Use the T-account approach to prepare the cash flow statement (optional - Appendix 11B).

REVIEW OF KEY CONCEPTS

A.   So far we have talked about the income statement, the balance sheet and the statement of retained earnings. There is a fourth statement which is an important component of a set of financial statements. This statement is called the *Statement of Cash Flows*.

Why do we need another financial statement? The Statement of Cash Flows focuses on the issue of **liquidity** (i.e. how much cash does the firm have, as opposed to profit or income, and how has this cash balance changed from the prior reporting period).

Why isn't the income statement enough to explain how liquid the company is based on net income or profits?

Profitability is not liquidity. A company can have a profit but not have a cent in the bank. This is because income is an **accrual measure** and includes, for example, sales which are on credit and are not represented by cash. The income statement also contains a number of non-cash credits or debits. For example, depreciation expense reduces income but it does not use cash. As well, cash from operations may be invested in current assets or used to reduce current liabilities. For example, new inventory may be purchased with cash, or cash may be used to pay suppliers (accounts payable). These transactions are all part of the operating cycle of the firm, and they affect the amount of cash which ultimately results from net income. They are accounted for in the section of the Statement known as **Cash flow from operations**.

The company has certain other activities, referred to as **Investing** and **Financing** activities, which relate to the non-current assets and liabilities on the balance sheet. **Investing** activities are those which relate to non-current assets, such as the purchase of new fixed assets or the sale of land. **Financing** activities relate to those which affect the non-current liability and equity side of the balance sheet. For example, the issuance or repayment of long-term debt or bonds, or the payment of dividends, or the redemption or issuance of stock.

The Statement of Cash Flows explains why liquidity (defined as cash) has changed from the prior period by **looking at the changes in all the other balance sheet accounts** (this of course includes the net income for the year as this is contained in retained earnings). It is necessary to have a separate financial statement to do this because there is an insufficient amount of detail on the balance sheet to explain the changes in the balance sheet accounts. (For example if the beginning Fixed Asset balance is $100K and the ending is $150K this does not necessarily mean that the company had fixed asset additions of $50K - there may have been additions of $200K and disposals of $150K. The Statement of Cash Flows gives this detail and also tells the reader how these investments were financed).

B.   There are two primary methods of constructing the statement of cash flows. The difference between the two methods lies in the approach to arriving at cash flows from operating activities. Beyond that, the other two sections, cash flows from investing activities, and cash flows from financing activities are constructed in the same manner using either approach.

    a.   **The direct method** is concerned only with the cash portion of each item in the income statement, such as cash receipts from customers, cash payments to suppliers, interest income etc.

    b.   **The indirect method** focuses on the non-cash transactions that affect net income. It is essentially a reconciliation of net income on the accrual basis to a cash measure of income, known as cash flows from operations. This approach adjusts for non-cash items, such as an increase in accounts receivable, which is subtracted from net income to arrive at cash flows from operations. The increase in accounts receivable is deducted because sales not collected in cash were included in the accrual-based net income figure.

> See the textbook example comparing cash flows from operating activities under both the direct and indirect method.

C.   It is very important to understand how operating activities affect cash. Cash flows from operating activities emphasize the flow of cash to and from the customers and suppliers; accrual accounting emphasizes the flow of goods and services. A major focus of the statement is to determine the **net cash flow** from operations.

D.   The **direct method** of computing cash flows from operations concentrates on the cash inflows associated with collections from customers, and the cash outflows associated with operations in the period. By analyzing changes in the non-cash **current assets** and the non-cash **current liabilities** on the balance sheet in terms of their effect on cash receipts and disbursements, it is possible to derive cash flows from operations.

> Review Exhibit 11-5 for the comparison of net income and net cash provided by operating activities utilizing the direct method. After you feel comfortable with the format and underlying concepts go back and review Exhibit 11-3 to see the direct method applied to the entire statement.

E.   The **indirect method** of determining **cash flows from operations** concentrates on the effects of changes to **net income** from non-cash **current asset** and non-cash **current liability** accounts, as well as adjusting for non-cash items.

1.   *Increases* in non-cash *asset* accounts and *decreases* in non-cash *liability* accounts are **deducted** from net income as a use of cash.

2.   *Decreases* in non-cash *asset* accounts and *increases* in non-cash *liability* accounts are **added** to net income as a source of cash.

3.   **Depreciation**, and other non-cash expenses, are **added back to net income under the indirect approach**. Even though depreciation does not involve cash it is an expense that is included in the accrual measure of net income, and so it must be added back as part of the conversion to cash flows from operations.

4.   Non-cash **gains and losses** on the disposal of non-current assets (e.g., disposal of equipment) or non-current liabilities (e.g., a bond redemption) must be adjusted in the reconciliation of net income on the accrual basis to cash flows. This is because the gain or loss is the difference between the proceeds (of disposal or cash used for redemption) and the book value of the non-current asset or liability. The gain or loss is *not* a cash item - *the **proceeds** are the cash item.* The

223

approach is to neutralize the gain or loss in the operations section (**deduct gains, add back losses**) and show the **proceeds** (the real cash effect) as a source of cash in the **investing** (for disposals of non-current assets) or **financing** (for redemption of non-current liabilities) section of the statement.

(Note: since gains and losses do not involve cash, no adjustments must be made in the operations section of the statement when constructing the statement of cash flows using the **direct** method - the proceeds, however, will still appear under investing or financing activities, as applicable)

F.   As was discussed earlier, determining cash flows from investing and financing activities are **identical** under either the direct or indirect method of constructing the statement of cash flows.

1.   Cash flows from **investing** activities deal primarily with changes in **long-term asset accounts** and the effect of these changes on cash.

a.   Any *increase* in a long-term asset account would be considered a *use* of cash and any *decrease* in a long-term asset account would be considered a *source* of cash.

2.   Cash flows from **financing** activities are concerned with the changes in **long-term liability and shareholders' equity accounts** and the effect of these changes on cash.

a.   Any *increase* in a long-term liability or equity account would be considered a *source* of cash and any *decrease* in a long-term liability or equity account would be considered a *use* of cash.

G.   When facts become complicated and confusing, use of **the T-account approach** to constructing the statement of cash flows can be helpful. The T-account approach systematically accounts for the change in each of the items on the balance sheet.

1.   Since the cash account is the focus of the statement, a T-account with the beginning and ending balance is established first. This same procedure is used for all other accounts.

2. Summary entries are made in each of the accounts to record the changes in the account balances over the period. When utilizing the indirect method, start with net income and consider all the non-cash accounts that would impact net income. Follow the same procedure for investing and financing activities.

3. The T-account approach for the direct method is similar to the indirect method. The exception is the need to recreate the summary journal entries for the year.

H. An **illustrated example** of the preparation of the statement of cash flows on the **indirect** basis will help to tie together the concepts in this chapter.

How do we prepare a statement of cash flows on the indirect basis?

1. Determine the change in liquidity (defined as **CASH**) from the prior period. This change is the amount which the statement should reconcile to at the end.

2. Determine the amount of cash which results from operations. This involves starting with net income and either adding back to net income all non-cash expenses (like depreciation expense, loss on the sale of capital assets, goodwill amortization, write-down of long-term investments, etc.) and deducting all non-cash revenue items, such as the gain on the sale of capital assets. We must also analyze the effect the change in the other current assets and liabilities, besides cash, has had on cash from operations. For example, if accounts receivable or inventory have increased from the prior period this is a use of cash. If inventory or receivables levels are lower, then this is a source of cash. If accounts payable have increased this is a source of cash. A decrease in payables is a use of cash. This exercise gives us *CASH FLOW FROM OPER-ATIONS*.

3. Analyze the change in each non-current balance sheet account. We do this by starting with the beginning balance and reconciling to the ending balance based on the other information which is made available to us. We want to determine the cash effect of each transaction that caused the account to change. This means that we show proceeds on disposal and **not** the historical acquisition cost of the capital asset as the item on the statement. If the account is a non-current asset account, changes are

reflected as **investing** activities. If the account is a non-current liability or equity account, changes are reflected as **financing** activities.

4. Place all relevant items (i.e. those affecting cash) from 2 and 3 above on the statement of cash flow directly after the section for cash flow from operations. For each financing or investing activity, indicate whether it is a *source* or *use* of cash, and reconcile to the end amount (the change in cash during the period).

Use the following data, and the checklist above to prepare a statement of cash flows on the indirect basis:

CRAIGHEAD LTD.
Comparative Balance Sheets
As at Dec. 31, 1989 and 1990

	1990	1989
Current Assets		
Cash	2,000	200
Accounts Receivable	60,000	69,000
Inventory	210,000	200,000
Noncurrent Assets		
Capital Assets	550,000	500,000
Accumulated Depreciation	(95,000)	(90,000)
Total Assets	727,000	679,200
Current Liabilities		
Bank loan	2,500	2,000
Accounts Payable	75,000	80,000
Noncurrent Liabilities		
Long-term debt	45,000	50,000
Equity		
Common	200,000	200,000
Preferred	150,000	100,000
Retained Earnings	254,500	247,200
Total Liab. & Equity	727,000	679,200

Other information:
1. Net income for 1990 was $64,300
2. Dividends of $57,000 were paid
3. Capital asset purchase - $100,000 in cash
4. Capital asset disposal - asset originally cost $50,000 and was half depreciated. Proceeds of $35,000 generated a gain on the income statement of $10,000.
5. Depreciation expense was $30,000
6. Issued preferred shares for $50,000
7. Repaid $5000 of long-term debt

Preparation of the Statement of Cash Flow

1. Calculate the change in liquidity (defined as **CASH**) from the balance sheets.

Beginning cash	$ 200
Ending cash	2 000
Increase	1 800

2. Analyze net income and non-cash items, as well as the changes in other current assets and liabilities to determined **Cash Flow From Operations.**

    Net income is $64,300

    Non-cash items?

    > Depreciation $30,000 (non-cash expense, so add back to income)
    >
    > Gain on disposal of capital assets $10,000 (non-cash revenue, so deduct from income)

    Other current asset and liability changes?

    > Accounts receivable decreased by $9,000 - this is a source of cash (add to net income)
    >
    > Inventory increased by $10,000 - this is a use of cash (deduct)
    >
    > Bank Loan increased by $500 - this is a source of cash (add)
    >
    > Accounts Payable decreased by $5000 - this is a use of cash (deduct)

    THIS INFORMATION IS REFLECTED IN THE SECTION OF THE STATEMENT ENTITLED CASH FLOW FROM OPERATIONS - SEE SOLUTION ON NEXT PAGE.

3. Analyze the change in the other non-current balance sheet accounts.

    INVESTING ACTIVITIES (noncurrent assets)

    a) Capital assets

beginning balance	$500,000	
additions	100,000	USE OF CASH
less disposals	50,000	THE PROCEEDS OF $35 000 ARE SOURCE CASH
ending balance	550,000	

    b) Accumulated Depreciation

beginning balance	90,000	
+ depreciation expense	30,000	REFLECTED ALREADY IN 2 ABOVE AS AN ADD BACK TO INCOME
less acc. dep. on disposal	25,000	USED WITH PROCEEDS AND COST TO CALCULATE GAIN ON DISPOSAL - PROCEEDS REFLECTED ABOVE, GAIN DEDUCTED FROM INCOME IN 2 ABOVE
ending balance	95,000	

    FINANCING ACTIVITIES (noncurrent liab. and equity)

    a) Long-term Debt

beginning balance	50,000	
repayment of debt	5,000	USE OF CASH
ending balance	45,000	

b) Common stock - no change

c) Preferred stock

beginning balance	100,000	
issue	50,000	SOURCE OF CASH
ending balance	150,000	

d) Retained Earnings

beginning balance	247,200	
add net income	64,300	DEALT WITH IN 2 ABOVE
less dividends	57,000	USE OF CASH
ending balance	254,500	

4.   Enter the relevant information on the statement and reconcile to the change in cash (an increase of $1800)

Craighead Ltd.
Statement of Cash Flows
For The Year Ended December 31,1990

Cash Flow from operations

Net income	$64,300	
add back non-cash expenses		
depreciation expense	30,000	
deduct non-cash gains		
gain on sale of capital assets	(10,000)	
Other current items		
sources of cash		
decrease in accounts receivable	9,000	
increase in bank loan	500	
uses of cash		
increase in inventory	(10,000)	
decrease in accounts payable	(5,000)	
Cash Flow from operations		78,800

Investing Activities

Proceeds on disposal of capital assets	35,000	
Purchase of capital assets	(100,000)	
Total Use of Cash From Investing Activities		(65,000)

Financing Activities

Issuance of Preferred Shares	50,000	
Reduction in LT Debt	(5,000)	
Payment of Dividends	(57,000)	
Total Use of Cash From Financing Activities		(12,000)

Increase in cash during the year (balances to the increase calculated in 1 above) | | $ 1,800

PRACTICE TEST QUESTIONS AND SOLUTIONS

I   **True or false** - For each of the following statements, enter a T or an F in the space provided to indicate whether the statement is true or false.

_____   1.   The statement of cash flows is an optional statement that may be included with the balance sheet, income statement, and the statement of retained earnings.

_____   2.   The statement of cash flows provides information about the operating, investing, and financing activities of the business.

_____   3.   Cash flow emphasizes the flow of cash to and from customers and suppliers; accrual accounting emphasizes the flow of goods and services.

_____   4.   While interesting, the cash flows from operations is not as important as the cash flows from investing and financing activities.

_____   5.   Using the **direct method** of determining cash flows from operations, depreciation expense would be added back to net income.

_____   6.   The statement of cash flows explains where cash came from during a period and where it was spent.

_____   7.   Dividends are paid out of after-tax income and would be classified as an operating activity.

_____   8.   The **direct** method of determining cash flows from operations focuses on receipts from customers, payments to suppliers, and cash payments for operating expenses.

_____   9.   Purchases of new equipment with cash obtained by selling long-term bonds would be classified as a financing activity because of the use of debt.

_____   10.   Major investing and financing activities not involving cash do not relate to the statement of cash flows and would not be referenced.

_____ 11. Amortization of a premium on bonds payable would be deducted from net income using the **indirect** method.

_____ 12. A decrease in accounts payable is considered a source of cash and added to net income using the **indirect** method.

_____ 13. Using the **indirect** method, a loss on the disposal of a capital asset would be added back to net income under the operating section, and cash from the sale of the asset would be included under cash flows from investing activities as a source of cash.

_____ 14. When adding back depreciation to net income under the **indirect** method use the difference between the beginning and ending accumulated depreciation.

_____ 15. The T-account approach is especially useful when there are a number of complex transactions to be dealt with.

II **Multiple choice** - For each of the following multiple choice questions, select the best answer and enter the identifying letter in the space provided.

_____ 1. Using the **direct** method, gains and losses on disposal of a capital asset would be classified as :

    a. Operating activity
    b. Investing activity
    c. Financing activity
    d. Not classified

_____ 2. Payment of dividends would be classified in the statement of cash flows as:

    a. Operating activity
    b. Investing activity
    c. Financing activity
    d. Not classified

3. Financing activities would not include:

   a. Sale of stock in the company
   b. Reduction in long-term liabilities
   c. Dividends paid
   d. Loss on early extinguishment of long-term debt

4. During the period, accounts receivable increased $4,000 on sales of $40,000. What would be the amount of cash collected from customers?

   a. $40,000
   b. $44,000
   c. $36,000
   d. $37,500

5. During the period the local frame store had the following information available:

Net income	$ 35,000
Increase in accounts receivable	2,000
Decrease in accounts payable	3,000
Depreciation expense	1,500
Decrease in prepaid expenses	2,000
Sale of stock investment at book value	1,500

   Cash flow from operations would be:

   a. $30,500
   b. $37,500
   c. $33,500
   d. $32,000

_____ 6. During 19X3, Seymore Fasteners sold investments in other companies for $100,000 and made purchases of capital assets for $225,000. Part of the asset purchase was financed by the sale of new stock for $175,000. Depreciation expense was $15,000 and retirement of long-term debt totalled $103,000. What was the cash flow from investing activities?

    a.   ($125,000)
    b.   ($225,000)
    c.   ($278,000)
    d.   ($110,000)

_____ 7. Losses on the early extinguishment of long-term debt should be _____ when calculating cash flows from operations using the **direct** method.

    a.   Added
    b.   Subtracted
    c.   Ignored
    d.   Added to net income

_____ 8. Beginning wages payable was $6,000. Payroll expense during the period was $14,500. If the ending balance in wages payable is $3,500, what was the amount of cash payments to employees during the period?

    a. $14,500
    b. $17,000
    c. $18,000
    d. $11,500

_____ 9. If Alpha Works had positive cash flows from operations of $68,000, negative cash flows from investing activities of $173,000, and a decrease in their cash account of $15,000, what was cash flow from financing activities?

    a. $ 95,000
    b. $173,000
    c. $105,000
    d. $ 90,000

_____ 10. Payment of dividends to shareholders would be classified as:

      a. Operating activity
      b. Investing activity
      c. Financing activity
      d. Not classified

_____ 11. Which of the following would not be considered a financing activity?

      a. Issuance of long-term bonds
      b. Dividend payments
      c. Repurchase of company common stock on the open market
      d. Gains on early retirement of long-term debt

III   Problems

Problem 1:
Indicate the effect of each of the following transactions on the cash balance . Use + for increase, - for decrease, and 0 for no change.

    a. Sale of goods for cash   _____
    b. Purchase of inventory on credit   _____
    c. Payment of accounts payable   _____
    d. Depreciation expense   _____
    e. Sale of capital asset for book value   _____
    f. Accrual of interest expense   _____
    g. Sale of merchandise on credit   _____
    h. Conversion of bonds to common stock _____

Chapter 11

Problem 2:

St. Louis Manufacturing Co.
Balance Sheet
12/31/X8

Assets:

Cash	$ 44,000	$ 29,000
Accounts receivables	68,000	38,000
Inventory	64,000	54,000
Prepaid expenses	4,000	-0-
Net capital assets	360,000	220,000
Total	$ 540,000	$ 341,000

Liabilities and Equity:

Accounts payable	$ 30,000	$ 20,000
Wages payable	3,000	3,000
Long-term debt	125,000	26,000
Capital stock	177,000	127,000
Retained earnings	205,000	165,000
Total	$ 540,000	$ 341,000

St. Louis Manufacturing Co.
Income Statement and Statement of Retained Earnings
For period ended 12/31/X8

Sales		$ 458,000
Less cost of goods sold:		
Inventory, 1/1/X8	$ 54,000	
Purchases	198,000	
Cost of goods available	$ 252,000	
Inventory 12/31/X8	64,000	
Cost of goods sold		188,000
Gross profit		$ 270,000
Operating expenses:		
Selling and administrative expense	$ 106,000	
Depreciation expense	20,000	
Property taxes	11,000	
Interest expense	6,250	
Salary expense	71,750	
Total operating expenses		$ 215,000
Net income		$ 55,000
Retained earnings 12/31/X7		165,000
Less dividends		(15,000)
Retained earnings 12/31/X8		$ 205,000

During the period St. Louis Manufacturing purchased machinery for $160,000. A portion of the purchase was financed through the sale of $50,000 in new stock and the acquisition of $99,000 in new long-term debt.

Required:

a. Calculate the cash flow from operations for 19X8 using the **direct** method.

b. Calculate the cash flow from operations for 19X8 using the **indirect** method.

c. Calculate the cash flows from investing activities for 19X8.

d. Calculate the cash flows from financing activities for 19X8.

Chapter 11

Problem 3:

The records of Concordia Corp. showed the following information in the balance sheet accounts at December 31, 19X1 and 19X2.

	19X2	19X1
Cash	$ 11,000	$ 10,000
Accounts receivable	24,000	19,000
Inventory	50,000	52,000
Prepaid expenses	4,000	3,000
Capital assets (net)	147,000	95,000
Long-term investments	0	10,000
Total Assets	$ 236,000	$ 189,000
Accounts payable	$ 8,000	$ 12,000
Wages payable	2,000	3,000
Long-term notes payable	48,000	39,000
Common stock	150,000	120,000
Retained earnings	28,000	15,000
Total liabilities and equity	$ 236,000	$ 189,000

Additional Information:

a. Net income was $ 24,000
b. Cash dividends of $11,000 were paid
c. Depreciation expense was $ 3,000
d. Common stock was given in exchange for capital assets costing $ 30,000
e. Capital assets were purchased for $ 25,000; a long-term note of $ 9,000 was given and the rest was paid in cash
f. There was no gain or loss on the sale of Long-term Investments.

Required:

Prepare a Statement of Cash Flows using the **indirect** method.

Problem 4:

The comparative balance sheet of McGill Corp. shows the following at December 31:

	19X2	19X1
Cash	$ 10,000	$ 8,000
Accounts receivable	18,000	10,000
Inventory	24,000	20,000
Capital assets	94,000	60,000
Less: accumulated depreciation	(14,000)	(10,000)
Long-term investments	10,000	24,000
Total assets	$ 142,000	$ 112,000
Accounts payable	$ 16,000	$ 12,000
Long-term notes payable	40,000	32,000
Common stock	60,000	50,000
Retained earnings	26,000	18,000
Total liabilities and equity	$ 142,000	$ 112,000

The **income statement** for 19X2 appears below:

Sales		$ 300,000
Cost of sales		200,000
Gross profit		100,000
Operating expenses except depreciation	$ 78,000	
Depreciation expense	6,000	84,000
Income from operations		16,000
Other gains (losses)		
Gain on disposal of capital assets	$ 2,000	
Loss on disposal of investments	(4,000)	(2,000)
Net income		$ 14,000

Additional Information:

a. Dividends were paid
b. Issued shares for cash, $ 10,000
c. Capital assets disposed of during the year cost $ 6,000 and had accumulated depreciation of $ 2,000
d. Ignore income taxes

Required:

Prepare a Statement of Cash Flows using the **indirect** approach

Chapter 11

For additional practice preparing a statement of cash flows using the **direct** method see Lotus Template files P11-42.wk1, P11-47.wk1, P11-49.wk1 and P11-61.wk1. For practice using the **indirect** method see files P11-43.wk1, P11-48.wk1 and P11-50.wk1.

CHAPTER 11 ANSWERS AND SOLUTIONS

I True and false

1. False   The statement of cash flows is a basic financial statement required to be presented in the set of audited financial statements.

2. True
3. True
4. False   The cash flows from operations is the focal point of the statement. It highlights an entity's ability to generate cash on an ongoing basis.

5. False   Depreciation expense is added back to net income using the indirect method. Depreciation expense is added back to operating expenses to determine cash payments for operating expenses under the indirect method only.

6. True
7. False   Dividends are considered payment to the shareholders as part of the financing function and are classified as such.

8. True
9. False   Purchase of new equipment is an investing activity, which uses cash, and the issuance of debt is a financing activity, which is a source of cash.

10. False   All major financing and investing activities should appear on the statement of cash flows.

11. True   Interest expense is less than the cash payments due to premium amortization, therefore, deduct the amortization in the adjustments to net income.

12. False   Using the indirect approach and studying the balance sheet changes shows that a decrease in a non-cash liability account is considered a use of cash.

13. True
14. False   This is not always possible because of adjustments to accumulated depreciation for the sale of a depreciable asset during the period. Look on the income statement for depreciation expense or adjust for the effect of the disposal on the change in acc. depreciation.

15. True

II Multiple choice

1. D   Gains and losses on disposal are non-cash transactions that are not considered when using the direct method. They affect cash flows from operations using the indirect method because of their effect on net income.

2. C   Payment of dividends is considered part of the financing function and would be shown under that heading.

3. D   Loss on early retirement of long-term debt would be added back to net income when using the indirect method of determining cash flows from operations. The cash paid to retire the debt would be part of financing activities.

4. C   If accounts receivable increased by $ 4,000, then $ 36,000 ($ 40,000-4000) was collected from customers.

5. C   Using the indirect method:

Net income	$35,000
(Increase) in accounts receivable	(2,000)
(Decrease) in accounts payable	(3,000)
Depreciation expense	1,500
Decrease in prepaid expense	2,000
Total	$33,500

6. A   The only two transactions that refer to investing activities would be the $100,000 receipt of cash for the sale of the equipment and the purchase of new equipment for $225,000. The net effect is a $125,000 cash outflow from investing activities. The stock issue, depreciation expense, and retirement of debt are distractors.

7. C   Just as gains and losses on the sale of an asset are ignored when using the direct method, so too are losses on the early extinguishment of long-term debt. These are all non-cash charges to net income.

8. B

Beg. balance wages payable	$ 6,000
add: Payroll expense	14,500
Total payroll to be made	20,500
less: end. balance wages payable	(3,500)
Cash payments for payroll	$17,000

Chapter 11

9. D   Remember, the change in cash is explained in the statement of cash flows by the activities above it.

Cash flow from operations	$ 68,000
Cash flow from investing activities	(173,000)
Cash flow from financing activities	**90,000**
Change in cash account	$(15,000)

10. C   Dividends are considered a "cost" of attracting and retaining shareholders for most businesses and are therefore considered part of the financing activity.

11. D   Gain on early retirement of bonds payable would not be considered using the direct method. The gain would be deducted from net income using the indirect method.

III Problems

Problem 1:

a.	+	e.	+
b.	0	f.	0
c.	-	g.	0
d.	0	h.	0

Problem 2:

a. Cash flows from operations - direct method.

Cash collections from customers (a*)		$428,000
Cash payments:		
To suppliers (b*)	$188,000	
To employees (c*)	71,750	
For taxes	11,000	
For interest	6,250	
For misc. selling & admin. (d*)	110,000	
Total cash payments		$387,000
Cash flows from operations		$ 41,000

(a*), (b*), (c*), (d*) see next page

(a*)

Sales	$ 458,000
+ Beginning accounts receivable	38,000
- Ending accounts receivable	(68,000)
Cash collected from customers	$ 428,000

(b*)

Beginning accounts payable	$ 20,000
+ Purchases	198,000
- Ending accounts payable	(30,000)
Cash payments to suppliers	$ 188,000

(c*)

Beginning salaries payable	$ 3,000
+ salary expense	71,750
- Ending salaries payable	(3,000)
Cash payments to employees	$ 71,750

(d*)

Beginning prepaid expenses	0
+ Payments (unknown)	?
- Selling and admin. expenses	(106,000)
= Ending balance prepaid expenses	$ 4,000
solving for the unknown: Payments	$ 110,000

b. Cash flows from operations - indirect method.

Net income	$ 55,000
Add back depreciation expense	20,000
Deduct increase in accounts receivable	(30,000)
Deduct increase in inventory	(10,000)
Deduct increase in prepaids	(4,000)
Add increase in accounts payable	10,000
Cash flow from operations	$ 41,000

Chapter 11

c. Cash flows from investing activities

Purchase of machinery	$ (160,000)
Cash flow from investing activities	$ (160,000)

d. Cash flows from financing activities

Sale of new stock	$ 50,000
Addition to long-term debt	99,000
Dividends paid	(15,000)
Cash flow from financing activities	$ 134,000

Problem 3:

Cash flow from operations:	
net income	$ 24,000
add back depreciation	3,000
add decrease in inventory	2,000
deduct increase in accounts receivable	(5,000)
deduct increase in prepaids	(1,000)
deduct increase in accounts payable	(4,000)
deduct decrease in wages payable	(1,000)
Cash flow from operations	$ 18,000
Investing activities:	
Proceeds on sale of l-t. investment	$ 10,000
Purchase of capital assets	(55,000)
	$ (45,000)
Financing activities:	
Issue of note	$ 9,000
Issue of common shares	30,000
Payment of dividends	(11,000)
	$ 28,000
Total Increase in Cash	$ 1,000

Problem 4:

Cash flow from operations:

Net income	$ 14,000
Add back depreciation	6,000
Add back loss on investments	4,000
Deduct gain on capital assets	(2,000)
Add increase in accounts payable	4,000
Deduct increase in accounts receivable	(8,000)
Deduct increase in inventory	(4,000)
Cash flow from operations	$ 14,000

Investing activities:

Proceeds on sale of capital assets	$ * 6,000
Proceeds on sale of investment	** 10,000
Purchase of capital assets	***(40,000)
	$ (24,000)

Financing activities:

Issue of note	$ 8,000
Issue of shares	10,000
Payment of dividend	(6,000)
	$ 12,000

Total Increase in cash	$ 2,000

* Gain of $2 on an asset which cost $6 (given) and acc. dep. of $2 (given), therefore: Proceeds = Gain + Net Book Value ($2 + [6-2])=$6

** Loss of $4 (given) - book value of $14 (from the balance sheet), therefore: Proceeds = Book value - Loss = $10

*** $ 40,000 additions obtained from looking at the change in capital assets of $34,000 and adjusting for the disposal which had a cost of $ 6,000 - gives addition of $ 40,000

Chapter 12

Shareholders' Equity

This chapter deals with the second element on the right-hand side of the balance sheet equation, shareholders' equity. Shareholders' equity represents the investment made by the shareholders, or owners, of the corporation and provides significant information concerning equity investment in the firm. Any user of financial statements should have a complete understanding of shareholders' equity and its composition. The following objectives will help you outline your study of this important and interesting section of the balance sheet.

1. Describe the rights of shareholders.
2. Differentiate among authorized, issued, and outstanding shares.
3. Explain the characteristics of preferred stock.
4. Discuss similarities and differences between bonds and preferred stock.
5. Identify the economic characteristics of stock splits and dividends.
6. Explain the accounting for stock splits.
7. Differentiate between the accounting for large-percentage and small-percentage stock dividends.
8. Account for treasury stock acquisitions.
9. Explain and record conversions of preferred stock into common stock.
10. Describe the motivation for and importance of restrictions on retained earnings.
11. Define and use the rate of return on common equity and book value per share.

REVIEW OF KEY CONCEPTS

A.   Shareholders' equity may be divided into two parts: paid-in capital, the original capital contributions by shareholders, and retained earnings, the cumulative amount of past earnings kept in the business for reinvestment.

1.   Unrecorded in the equity section of the balance sheet, but still of great importance are shareholders' rights. These include: the right to vote, share in corporate profits, share residually in corporate assets upon liquidation, and acquire more shares of subsequent issues of stock.

   a.   An effective tool available to the shareholder is the **corporate proxy**, which gives the shareholder the ability to transfer voting rights to another individual, or group of individuals, facilitating voting "blocks" on issues of concern to the shareholders.

   b.   In order not to intentionally dilute the voting and earnings power of a shareholder, the corporation may grant its shareholders a **preemptive right** which is the right to acquire a pro-rata share of any new stock issued.

2.   One of the most important features concerning shareholders' rights is **limited liability**. This limits shareholder exposure in such things as lawsuits, liquidations of corporate liabilities, etc. to the amount of the shareholders' investment.

3.   Upon incorporation (either federally under the terms of the Canada Business Corporations Act or under provincial charter), a corporation issues shares of stock to represent ownership interest in the entity. These shares, listed in shareholders' equity, are referenced as follows:

   a.   **Authorized shares** - the total number of shares that may legally be issued under the articles of incorporation (the CBCA grants an unlimited amount of authorized capital).

   b.   **Issued shares** - this represents the shares sold to shareholders.

   c.   **Outstanding shares** - this represents the shares issued and still held by shareholders.

B.   **Preferred stock** is a class of stock that gives specific rights and privileges to the holder. If the shares have a par value, dividends are usually stated as a given percentage of par value, otherwise they may be stated as a dollar amount per share. Preferred shareholders are entitled to receive dividends before they are distributed to common shareholders. Preferred shareholders also have preference over common shareholders upon liquidation of assets. Other preferred stock features of importance include: cumulative and non-cumulative, participating and nonparticipating, callable, and convertible.

1.   **Cumulative** preferred shares give the holder the right to receive all accumulated unpaid past dividends before any distributions are made to common shareholders. This **arrearage** is noted in the financial statements. Dividends in arrears must be paid to preferred shareholders upon liquidation of assets before any distributions may be made to common shareholders. Unpaid cumulative dividends (i.e. dividends in arrears) are not an accounting liability until they are declared.

> See the example on page 551 of the text

2.   Preferred shares usually have a **liquidating value** printed on the stock certificate. If the shares are par value shares, the liquidating value is usually equal to the par value. Distribution of liquidated assets is accomplished according to a priority of claims, starting with secured liabilities and proceeding to the residual claims of the common shareholders. This liquidating value provision assures the holder a preference in asset distribution superior to those of common shareholders.

> See Exhibit 12-1 on page 553 of the text

3.   **Callable preferred** shares give the company the option of repurchasing the shares at a **call price**. The call price is generally in excess of the original issue price.

4. **Convertible preferred** shares give the shareholder the option of converting preferred into common stock , based upon an established conversion ratio. This is normally done when the yield on the common stock exceeds the yield on the preferred. This is an attractive share feature and increases the issue price of the preferred share in excess of a preferred share with no convertibility feature.

C. Companies have the option of retaining earnings for future corporate growth or distributing the earnings in the form of dividends. The ratio of distribution to retention is called their dividend policy. Dividends are normally distributed in the form of cash. There are three dates important to the distribution of dividends: date of declaration, date of record, and payment date.

1. **Date of declaration** is the date a dividend is declared by the board of directors. On this date the dividend becomes a liability to the corporation and is recorded in the records as such.

2. **Date of record** is the cut-off date for determining who will receive the dividend declared by the board.

3. **Payment date** is the date on which the company distributes the dividend to the shareholder on the date of record.

D. Distributions to shareholders is not limited to distributions in cash. For a variety of reasons a company may wish to make distributions to current shareholders in the form of additional stock. These stock distributions normally take the form of a stock split or a stock dividend.

1. A **stock split** is the issuance of additional shares to existing shareholders without requiring payment in return. Par value per share is usually adjusted to maintain the same total par value for the stock. With a split the same relative voting power still exists. The rationale for a stock split includes keeping the market price of the stock within a range deemed desirable by management.

See the text example on page 560 of the different methods of accounting for a stock split

2. **Stock dividends** are distributions of stock to existing shareholders, as well. Accounting for a stock dividend depends on whether the distribution is classified as a *large-stock dividend* or a *small-stock dividend*

    a. **Large-stock dividends**, generally distributions of 20% or more of outstanding stock, are accounted for in the same manner as stock splits. If the company has **par value** shares, an amount equal to the number of shares in the stock dividend multiplied by the par value of the stock distributed, is transferred from retained earnings to common stock. If the company is incorporated under the CBCA and has **no par value** shares then no entry is made, just as in the case of a stock split.

    b. A **small stock dividend**, a distribution of less than 20% of the outstanding shares, is accounted for at the fair market value of the firm's shares on the date of declaration. An amount equal to the number of shares issued in the distribution multiplied by the fair market value of each share on the date of declaration is debited to retained earnings. If the firm has **par value** shares, the total dollar amount transferred from retained earnings must be split between common stock and contributed surplus. The amount related to par value goes to common stock and the excess goes to contributed surplus. If the firm has **no par value** shares, the same amount is debited to retained earnings as with par value shares but this time all of it goes to the common stock account (i.e. there is no need to split the amount since there is no par value).

Before continuing, see the examples on pages 560-564 of the text illustrating the proper methods of accounting for stock splits and stock dividends

E. Under certain circumstances a company will repurchase its own stock on the open market. Shares repurchased in this manner are called **treasury shares.** Acquisition of stock for treasury is done for a variety of reasons, such as retirement of a portion of outstanding shares, or to have shares available for future stock bonuses or option plans.

1. Shares repurchased and retired are valued at the historical average issue price of the stock (i.e. as calculated from book values in the stock account and contributed surplus, if applicable). If the repurchase price exceeds the historical average issue price on the books, the excess is charged against retained earnings.

2. Shares repurchased and held for later reissue are accumulated at the repurchase price in a contra-shareholders' equity account, called treasury stock. Common stock and contributed surplus are not affected.

> See the examples on page 569 of the text relating to the retirement of shares and treasury shares being held for reissue

F. For many non-cash transactions fair market value is used as the benchmark. When stock is exchanged for non-cash assets the fair market value of the asset or the stock, *whichever is most objectively determined*, becomes the basis for recording the exchange. The same valuation should be used by both parties to the exchange.

> See the exhibit on page 573 of the text

G. Circumstances arise where it may be desirable for the investor to exchange bonds or preferred stock for common equity in the same company. **Convertible preferred stock** facilitates this type of transaction. When conversion takes place there are no gains or losses recognized. The accounting for the conversion is simply to reduce preferred stock and to increase common stock (and contributed surplus, if applicable).

See Exhibit 12-2 on page 574 of the text

H.   The CBCA restricts a firm's ability to pay dividends if it would reduce shareholders' equity to a level below paid-in capital. Contractual obligations may restrict a firms ability to pay dividends as well. A third type of restriction would be imposed by management itself in the form of an appropriation of retained earnings. This appropriation of retained earnings may be segregated from unrestricted retained earnings on the face of the balance sheet and referenced in a note, or simply referenced in a note. This appropriation signals management's intention to restrict potential dividend distributions to unrestricted retained earnings.

I.   **Stock options** are the rights to purchase specific amounts of corporate stock during some future time period, for a specified price. Options are often used as a form of compensation for key employees.

     a.   From an accounting point-of-view, options are not recorded until exercised, but the notes to the financial statements must disclose the type and number of outstanding options at any point in time.

     b.   This accounting treatment is criticized on the grounds that options are a part of management compensation and they should be recorded when they are issued. Although this is possible, this would involve the calculation of a value for the options at the issuance date. This type of calculation is very subjective in nature and, as a result, accountants have shied away from regulating this approach to accounting for stock options.

J.   A good indicator of how well management is utilizing invested capital is the **rate of return on common equity**. This rate focuses on a return based on the book value of common equity and varies from industry to industry. **Book value per share of common stock** is often calculated to present common equity on a per share basis. This allows the reader to compare book value to the current market price of the stock. This comparison acts as a starting point for questions as to why a differential between the two values may exist.

$$\text{Return on common equity} = \frac{\text{Net income - preferred dividends}}{\text{Average common equity}}$$

$$\text{Book value per share of common stock} = \frac{\text{Total shareholders' equity - Book value of preferred stock}}{\text{Number of common shares outstand.}}$$

PRACTICE TEST QUESTIONS AND SOLUTIONS

I   **True or false** - For each of the following statements, enter a T or an F in the space provided to indicate whether the statement is true or false.

_____ 1.   The owners of the business have a superior interest in the assets of the firm upon liquidation.

_____ 2.   Corporations are entities created by an incorporating charter which exist separately from the owners.

_____ 3.   If a firm has cumulative preferred stock the preferred shareholders will receive all dividends in arrears before distributions are made to the common shareholders.

_____ 4.   Common dividends are recorded as a liability of the corporation, if not paid by the specified payment date.

_____ 5.   A firm may decide to split its stock if the market price of the stock exceeds the price range of the firm's target shareholders.

251

_____ 6. When a firm splits its stock, the market value of the shares in the split must be transferred to common stock from retained earnings.

_____ 7. When an investor receives a stock dividend it is recorded in the investors records at the current fair market value on the date of the distribution.

_____ 8. Treasury stock held for redistribution is held in a separate contra-equity account at the repurchased value.

_____ 9. Stock exchanged in a non-cash transaction should be valued at the book value of the asset received.

_____ 10. Conversion of preferred stock to common stock is considered a "transaction" and triggers recognition of any gains or losses by the issuer.

_____ 11. An appropriation of retained earnings for construction of a new plant indicates a fund has been created for that purpose.

_____ 12. Stock options are often used as compensation to key employees.

_____ 13. Participating preferred stock receives additional distributions of earnings after the normal preferred dividend is paid.

_____ 14. Professional corporations, like other corporations, enjoy limited liability.

_____ 15. Shareholders may band together through the use of a corporate proxy to elect members to the board of directors that are sympathetic to their points of view.

II   **Multiple Choice -** For the following multiple choice questions, select the best answer and enter the identifying letter in the space provided.

_____   1.   Small stock dividends are generally distributions of _____ of the outstanding stock.

        a.   More than 50%
        b.   Less than 20%
        c.   Less than 50%
        d.   More than 20%

_____   2.   Upon liquidation of assets, which of the following is correct as to priority of claims?

        a.   Liabilities, common shareholders, preferred shareholders
        b.   Preferred shareholders, common shareholders, liabilities
        c.   Liabilities, preferred shareholders, common shareholders
        d.   Common shareholders, preferred shareholders, liabilities

_____   3.   When a small stock dividend occurs:

        a.   Common stock is debited
        b.   Retained earnings are reduced by the par value of the common stock
        c.   Retained earnings are increased by the market value of the stock
        d.   Retained earnings are reduced by the market value of the stock

_____   4.   On Dec. 31, 19X1 Gildehaus Bakeries had 10,000 shares of $10 par common stock outstanding and retained earnings of $4,000,000. The board of directors declared a 2-1 stock split because the stock price had reached a high of $ 82. What will be the effect on total shareholders' equity as a result of this split?

        a.   -0-
        b. $82,000 reduction
        c. $100,000 reduction
        d. $720,000 increase

Chapter 12

_____ 5. Spinnaker Sails had $750,000 in total shareholders' equity, 10,000 shares of $15 par value common stock, contributed surplus of $450,000, and retained earnings of $200,000. What is the balance in the treasury stock account?

    a. $27,500
    b. $50,000
    c.   -0-
    d. $25,000

_____ 6. C & C Boat Builders repurchased 10% of their 100,000 outstanding $10 par value common shares for retirement. Before the repurchase, contributed surplus was $500,000, retained earnings were $650,000 and per share market price was $17. What was the balance in Retained Earnings after the repurchase?

    a. $580,000
    b. $670,000
    c. $630,000
    d. $640,000

_____ 7. Holman Industries exchanged 1,000 shares of its common stock for a parcel of land owner by Martin Properties. The stock was not actively traded on the market but carried an average book value of $10 per share. The fair market value of the land was appraised at $150,000. What is the journal entry Holman will make on its books to record this non-cash transfer?

    a.

Land	100,000	
Common stock		100,000

    b.

Land	150,000	
Common stock		100,000
Paid-in capital		50,000

    c.

Land	150,000	
Common stock		150,000

    d.   No entry until the land is sold

8. Lenk's board of directors declared a dividend on October 1, 19X2 of $4.30 per share to stockholders of record Dec. 31, 19X2. The dividend would be paid on Jan. 15, 19X3. Lenk's year ends Nov. 30. The corporation will record a liability on:

    a. Jan. 15
    b. Dec. 31
    c. Nov. 30
    d. Oct. 1

9. The following information was made available for your inspection:

Net income	$ 2,000,000
Preferred dividends	500,000
Beg. bal. shareholders' equity	16,000,000
End. bal. shareholders' equity	20,000,000
Book value of preferred stock	5,000,000
Liquidating value of preferred	5,500,000

    What is the rate of return on the common equity?

    a. 13%
    b. 12%
    c. 11%
    d. 10%

10. A corporation has total shareholders' equity of $1,500,000. Of that total, retained earnings is $800,000. On September 1, the board of directors voted to restrict $400,000 of retained earnings for two years during the construction of a new plant. What is the maximum amount the board may distribute as dividends?

    a. $600,000
    b. $800,000
    c. $400,000
    d. -0-

Chapter 12

III   Problems

Problem 1:

The following information is available for operations in 19X3:

Preferred stock, $100 par, 8%, cumulative, nonparticipating. 10,000 shares issued and outstanding.	$ 1,000,000
Common stock, $1 par value, 1,000,000 shares authorized, issued and outstanding	1,000,000
Contributed surplus	490,000
Retained Earnings	400,000
Total Shareholders' Equity	$ 2,890,000

Earning's history - 19X4 through 19X9:

Year	Net income
19X4	$(200,000)
19X5	(100,000)
19X6	-0-
19X7	400,000
19X8	600,000
19X9	900,000

The board of directors declared total dividend distributions of $240,000 in 19X7, $360,000 in 19X8, and $540,000 in 19X9.

Required:

a.   What was the total amount the company was in arrears in 19X6?
b.   What was the total amount of common stock dividends paid?
c.   What is the balance in Retained Earnings at the end of year 19X9?

Problem 2:

On March 1, 19X4, the board of directors declared a 10% stock dividend. At the time of the declaration there were 725,000 $10 par value common shares outstanding with a fair market value of $32 per share. Retained earnings was $7,350,000 and contributed surplus totalled $10,875,000.

Required:

a.   Record the journal entry recognizing the distribution of the stock dividend.

b.   Assume the same facts except that the board declared a 2-1 stock split. Show the shareholders' equity section before and after the split.

c.   Assume the same facts again except in this case the board declared a 50% stock dividend. Show the shareholders' equity section before and after the stock dividend.

Problem 3:

On January 1, 19X3, Magnet Inc. issued 10,000 stock options to certain key members of management. Each option granted the holder the right to purchase 1 Class A share at an exercise price of $ 21 (the market price on January 1, 19X3) any time up to January 1, 19X8. On December 31, 19X5, 5000 of these options were exercised when the market price was $ 30.

Required:

a.   Prepare the journal entry to record the exercise of the option on December 31, 19X5.

b.   Assume that the Class A shares have a par value of $ 20 per share. Prepare the appropriate journal entry to record the exercise of the option on December 31, 19X5.

> **For additional practice using financial ratios see Lotus Template file P12-34.wk1. For practice preparing the equity section of the balance sheet see file P12-36.wk1.**

CHAPTER 12 ANSWERS AND SOLUTIONS

I   True and false

1.   False   The owners are the common shareholders and they have a residual interest in liquidated assets.

2.   True

3.   True

4.   False   Dividends become a liability of the corporation on the date they are declared by the board of directors.

5.   True

6.   False   Par value and the number of shares outstanding are adjusted for the split.   Paid-in capital and Retained Earnings are not affected. The situation depicted in the question applies to a small stock dividend.

7.   False   Only a memo entry is made. The stock dividend does affect the average book value per share used to compute gains and losses on disposal of the stock.

8.   True

9.   False   The basis should be the asset with the most objectively determined fair market value.

10.   False   A transfer is made between preferred and common stock according to the conversion provisions. No gains or losses are recognized.

11.   False   Appropriations of retained earnings signals managements intention to segregate a portion of retained earnings from availability for dividend distribution.

12.   True

13.   True

14.   False   Professional corporations share many of the same features as other corporate entities. However, limited liability is not available to professional corporations.

15.   True

II   Multiple choice.

1.   B

2.   C   Order of priority on distribution of liquidated assets starts with secured creditors, unsecured creditors, preferred shareholders, and finally common shareholders.

3.   D   Small stock dividends are treated basically the same as cash dividends with the substitution of market value of the stock as the benchmark for valuing the reduction in retained earnings.

4.   A   Total shareholders' equity is not affected by a stock split. Par value and the number of shares outstanding are adjusted for the effect of the split.

5. B Remember, treasury stock is held in a contra-equity account thus reducing total stockholders equity by the amount of the treasury stock.

Common stock	$150,000
Contributed surplus	450,000
Retained earnings	200,000
Treasury stock	(50,000)
Total shareholders equity	$750,000

6. C

$17 market price

less: 15* average value per share

$ 2 per share difference to be taken from retained earnings.

* this value comes from the $ 10 par value plus $ 5 average value in contributed surplus per share ($ 500,000 cont. surplus/100,000 shares = $ 5/sh)

$2 x 10,000 shares retired = $20,000 reduction in retained earnings

Beg. bal. retained earnings	$650,000
Reduction	20,000
End. bal. retained earnings	$630,000

7. C When a non-cash transfer occurs, the value for the asset with the most objectively determined value is used to value the transaction. In this case, the appraised value of the property is the most objectively determined value and so it is used.

8. D The liability exists on the declaration date. The entry would be:

Retained earnings	xxxx
Dividends payable	xxxx

9. B

Beginning shareholders' equity	16,000,000
less: liquidating value* preferred stock	5,500,000
Beginning balance common equity	10,500,000

* use liquidating value instead of book value whenever it exceeds book value.

Ending shareholders' equity	20,000,000
less: liquidating value preferred stock	5,500,000
Ending balance common equity	14,500,000

Avg. common equity = (10,500,000 + 14,500,000)/2 = $12,500,000

$$\frac{2,000,000 - 500,000}{12,500,000} = 12\%$$

Chapter 12

10.   C   Total retained earnings less the amount restricted from distribution is considered unrestricted retained earnings and remains available for *potential* distribution as dividends.

III   Problems

Problem 1:

Yr.	Net Income	Preferred Declared	Preferred In arrears	Common Dividends	Ret. Earn. Balance
X4	(200,000)	-0-	80,000	-0-	200,000
X5	(100,000)	-0-	160,000	-0-	100,000
X6	-0-	-0-	240,000	-0-	100,000
X7	400,000	240,000	80,000	-0-	260,000
X8	600,000	160,000	-0-	200,000	500,000
X9	900,000	80,000	-0-	460,000	860,000
				660,000	

answers: a. $ 240,000
              b. $ 660,000
              c. $ 860,000

Problem 2:

a. Retained earnings (725,000 x .10 x $32) 2,320,000
            Common stock (72,500 x $10)   725,000
            Contributed surplus   1,595,000

b.

	Before	After
Common stock	$ 7,250,000	$ 7,250,000
Contributed surplus	10,875,000	10,875,000
Retained earnings	7,350,000	7,350,000
Total Shareholders' equity	$25,475,000	$25,475,000

Note: The only change occurs to par value and the number of shares outstanding.

c.

	Before	After
Common stock	$ 7,250,000	$ *10,875,000
Contributed surplus	10,875,000	7,250,000
Retained earnings	7,350,000	7,350,000
Total equity	$ 25,475,000	$ 25,475,000

* the additional amount comes from contributed surplus

Problem 3:

a. option exercise - **no par value shares**

DR Cash (5,000 x $21 exercise price)	105,000	
CR Class A shares		105,000

b. option exercise - **par value shares**

DR Cash	105,000	
CR Class A shares ($ 20 x 5000)		100,000
CR Contributed surplus		5,000

Chapter 13

> ## Intercorporate Investments, Including Consolidations

Astute resource management often results in companies investing in the shares of other companies. These investments may take the form of short-term investments of idle cash or companies may invest in other companies on a longer term basis. Whatever the case, it is necessary for a manager to be familiar with the proper accounting practices and procedures associated with short and long-term investments. Use the following objectives as focal points in your study of this material.

1. Account for temporary (short-term) investments in debt securities and equity securities.
2. Explain the accounting for long-term investments in bonds.
3. Contrast the equity and cost methods of accounting for long-term investments in equity securities.
4. Explain how equity-method investments affect the statement of cash flows.
5. Explain the preparation of consolidated financial statements.
6. Describe the use of non-controlling (minority) interests in consolidated financial statements.
7. Explain why goodwill arises and how to account for it.
8. Contrast the purchase method and the pooling-of-interests method of accounting for business combinations (Appendix 13).

REVIEW OF KEY CONCEPTS

A. Proper management of assets is critical to the success of a firm. Cash must be available to meet obligations as they come due but not be so "plentiful" that it lies idle and unproductive. Both temporary and long-term investments are used to invest excess cash. A company may hold shares in another company and classify some as temporary investments, and others as long-term investments. The critical difference relates to **management intention**. If management **intends** to turn the shares into cash in the short-term (usually within one year) than the investment is **temporary** in nature. On the other hand, if management purchases an investment and has no intention of selling it in the short-term, then it is classified as a **long-term investment**.

B. Temporary investments in highly liquid, stable securities, may be held in a portfolio of both debt or equity securities. These securities are normally classified on the balance sheet directly under Cash.

1. **Short-term debt securities** are investments with a maturity of one year or less. Examples include certificates of deposit, commercial paper and treasury bills. Short-term debt securities are *carried at acquisition cost* and are not adjusted to present value. They are only written down if a decline in value is judged to be permanent.

2. **Short-term equity securities** are investments in stocks of another company. Generally, these investments are traded on an organized exchange ensuring a high degree of liquidity. Investments in equity securities, which are expected to be held for one year or less, are classified as temporary (short-term) and are carried at original cost. At the end of the period the *total* short-term equity portfolio is valued at the **lower-of-cost-and-market**. Any reduction in the value of the portfolio is charged against income of the period. Any subsequent recovery of portfolio value is *limited to the level of the original investment.*

> See the example on pages 599-600 of the text

C. Investments in long-term debt securities are carried on the balance sheet at **book value** (face value plus or minus the unamortized discount or premium). Any premium or discount from the face value of the investment is amortized over the life of the investment. Early extinguishment of long-term debt held as an investment involves the removal of its book value on the date of disposal. A gain or loss on extinguishment will arise if the proceeds received on disposal are greater (a gain) or less (a loss) than the book value of the investment. From the investor's viewpoint:

1. Discount amortization *increases* interest revenue.

2. Premium amortization *decreases* interest revenue.

See Exhibits 13-1 and 13-2 on pages 601
and 602 of the text

See the text examples of the journal entries by both the
investor (page 602) and the issuer (page 603)

D. Once an investment in equity securities has been classified as a **long-term investment**, accounting for the investment depends on the degree of control exercised by the investor over the investee. If the investor holds the shares passively (i.e. does not participate in or influence the investee's business decisions), then we use the **cost method**. If, on the other hand, the investor exerts *significant* influence over the investee (for example, the investor has a representative on the investee's board of directors), then we use the **equity method**.

1. The **cost method** records the investment at acquisition cost. This method is utilized when the level of investment is generally below 20% of the outstanding stock of the investee, and the investor is not deemed to exercise significant influence. Dividends are recorded as investment income when received.

2.   The **equity method** is used when the investment is greater than 20% and the investor is **deemed to exercise significant influence**.

     a.   Income or losses of the investee, in proportion to the degree of ownership, are recorded as additions to, or subtractions from, the investor's intercorporate investment account.

     b.   Dividends received from the investee are used to reduce the investment account. Theoretically this reduction is based on the belief that dividends are considered a partial return of invested capital.

It should be noted that the 20% reference is merely a **guideline** - the critical criterion relates to the presence, or not, of **significant influence**. An investor may hold less than 20% but have significant influence. In this case, the investor would account for its investment using the equity method. On the other hand, the investor may hold more than 20%, but have no influence over the investee, and the cost method will be used to account for the investment.

Before continuing to the discussion on consolidated financial statements, it would be a good idea to review the textbook examples on pages 605 and 606 of the accounting for long-term investments using the cost and equity methods.

---

3.   When using the **indirect method** of presenting the statement of cash flows the proportionate share of investee earnings will be included in the investor's net income. To reach cash flows from operations the difference between the proportionate share of investee earnings and dividends received must be subtracted from the investor's net income if the investee had a profit. If the investee suffered a loss, the adjustment must add back the loss plus any dividends received during the period.

E.   When a company holds **more than 50%** of the outstanding voting stock of another corporation as an investment, we say that the investor controls the investee and **consolidated statements** showing the financial position and income of both entities as one are normally prepared. In this relationship the controlling company is known as the **parent company**, and the investee is known as the **subsidiary company.**

Chapter 13

1.	At the time of acquisition, the investment is recorded in the parent's books as an asset at the acquisition price. No entry is made in the investee's records because the purchase is made in the open market and does not affect the investee's books.

2.	When consolidated statements are prepared, all evidence of ownership, both in the parent's investment account and the subsidiary's shareholders' equity account are eliminated, leaving a summation of the individual assets, liabilities, and results of operations for the consolidated unit.

See the example on page 611 of the text

3.	Earnings and dividend distributions of the subsidiary are recorded in the parent's books using the **equity method**. When consolidated statements are prepared, the updated balance in the investment account is removed through the use of eliminating entries on the consolidated worksheet.

	a.	When eliminating entries are prepared, intercompany receivables, payables, and costs and revenues, are eliminated and intercompany transfers of inventory are carried at cost.

	b.	No separate books exist for the consolidated entity. All consolidation activity, including eliminating entries, are carried out on the consolidation worksheet.

4.	For companies that have ownership interests in excess of 50%, but less than 100%, minority interests must be recognized in the consolidated financial statements. **Minority interests** (also known as Non-controlling Interests) represent the ownership interests of non-majority shareholders in the assets and earnings of the consolidated entity. The consolidation process combines 100% of the subsidiary's assets and earnings (after intercompany adjustments) with those of the parent. The minority interest recognizes that, although the parent has access to 100% of the net assets of the subsidiary, the minority shareholders have legal residual claim to a proportion of the subsidiary's assets.

> See the example of a consolidated income statement with minority interests on page 616 of the text

F.   When a business purchases the net identifiable assets of another business at a price in excess of the fair value of the purchased assets, the difference is called **purchased goodwill**.

1.   For consolidated statement purposes goodwill is the remainder after the parent's investment at the purchase price and the subsidiary's shareholders' equity account are eliminated on the consolidated worksheet. Goodwill is carried on the consolidated statements as an intangible asset and it is usually amortized straight-line over a period not to exceed forty years.

2.   For consolidation purposes, when a difference exists between the fair market value of the identifiable assets acquired and their book values, each asset is revalued to fair market at the date of the acquisition. Any difference that remains between the total for the revalued individual assets and purchase price is classified as goodwill.

3.   Goodwill is the result of a number of factors that may cause a firm to enjoy "abnormal" earnings relative to others in the industry with a similar financial structure. Although goodwill may exist in a firm, it is only recognized as an intangible asset under GAAP when it is **purchased**. This means that internally created goodwill is not recognized on the books of the company that has created it. This internally generated goodwill can only show up on the books of a company that purchases the company that has created the goodwill. (This may seem unfair - however, we have no *objective* way to value internally generated goodwill.)

> See the textbook example on page 619 of valuing goodwill based upon normal and abnormal earnings levels

Before continuing, carefully review Exhibit 13-5 on page 625 of the text.

G.   Depending on the circumstances surrounding a business combination, the purchase method or the pooling-of-interests method may be used to value the assets associated with the combination. This valuation can have a significant impact on net income, as well as the balance sheet values of the individual assets.

  1.   **The purchase method** values the individual assets at fair market value on the date of the acquisition. This adjustment in value may lead to higher depreciation charges and a reduction in income through the amortization of goodwill. When consolidated statements are prepared under the purchase method, the subsidiary shareholders' equity is eliminated leaving only the retained earnings of the parent as part of the consolidated statements.

  2.   **The pooling-of-interests method** recognizes the combination of two or more entities by the exchange of voting common stock. Assets and liabilities are carried at book value after the pooling, eliminating the creation of purchased goodwill. Retained earnings of the two entities are combined on the consolidated balance sheet.

    a.   Consolidation of shareholders' equity under pooling requires any difference between the par value of the parent's stock and that of the subsidiary to be adjusted to the parent's par. This requires that a transfer be made between additional paid-in capital and common stock to effect the adjustment.

    b.   Under the pooling-of-interest method, income for the entire year, regardless of the date of combination, is included in consolidated results. The purchase method only allows income from the date of acquisition to be included in the consolidated statements.

In Canada, use of the pooling method is **very** rare. The following conditions must be met in order for a business combination to qualify as a pooling:

a.   It is impossible to identify an acquirer.

b.   Each company issues voting common shares (not cash) in exchange for substantially all (normally, at least 90%) of the voting common shares of the other company.

c.   The acquisition occurs in a single transaction.

See Exhibit 13-6 on page 631 of the text for a comparison of the purchase and pooling methods

---

PRACTICE TEST QUESTIONS AND SOLUTIONS

I   True and false - For each of the following statements, enter a T or an F in the space provided to indicate whether the statement is true or false.

_____   1.   An investment in short-term debt securities would be listed on the balance sheet as a current asset.

_____   2.   When determining the value of a short-term investment portfolio each security in the portfolio is analyzed and valued at the lower-of-cost-and-market .

_____   3.   Dividends received from an investment of less than 20% in the stock of another company would be credited to the investment account.

_____   4.   A company that uses the indirect method of determining cash flows from operations, and which has equity affiliates, would deduct the affiliate's earnings from net income.

_____   5.   A company accounting for investments under the equity method is assumed to exercise significant influence over the investee.

_____ 6. Consolidated financial statements would eliminate the parent's investment in the subsidiary.

_____ 7. Minority interests are shown on the face of the consolidated financial statements.

_____ 8. Goodwill is the difference between the purchase price and the fair value of the assets acquired when acquiring another company.

_____ 9. Companies that issue consolidated statements are required by GAAP to maintain a separate set of consolidated books.

_____ 10. For consolidated reporting purposes, assets of the subsidiary are individually identified and revalued to fair market value on the date of the acquisition. Any unallocated difference between purchase price and fair market value of the individual assets is considered goodwill.

_____ 11. GAAP requires purchased goodwill to be amortized to net income over a period not to exceed 40 years.

_____ 12. If a company holds greater than 50% of another company's stock as an investment and has significant influence, they would normally account for the investment using the cost method.

_____ 13. When a company has interests in another company of greater than 20% but less than 50%, dividends received from the investee would be deducted from the investment account.

_____ 14. When consolidated statements are prepared, the investment in the subsidiary on the parent's books and shareholders' equity on the subsidiary's books are eliminated.

_____ 15. Amortization of bond discounts by the investor decreases interest revenue.

_____ 16. Long-term investments in debt securities are presented on the statements at acquisition cost.

_____ 17. A company using the pooling-of-interest method of accounting for a combination will adjust the identifiable assets of the subsidiary to fair market value on the date of the combination for consolidation purposes.

_____ 18. A criticism of the pooling method is that it ignores the asset values on which the parties have traded and substitutes a wholly irrelevant figure - the amount on the seller's books.

II **Multiple choice -** For the following multiple choice problems, select the best answer and enter the identifying letter in the space provided.

1. A company paid $1,750,000 for a company that had a net book value of $1,250,000. The difference is referred to as:

    a. A long-term investment
    b. Goodwill
    c. Excess over book valuation
    d. Investment coverage·

2. Harlan Industries purchased 50% of Hart Tool and Die's common stock for $2,000,000 on December 31, 19X4. Hart had income in 19X5 of $120,000 and paid 30% of the earnings as dividends. What will be the balance in Harlan Industries investment account after adjusting for these activities?

    a. $2,000,000
    b. $2,042,000
    c. $2,060,000
    d. $2,018,000

Chapter 13

3.   On December 31, 19X6, Walker Engineering repurchased on the open market all of its outstanding bonds. The bonds had a face value of $5,000 each, a 12% coupon rate, and 10 years left to maturity. Walker paid $5,250 for each of the outstanding bonds. At the time of the repurchase you held 100 of the bonds which had a book value of $511,000. · What is the amount of your gain or loss on the early extinguishment of the bonds?

    a. $25,000
    b. $16,255
    c. $36,000
    d. $14,000

4.   Your company accounts for its investment in other companies' stocks using the cost method. During 19X4, your company received $5,000 in dividends as a result of these investments. The journal entry to record the receipt of these dividends would include:

    a.   A credit to long-term investments
    b.   A debit to dividend revenue
    c.   A credit to dividend revenue
    d.   A credit to cash

5.   On January 1, 19X3, Moore Steel purchased 100% of Markland Transportation for $875,000. For 19X3 Markland Transportation had earnings of $65,000. If Moore were to prepare consolidated statements for 19X3, how much of Moore's investment would be eliminated?

    a. $940,000
    b. $875,000
    c.   -0-
    d. $ 65,000

6. In 19X1, Block Inc. purchased the assets of Snow Processing for $2,500,000. The following data was available concerning Snow at the time of the acquisition:

	Book Value	Market Value
Cash	$ 100,000	$ 100,000
Accounts receivable	400,000	400,000
Inventory	600,000	800,000
Net capital assets	1,000,000	900,000
Total	$ 2,100,000	$ 2,200,000

If consolidated statements are prepared upon completion of the acquisition, how much will appear as goodwill?

a. $400.000
b. $300,000
c. $200,000
d. $100,000

7. Nichols' Antiques enjoy an enviable reputation in River City. Nick Nichols decided to retire and become a ski "bum" and he put the business up for sale. The fair market value of the identifiable assets, less liabilities was $650,000. Nichols' Antiques is expected to earn $15,000 per year more than another business of the same type and financial structure. You have assessed an earnings multiple of 7 (a capitalization rate of 14.3%) to be used for valuation of these extraordinary returns. What is the most you would be willing to pay for Nichols' Antiques?

a. $650,000
b. $652,142
c. $755,000
d. $712,480

8. When two or more companies exchange voting stock in a single transaction sufficient enough to qualify for pooling-of-assets, at what value will the assets be recorded on the consolidated balance sheet?

a. Fair market value at the date of the pooling
b. Book value prior to the pooling
c. Lower-of-cost-or-market at balance sheet date
d. Historical cost at the date of pooling

Chapter 13

9.   When comparing purchase and pooling methods of accounting which of the following is true?

    a.   Asset values will be higher under pooling because of revaluation to generally higher fair market value.

    b.   Retained earnings on the consolidated statements will be lower because the purchase method does not include retained earnings of the subsidiary.

    c.   Both purchase and pooling methods include earnings from the beginning of the period in the consolidated statements.

    d.   Under the pooling method depreciation expense is based upon fair market values at the date of the acquisition.

10.   During 19X4, your company purchased the assets of another company. Goodwill of $5,280,000 was recorded as a result of the transaction. You have decided to amortize the goodwill over the maximum time available according to GAAP. What is your amortization expense for the first year?

    a. $211,200
    b. $528,000
    c. $264,000
    d. $132,000

III   Problems

Problem 1:

On December 31 the following information was available concerning the company's short-term investment portfolio:

Description	Book value	Market value
Hutson-Orf Department Stores	$ 750,000	$ 804,000
Wind Dancer Sailboards	225,000	197,000
Tilt-eze Trailer Mfg.	500,000	613,000
Eastern Shore Fisheries	700,000	550,000
Skipjack Reproductions	125,000	125,000

Required:

a. Compute the balance to be reported for temporary investments on the balance sheet.

b. Prepare the journal entry necessary to adjust the balance in the temporary investment account.

c. If during the following year the fair market value of the portfolio were to rise to $2,305,000, what would be the journal entry to reflect this change?

Problem 2:

Clifton Forge acquired a 32% interest in West Virginia Mining for $1,410,000. During the following year West Virginia Mining had net income of $500,000 and distributed cash dividends of $150,000.

Required:

a. Compute the book value of Clifton Forge's investment in West Virginia Mining at the end of the period using the **equity method**.

b. Compute the book value of Clifton Forge's investment in West Virginia Mining at the end of the period using the **cost method**.

c. Compute the increase in Clifton Forge shareholders' equity account by the **equity method** as a result of West Virginia Mining's operations during the period.

d. Compute the increase in Clifton Forge shareholders' equity account by the **cost method** as a result of West Virginia Mining's operations during the period.

Problem 3:

Jolt Dairy Products recently acquired an 80% voting interest in Jen and Barry's Ice Cream for the amount shown in the investment account. (in thousands)

Description	Jolt	J&B
Cash and other assets	$500	$550
Investment in J&B	500	-
Accounts payable, etc.	200	100
Shareholders' equity	800	450

Chapter 13

Required:

a.   Compute the minority interest.

b.   Compute consolidated shareholders' equity.

c.   Compute consolidated cash and other assets.

d.   Compute consolidated net income for the first year after acquisition if Jolt earned $80,000 and J&B earned $54,000.

For additional practice accounting for temporary investments see Lotus Template P13-25.wk1. For practice accounting for bonds on the investor's books see files P13-26.wk1 and P13-27.wk1. For practice accounting for long-term investments see files P13-28.wk1 (cost and equity methods) and P13-44.wk1 (consolidated financial statements).

CHAPTER 13 ANSWERS AND SOLUTIONS

I   True and false

1.   True

2.   False   The total value of the portfolio at market is compared to cost. The lower value of the two is reported on the balance sheet.

3.   False   An investment of less than 20% is not normally considered to have significant influence and would be recorded by the investor using the cost method. Dividends determine investment income.

4.   False   If the investee is profitable, the investor must deduct the excess of their share of the profits over the dividends received from net income. If the investee suffered a loss, the investor must add back the loss plus the amount of any dividends received during the period.

5.   True

6.   True

7.   True

8.   True

9.   False   Consolidated statements are prepared from the individual companies' records and consolidated through the use of a consolidation worksheet.

10.   True
11.   True
12.   False   An investment of greater than 50% would usually be accounted for as a consolidation.
13.   True   Under the equity method dividends are considered as a partial return of capital.
14.   True
15.   False   Amortization of a discount by the **investor** increases interest revenue. This is done to equate the effective interest rate (which is greater than the stated rate) on the date of the original transaction with the bond's stated rate of interest.
16.   False   Investments in long-term bonds are normally shown on the statements at book value (face value - a discount or + a premium).
17.   False   Assets are carried at book value in a pooling.
18.   True

II   Multiple choice

1.   B   From the text, "Such excess of purchase price over fair market value is called goodwill or purchased goodwill."

2.   B   The equity method adds the proportionate share of the investee's income to the investor's investment account and subtracts the proportionate share of dividends received from that same account.

Investee earnings share (120,000 x .50)	$ 60,000
Less: proportionate share of dividends	18,000
Net addition to investment account	$ 42,000

3.   D

Book value	$511,000
Repurchase price	525,000
Gain on early extinguishment	$ 14,000

4.   C   Using the cost method any dividends received would be recorded as dividend revenue. The investment account would be unaffected.

Chapter 13

5.   A   For consolidation purposes, the investment account of the parent would be eliminated. This would include the original value of the investment and any share of net earnings that are part of the account. P uses the equity method to account for S.

Original investment	$ 875,000
plus: sub's earnings	65,000
Total	$ 940,000

6.   B   Goodwill for consolidated purposes is the difference between the purchase price ($2,500,000) and the net identifiable assets adjusted to fair value ($ 2,200,000) on the date of the original transaction.

7.   C

Excess annual earnings	$ 15,000
x earnings multiplier	x 7
Max. price for excess earnings	$105,000

Fair value of net identifiable assets	$650,000
plus: Excess earnings premium	105,000
Maximum purchase price	$755,000

8.   B   Using the pooling-of-interest method, assets are carried at book value prior to the combination.

9.   B   See the tables in the textbook that summarize the difference between purchase and pooling on the balance sheet and the income statement.

10. D.   GAAP indicates that goodwill should be amortized over a period not exceeding 40 years.

$$\frac{\$5,280,000}{40} = \$132,000 \text{ annual goodwill amortization}$$

III   Problems

Problem 1:

a.   For short-term investments the whole portfolio is valued at lower-of-cost-and-market (which is market) on the balance sheet date.

Book value	Market value
$2,300,000	**$2,289,000**

b.   Unrealized loss on temporary investments   11,0(
         Allow. to reduce temporary investments

c.   Unrealized gains are limited up to the amount of the or
investment.

       Allow. to reduce temporary investments   11,0
         Unrealized gain on temporary investments

Problem 2:

a.   Proportionate share of earnings: ($500,000 x .32)
Proportionate share of dividends: ($150,000 x .32)
Net addition to investment account
plus: Beg. balance investment account
Ending value investment account

b. $1,410,000

c. $500,000 x .32 = $160,000

d. $150,000 x .32 = $ 48,000

Problem 3:

a.   minority interest: $450,000 x .20 = $90,000

b.   Only the shareholders' equity of the parent is include
consolidated statements. The parent's investment acc
subsidiary's shareholders' equity accounts are elimina
consolidated worksheet. The balance in the consolida
equity would be $800,000.

c. $500,000 + $550,000 = $1,050

d.   Parent's earnings + Sub. earnings - Minority interest
Consolidated Net Income

       $80,000 + $54,000 - .20(54,000) = $123,200

**Income Taxes,
Including
Interperiod
Allocation**

ute users of financial statement information are aware of potential differences that
st between the company's income tax liability, and the income tax expense reported
GAAP based financial statements. This situation exists because some revenue and
ense items are treated differently under income tax regulation than under GAAP.
AP is based on a few fundamental concepts, one of which is the matching
nciple. Tax regulation, on the other hand, is a function of government policy. Given
, it is understandable that differences would exist between the two systems. It is
portant to understand the nature of these differences, and how they affect financial
orting. The following objectives highlight the key concepts in this chapter:

1. Identify timing and permanent differences between tax rules and GAAP.
2. Explain how timing differences create deferred taxes.
3. Contrast tax capital cost allowance (CCA) and straight-line depreciation.
4. Explain why interperiod tax allocation is generally accepted.
5. Distinguish tax credits and tax deductions.
6. Illustrate the importance of loss carry-overs (LCOs).
7. Differentiate the flow-through and deferral accounting methods for
   investment tax credits (Appendix 14A).

REVIEW OF KEY CONCEPTS

A. Deferred income taxes result primarily from the mandated use of accrual accounting concepts for GAAP prepared financial statements, and the reliance for tax purposes on a mainly cash basis approach to computing income. The differences between accounting and taxable income can be classified as either permanent differences or temporary differences.

1. **Permanent differences** are revenue or expense items which are recognized for either tax or financial reporting purposes *but not for both.* Examples of permanent differences include non-taxable dividends, the non-taxable portion of capital gains or cumulative eligible capital (e.g., one quarter of goodwill is never deductible).

2. **Timing differences** are revenue or expense items which are included in both accounting and taxable income but at different times. For example, capital cost allowance is normally higher in an asset's early years than depreciation expense. In the later years, the opposite is true. We say that timing differences "reverse" (at least in theory) over the asset's life, so that the expense or revenue is eventually the same under both systems (i.e. over a long period of time the same total revenues and the same total expenses are included in each system).

3. In an effort to match expenses with revenues, GAAP requires that the tax expense on the financial statements be equal to the tax costs that are, or will eventually be, incurred as a result of the taxable activity in that period (even if it will only be taxed later). The amount of tax a company is required to pay in any given year is based on its taxable income (which is different from GAAP income by the amount of the timing differences). If the tax liability is less than the tax expense (often because the CCA deduction is greater than depreciation expense), we have **deferred income taxes**. Deferred income taxes of this nature appear on the liability side of the balance sheet.

See Exhibit 14-4 on page 660 of the text

B.   The primary method of calculating depreciation for tax purposes is **Capital Cost Allowance (CCA)** and it was studied in Chapter 9. The significant features of this system include:

   1.   Assets are classified according to predetermined asset classes. In the year of acquisition, the company may only deduct up to one-half of the CCA on that asset.

   2.   The asset classes have predetermined CCA rates. Most of these rates are applied using the declining balance method (i.e. they are applied on an accelerated basis). A company may claim any amount equal to or less than the eligible maximum CCA based on the predetermined rates and classes (and taking into account the half-year rule for new assets).

> See Exhibit 14-1 on page 656 of the text

C.   **Tax Deferral** (interperiod tax allocation) measures reported net income as if pretax accounting income (excluding permanent differences) were subject to the full current tax rate, even though a more advantageous accounting method was used for tax purposes.

   1.   Financial statement income tax expense is composed of two elements: **current**, which is the portion which is currently payable according to the company's tax return, and **deferred income taxes**, which are potential future tax payments arising from timing differences. Deferred taxes are potential future payments because they will only actually be paid if the company is taxable when it files future tax returns.

   2.   Tax deferral has a smoothing effect on reported financial statement income because tax expense matches accounting income instead of being equal to the amount of the firm's actual tax liability.

3.   Growth companies that continually add to long-term assets have the potential of never discharging their deferred tax liability (because the amount of CCA always exceeds the amount of depreciation expense). This creates a situation where the deferred tax liability either stays the same, or actually increases, throughout the growth period. This result is criticized by some as a weakness of comprehensive tax allocation or tax deferral.

See Exhibit 14-7 on page 663 of the text

D.   Canadian tax laws are often designed with the dual purpose of raising revenue and acting as a tool to be used by the federal government in advancing specific social and economic goals (e.g., encouraging companies to invest in pollution-control equipment). Tax credits and government grants are two such examples.

1.   **Grants** are given by the federal and provincial governments to encourage companies to engage in activities that benefit Canadians. The receipt of these grants poses no special accounting problems. They are usually taken into income in the year received unless the grant applies to a fixed future period, in which case it is taken into income over this longer period of time. One exception to this treatment are grants received by companies to encourage them to purchase capital assets. Under these circumstances, GAAP requires that the grant be deducted from the cost of the asset, thereby reducing the asset base to be depreciated over future periods.

2.   **Tax credits** are a *direct reduction* of the tax liability. Tax credits are not to be confused with tax deductions, which are reductions in arriving at taxable income. **Investment tax credits** are a specific type of tax credit given by the government in order to encourage company investment in certain capital assets. The company may reduce its tax liability by the amount of the investment tax credit. If the company has no taxable income for an extended period of time (i.e. it is not profitable), it is possible for the tax credit to expire. In Canada, GAAP

requires companies to account for investment tax credits using the **deferral method**. This method sets the investment tax credit up as a deferred credit on the liability side of the balance sheet and amortizes it to income (as a credit to income tax expense) over the life of the capital asset.

E.   When a company incurs a loss for tax purposes it may do a **loss carry-over** which permits the company to either obtain a refund of past income taxes (a **loss carry-back**) or to reduce income taxes as they arise in the future (**a loss carry-forward**. Under Canadian tax law, losses may be carried back three years or forward seven years.

1.   If a company can not carry all or part of the loss back (i.e. the loss is greater than the last three years of taxable income, or there are no past profits in the last three years), then it will carry the loss forward. If the company already has deferred taxes on the balance sheet, then the company will likely elect not to claim CCA in the future so that it can **drawdown** its deferred taxes. This enables the company to benefit from the loss by reducing future taxes, and by saving the CCA (which does not expire) as a future deduction after the loss carry-forward has expired.

When a company elects to drawdown its deferred taxes, it will normally recognize the benefit in the year of the loss. This reduces the loss and correctly matches revenues and expenses in the same accounting period. If a company does not have deferred taxes available to be drawn down, then it can only recognize the benefit in the year of the loss if it has **virtual certainty**. Virtual certainty relates to management's certainty regarding whether the company will have sufficient taxable income over the next seven years to use the loss. GAAP suggests that virtual certainty only exists if *all three* of the following conditions can be met:

i)   the reason for the loss can be identified
ii)   the company has a long history of profitability
iii)   there is little doubt that future taxable income will exceed the current loss

If the company has virtual certainty, it may recognize the benefit in the year of the loss. If virtual certainty does not exist then management will disclose the amount of the loss carry-forward in the notes to the financial statements.

F.   There are two approaches to accounting for investment tax credits:

      1.   **Flow-through method** - the investment tax credit is taken into income one hundred percent in the year of the acquisition of the capital asset. This method is acceptable for purposes of GAAP in the United States but it is not allowed in Canada.

      2.   **Deferral method** - the investment tax credit is amortized to income (as a reduction in tax expense) over the life of the capital asset to which it relates. This is the required approach in Canada.

PRACTICE TEST QUESTIONS AND SOLUTIONS

I   **True or False** - For each of the following statements, enter a T or an F in the space provided to indicate whether the statement is true or false.

      _____   1.   Definitions used by taxing authorities to determine taxable income conform to the definitions used by GAAP to determine accounting income for financial reporting purposes.

      _____   2.   Under GAAP, income tax expense on the income statement is always equal to the amount of income taxes payable for the same period.

      _____   3.   Use of the actual tax amount paid to the government tends to distort the level and pattern of reported earnings for financial statement purposes.

      _____   4.   A loss for tax purposes can only be used by a company if it has paid taxes in the three years prior to the year of the loss.

      _____   5.   Deferred taxes on the balance sheet of a growth company have the potential of accumulating to enormous amounts that will not diminish unless the company discontinues replacement of old facilities used in its operations.

_____ 6. Use of accelerated depreciation for tax purposes and straight-line for financial reporting purposes will not give rise to deferred taxes on the financial statements.

_____ 7. A company must always claim the maximum amount of CCA in any given year.

_____ 8. When utilizing CCA, the asset classes and depreciation rates are predetermined.

_____ 9. If a new capital asset is acquired in the first month of the year, the company may only claim 11 months of CCA on the asset.

_____ 10. Income tax expense on the income statement for shareholders is based on the revenue and expenses on that statement, not those on the tax statement.

_____ 11. A category of timing difference would be expenses that are deducted for income tax purposes later than they are deducted for financial statement purposes, such as those related to product warranties.

_____ 12. An example of a permanent difference would be three-quarters of a capital gain on the sale of an asset.

_____ 13. Tax credits are reductions in taxable income before application of the marginal tax rate.

_____ 14. Advocates of the deferral method maintain the amount of the tax credit is more closely associated with the period of use of the capital asset qualifying for the credit than with the period in which the tax credit was received by the company.

II   **Multiple choice -** For the following multiple choice questions, select the best answer and enter the identifying letter in the space provided.

1.   When calculating taxable income for income tax purposes, revenues and expenses are accumulated primarily on:

   a.   An accrual basis.
   b.   A cash basis.
   c.   Either, depending on the basis used for financial statement purposes.
   d.   The basis of CTAG (Canadian Tax Accounting Guidelines).

2.   An example of a permanent difference would be:

   a.   Straight-line depreciation
   b.   Amortization of goodwill
   c.   Dividends received from an investment in another company
   d.   Receipts from service contracts

3.   For many assets, CCA accelerates depreciation even faster than traditional methods of depreciation because,

   a.   The recovery periods are longer than the useful lives.
   b.   The recovery periods are the same as the useful lives.
   c.   The recovery periods are shorter than the useful lives.
   d.   There is no residual value used with CCA.

4.   Pizza Wonder purchased a delivery vehicle for $28,000. It is the company's first class 10 asset, and it is subject to CCA at an accelerated rate of 30%. It is expected to have a useful life of 7 years, and a salvage value of $7,000. What is the maximum amount of CCA the company can claim this year?

   a. $8,400
   b. $4,200
   c. $3,000
   d. $1,500

Chapter 14

5. While rummaging through company records you came across the following information:

Year	Tax expense per F/S	Taxes payable per return
1	$ 50	$ 20
2	60	40
3	70	100
4	80	100

The balance in the deferred tax liability account at the end of **year 3** would be:

a. $30
b. $50
c. $20
d. $80

6. At the beginning of 19X2, Hagan Ceramics purchased a piece of equipment for $150,000 subject to a 10% investment tax credit. Expected useful life of the machine was 5 years. Hagan was in the 40% tax bracket and had income of $75,000 per year for 19X2 and 19X3. Hagan's accountant uses the deferral method of allocating the investment tax credit. What is the impact of the investment tax credit on income tax expense in 19X3?

a. 0
b. $3,000
c. $1,500
d. $1,200

7. Income tax expense for financial statement purposes is generally composed of:

a. Income tax payable and the addition to/subtraction from deferred taxes.
b. Income tax payable and the balance in the deferred tax liability account.
c. Income tax payable.
d. The amount of the addition to the deferred tax liability account.

8.   In 19X7, Murabito Yacht Sales had taxable income of $1,200,000. Murabito is in the 40% tax bracket and had $100,000 in available tax credits. Penny Bryant, the company accountant is an advocate of using flow-through accounting for tax credits. What is Murabito Yacht Sales net income for 19X7?

      a. $775,000
      b. $760,000
      c. $820,000
      d. $660,000

9.   In the first year of operations, Lambert Ltd. had income before depreciation of $ 100,000. Depreciation expense was $ 10,000 for the year. The company had two assets; a truck that cost $ 80,000 (classified as a Class 10 asset (30% depreciation) for tax purposes) and a computer that cost $ 20,000 (considered a Class 8 asset (20%) for tax purposes). The company claimed the maximum amount of CCA available for the year. The tax rate was 40%. What was the balance in the deferred tax account at the end of the first year.

      a. $ 1,600
      b. $ 2,400
      c. $ 7,200
      d. $10,800

III Problems

Problem 1:
Harlan Industries on the last day of 19X3, purchased equipment that qualified for a 10% investment tax credit. The equipment cost $125,000 and had an estimated useful life of 5 years. The corporate income before income tax was:

19X3	$40,000
19X4	$70,000
19X5	$50,000

Assume a 40% income tax rate during all three years and also that it is company policy not to book depreciation in the year of acquisition for any asset acquired during the last six months of the year.

Chapter 14

Required:

a. Compute net income for each year if the flow-through method is used to account for the investment tax credit.

b. Compute net income for each year if the deferral method is used to account for the investment tax credit.

c. Compute the amount of the deferred investment tax credit at the end of 19X5 assuming use of the deferral method.

Problem 2:

On January 1 19X1, Techno Ltd. purchased 15 portable computers for the office. The total price was $175,000 and they had an expected useful life of 10 years with a residual value of zero. The computers are classified as Class 8 assets (20% CCA rate) for tax purposes. Straight-line depreciation is used for financial statement purposes. The expected tax bracket is 40%.

Required:

a. Compute depreciation for financial statement purposes for the first five years.

b. Compute the maximum allowable CCA for tax purposes for the first five years.

c. Compute the deferred tax liability at the end of each year.

Problem 3:

Preville Ltd., a taxable Canadian corporation, provided you with the following information:

		Year 14
Net accounting loss before tax effects	$	50,000
Amount of depreciation deducted		40,000
CCA claimed for tax purposes		60,000*

* the company has elected to claim the full amount of CCA in the current year due to the fact that taxable income in the prior three years is sufficient to absorb the loss in year 14

290

Prior taxable income:

Year 13	$	40,000
Year 12		20,000
Year 11		10,000

Assume the income tax rate is 40% in all the years.

Required:
Calculate the loss for tax purposes, and prepare the journal entry to recognize the tax recovery arising from loss carry-backs to prior years.

Problem 4:
The St. Lawrence Boat Company Ltd., a taxable Canadian corporation, provided you with the following information:

	Year 1	Year 2
Net income before tax	$ 38,200	$ 49,200
Depreciation deducted	32,000	30,000
CCA claimed	40,000	32,000
Dividends from other taxable Canadian Corporations*	2,000	4,000

* the company uses the cost method to account for its investment in other corporations

Required:
a. Calculate the taxable income for the St. Lawrence Boat Company Ltd. for each of years 1 and 2.

b. Calculate the income tax payable with respect to each year. Assume a 40% tax rate.

c. Calculate the income tax expense that will appear on each of the year 1 and year 2 income statements.

d. Calculate the deferred tax balance at the end of each year.

For additional practice with deferred income taxes see Lotus Template file P14-41.wk1.

CHAPTER 14 ANSWERS AND SOLUTIONS

I True and False

1. False   The subject of the bulk of this chapter concerns the differences between revenue and expense items for tax purposes and for financial statement purposes. Examples include methods of depreciation, non-taxable dividends, and the timing of reporting revenues in completed-contract vs. percentage-of-completion methods of revenue recognition.

2. False   Tax expense is based on accounting income, not taxable income. Taxes payable can only equal tax expense if there are no timing differences.

3. True   Under the taxes payable method, no matching is achieved between income and tax expense unless there are no timing differences.

4. False   Losses for tax purposes may be carried back three years and forward seven years.

5. True

6. False   The difference between straight-line and accelerated depreciation is an example of a timing difference that would be reported as a deferred tax liability.

7. False   CCA is the maximum amount a company can claim for the year but the company may claim less, or none at all if the company is drawing down its deferred taxes or if it has a loss for tax purposes.

8. True

9. False   In the year of acquisition assets are subject to the half-year rule.

10. True

11. True

12. False   Three-quarters of a capital gain is taxable - it is the one-quarter which is nontaxable and which generates a permanent difference.

13. False   Tax credits are direct reductions of income tax due. Tax deductions are reductions of taxable income.

14. True

II Multiple Choice

1. B.   Much of accounting for tax purposes is on the cash basis. Examples include recognition of warranty expense only when warranty outlays have been made, and the taxability of cash received in advance for work to be done in the next accounting period.

2. C.   Dividends received from other taxable Canadian corporations are not taxable because they come out of after-tax earnings which are taxed in the hands of the investee. If these dividends were taxed it would be double taxation.

3. C.   The method of depreciation may be the same for CCA and financial statement purposes, but assets generally have a shorter life for tax purposes due to the higher (accelerated) rates of depreciation.

4. B.   Remember, CCA does not deduct residual value when computing depreciation expense.

$28,000 x .30 x 1/2* = $4,200

* remember the half-year rule in the year of acquisition

5. C.   The balance in the deferred tax liability account is cumulative.

Yr.	Fin. stmt.	Tax return	Diff.	Cum.bal.
1	50	20	30	30
2	60	40	20	50
3	70	100	(30)	**20**

6. B. $150,000 x .10 = $15,000

$ 15,000/ 5 = $3,000

The acquisition cost of the equipment is multiplied by the investment tax credit percentage to arrive at the dollar value of the tax credit. This tax credit is then divided by the useful life of the asset to determine the amount of tax credit used to reduce income taxes for that period.

7. A.   Income tax expense for financial statement purposes is composed of two elements: income tax payable for the current period and the addition to/subtraction from the deferred tax liability account.

B. is incorrect because the balance in the deferred tax liability account is cumulative.

C. is incorrect because of the adjustment necessary to the deferred tax liability account if timing differences exist.

8. C.

$1,200,000	tax. income	$1,200,000	tax. income
x .40	tax rate	- 380,000	tax due
$ 480,000	unadj. tax liab.	$ 820,000	net income
- 100,000	tax credit avail.		
$ 380,000	tax due		

Chapter 14

9. A.   Capital Cost Allowance:

$ 80,000 x 1/2* x .30 =	$ 12,000
$ 20,000 x 1/2* x .20 =	$ 2,000
Total CCA	$ 14,000

* half-year rule

Depreciation	$ 10,000
CCA	$ 14,000
Timing difference	$ 4,000

Timing difference x tax rate = $ 4,000 x .40 = **$ 1,600**

III Problems

Problem 1:

a.

	19X3	19X4	19X5
Pretax income	$ 40,000	$ 70,000	$ 50,000
Less income tax (40%)	16,000	28,000	20,000
Income before tax credit	$ 24,000	$ 42,000	$ 30,000
Add tax credit (flow-through)	12,500	- 0 -	- 0 -
Net income	$36,500	$ 42,000	$ 30,000

b.

	19X3	19X4	19X5
Income before credit	$ 24,000	$ 42,000	$ 30,000
Add tax credit (deferral $12,500/5 yrs.)	- 0* -	2,500	2,500
Net income	$ 24,000	$ 44,500	$ 32,500

* the amortization of the investment tax credit in the deferral method should match the depreciation policy - if the firm doesn't depreciate the asset in 19X3, it should not amortize the investment tax credit either (note this is an accounting "matching" issue only - the cash flow effects of the investment tax credit are unaffected).

c.
deferred income tax credit end of 19X5:

Beg. Bal. deferred tax credit	$12,500
less: 19X3 adjustment	-0-
19X4 adjustment	2,500
19X5 adjustment	2,500
End. Bal. deferred tax credit	$ 7,500

Problem 2:
a. Depreciation expense each year = $ 175,000/10 years = $ 17,500/year

b. CCA

Year	Rate	**CCA**	UCC*
1	1/2 x .20 x $ 175,000	$ 17,500	$ 157,500
2	.20 x $ 157,500	$ 31,500	$ 126,000
3	.20 x $ 126,000	$ 25,200	$ 100,800
4	.20 x $ 100,800	$ 20,160	$ 80,640
5	.20 x $ 80,640	$ 16,128	$ 64,512

* UCC is the undepreciated capital cost - the asset's book value for tax purposes.

c.

year	dep. exp.	CCA	tim. dif.*	cum.t.d.*	rate	d.t.liab.*
1	$ 17,500	$ 17,500	- 0 -	- 0 -	40%	- 0 -
2	17,500	31,500	$ 14,000	$ 14,000	40%	$ 5,600
3	17,500	25,200	7,700	21,700	40%	8,680
4	17,500	20,160	2,660	24,360	40%	9,744
5	17,500	16,128	**(1,372)	22,988	40%	9,195

*   tim. dif. = timing difference, cum.t.d. = cumultaive timing difference, d.t. liab. = deferred tax liability.
** the timing differences start to reverse in year 5, that is depreciation expense exceeds CCA starting in year 5)

Problem 3:
calculation of loss for tax purposes:

net accounting loss (includes depreciation) $	(50,000)
add back depreciation	40,000
deduct CCA	(60,000)
loss for tax purposes $	(70,000)

entry:
DR Income Taxes Recoverable (.4 x $ 70,000)   28,000
      CR Tax expense (.4 x $ 50,000)   20,000
      CR Deferred income taxes* (.4 x $ 20,000)   8,000
* timing difference between depreciation expense ($40,000) and CCA ($60,000)

Chapter 14

Problem 4:

a.

	Year 1	Year 2
Net income before tax	$ 38,200	$ 49,200
Less permanent difference*	2,000	4,000
Add back deprectaion expense	32,000	30,000
Less CCA	40,000	32,000
Taxable income	$ 28,200	$ 43,200

* non-taxable dividends included in net
income before tax

b.

Taxes payable (taxable income x 40%)	$ 11,280	$ 17,280

c.

Net income before tax	$ 38,200	$ 49,200
Less permanent difference*	2,000	4,000
Financial statement income subject to tax at 40%	$ 36,200	$ 45,200
Tax expense	14,480	18,080
Net income	$ 21,720	$ 27,120

* non-taxable dividends included in net
income before tax

d.

Taxes payable	$ 11,280	$17,280
Tax expense	14,480	18,080
Deferred taxes for the year	$ 3,200	$ 800
Cumulative balance, Deferred Tax	$ 3,200	$ 4,000

Chapter 15

> ## Analysis of
> ## Financial
> ## Statements

Much of the text has focused on the theories and practices associated with financial statement preparation. This chapter shifts the focus to understanding some of the analytical tools available for financial statement analysis. Attention is also given to understanding when special disclosure of nonrecurring items is necessary in order to facilitate meaningful analysis. The following objectives should help enhance your understanding of the basic concepts associated with financial statement analysis.

1. Describe many sources of financial and operating information about company performance.
2. Explain the different objectives of debt and equity investors in analyzing information.
3. Describe trend analysis and approaches to analyzing the components of a business.
4. Review the basic financial ratios.
5. Explain the relationship between ROA and ROE in evaluating corporate performance.
6. Calculate EPS when preferred stock exists, shares outstanding change during the year, and dilution is a possibility.
7. Characterize special items, extraordinary items, and discontinued operations.
8. Explain the importance of efficient markets to accounting disclosures.
9. Explain some effects on financial statements from translating foreign currencies.

Chapter 15

REVIEW OF KEY CONCEPTS

A.   Much of the financial information concerning a company is available in its annual report. However, in order to gain a more complete and timely understanding of an entity, analysis should go beyond the confines of the published statements. Other sources include the company's annual filings with the securities commissions (e.g., the Annual Information Form required by many Canadian commissions or the 10K report which is required by the United States Securities and Exchange Commission), government reports, pro forma statements, Dun & Bradstreet credit ratings and less formal sources, such as newspaper and magazine articles, and interviews with corporate executives.

B.   The objective of financial statement analysis, generally, is to gain a deeper understanding of the trends and issues facing the firm and how these affect risk and profitability. Investors who are interested in capital gains often analyze past results in an effort to assess future profitability and future growth potential and how these will affect future stock price and dividend yield. Creditors (both long and short-term) use financial statement analysis to assess risk and the likelihood of the firm being able to meet its future obligations.

C.   Financial statement analysis is most useful when the results are viewed comparatively, that is the results of analysis must be compared to the results of prior years' (trend analysis), to a bench mark, or to the results of comparable other corporations (cross-sectional analysis).

    1.   **Trend analysis** focuses on changes that have occurred in the different financial statement components over time. In order for this analysis to be meaningful, changes in both the amounts and percentage changes should be considered.

> See Exhibit 15-1 on page 695, and
> Exhibit 15-2 on page 696 of the text

2.	**Common-size** statements restate the financial statement components to percentage relationships. This is done in order to facilitate comparative analysis of the financial statements from companies of different sizes. Common-size statements are also useful when analyzing data covering several periods for a single company.

a.	Balance sheet percentages are based on *total assets* = 100%.

b.	Income statement percentages are based on *sales* = 100%.

> See Exhibit 15-4 on page 698 of the text

3.	Since companies today are not limited to single products and single locations, analysis of business segments is important in understanding the financial position and profitability of the whole entity.

a.	An **industry segment** is a product or service, or a group of related products or services. The CICA requires companies to either disclose information about significant industry segments separately, or to state that the company deals in one "dominant industry" and that segmented disclosure is not necessary.

b.	The CICA also requires a company to disclose significant **geographic segments**.

c.	A segment (industry or geographic) is normally considered significant if its revenues or operating profits are 10 percent of total revenues or total operating profits respectively, or if identifiable assets of the segment are 10 percent of total corporate assets.

d.	Segment disclosure according to GAAP includes disclosure of segment revenues, segment operating profit or loss, and the total carrying amount of the assets which can be identified with the segment.

e.   GAAP also requires a company to disclose the amount of its sales of products and services to foreign customers if the sales are significant (i.e. if foreign sales exceed 10 percent of total sales).

See Exhibit 15-5 on page 699 of the text for examples of segment and geographic disclosure

---

4.   The section of the annual report called **management's discussion and analysis** details management's explanations for major changes in the financial results. It is also used by management to communicate future plans and strategy. This is an important source of information about the firm both because of its future orientation and because it reflects corporate personality and management priorities. The auditors review this section of the annual report to ensure that it is consistent with the audited information.

See Exhibit 15-7 on page 702 of the text

D.   Ratio analysis uses the relationship between different elements of the financial statements to assist in making decisions concerning the operational and financial performance of a firm. The most popular ratios used by analysts are grouped as short-term liquidity ratios, long-term solvency ratios, profitability ratios and market price and dividend ratios.

1.   **Short-term liquidity ratios** deal with a firm's ability to satisfy its short-term obligations as they come due. These ratios are the current ratio, the quick ratio, average collection period in days, and inventory turnover.

a.   The **current ratio** gives the reader an idea of the entity's ability to pay current obligations, normally through the use of current assets, as they mature.

b.   **The quick ratio** is an indicator of an entity's ability to quickly generate cash to meet current obligations without liquidating inventory, generally the least liquid of the current assets.

c.   **Average collection period** is an indicator of how many days sales are tied up in receivables and, therefore, how long it is taking to turn receivables into cash. A longer collection period may indicate a less aggressive collection department, or it may reflect an intentional shift in policy by management. In the latter case, management may have modified the collection terms in order to match the terms offered by a competitor.

d.   **Inventory turnover** is an indicator of how quickly inventory is being sold and turned into a more liquid asset, cash or accounts receivable. A slowing of inventory turnover could indicate an inventory build-up which in turn could affect the quick ratio and total asset turnover.

2.   **Long-term solvency ratios** give an indication of a firm's ability to repay long-term creditors. Generally speaking, the more debt a firm carries in its capital structure, in relation to contributed capital, the greater the degree of risk that may be associated with expected future profits. These ratios include: total-debt-to-total-assets, total-debt-to-equity, and interest coverage.

a.   **Total-debt-to-total-assets** provides an indication of how many of the firm's assets have been acquired through the use of outside financing. The more funding provided by debt the greater the fixed interest obligation and the higher the risk the company may default on its debt payments.

b.   **Total-debt-to-equity** is another indicator of risk. The higher the debt-to-equity ratio, the greater the risk, but also the greater the potential for the positive effects of financial leverage. The higher the firm is levered with debt, the higher the return for the shareholders if the firm's return on its assets exceeds the cost of its debt. On the other hand, shareholders will be negatively affected if the opposite takes place and the company generates a lower return on its assets than the cost of its debt.

        c.   **Interest coverage** gives the analyst an indication of the firm's ability to generate sufficient income from operations to cover the interest on outstanding debt obligations. The higher the coverage ratio, the less risk there is associated with potential default. A benchmark coverage of five is considered a minimum.

3.   **Profitability ratios** include return on sales, return on assets, total asset turnover, return on shareholders' equity, and earnings per share.

        a.   **Return on sales** is the traditional net profit percentage. It indicates the degree of profitability from the period's operations. When multiplied by the total asset turnover it helps determine the return on assets for the period.

        b.   **Return on assets (ROA)** provides an indication of the income generated as a result of the mix of assets employed. A poor ROA could be caused by a number of factors, such as low asset turnover and/or a poor return on sales.

        c.   **Total asset turnover** provides information about how well the assets are being utilized to generate sales. A low total asset turnover could be the result of poor sales performance due to an excess, or inappropriate mix, of assets for the level of sales generated.

        d.   **Return on equity (ROE)** is an indication of how well the invested capital is being utilized to produce a return for the shareholders. ROE is similar in nature to ROA unless a portion of the assets have been financed, or leveraged, through the use of debt. If this is the case, the return to the shareholders, measured by ROE will be "magnified", either positively or negatively, depending on whether ROA is greater or less than the cost of debt.

        e.   **Earnings per share (EPS)** is a measure of profitability which allocates net income to each share of common stock outstanding.

4.   **Market price and dividend ratios** are of particular interest to investors. These ratios give an indication of the market's assessment of risk and return, as well as providing an indication of management's dividend policy relative to the level of corporate earnings. Theses ratios include: price-earnings, dividend-yield, and dividend-payout.

See Exhibit 15-8 on page 704 of the text for a detailed list of
the typical financial ratios

E. Management is often judged on its **operational performance**, the day-to-day ability to generate revenues and control expenses, and its **financial performance**, the ability to obtain cash and employ it for the benefit of the entity. Ratio analysis can be utilized to judge these performances.

   1. **Operational performance** should be judged separately from financial performance. A good measure of operating performance is the **pretax operating rate of return on total assets (ROA)** which is the ratio of operating income (i.e. before interest expense) before taxes divided by the average total assets available to the firm.

      a. Another way to determine ROA is to multiply the **operating income percentage on sales** by the **total asset turnover**.

Pretax operating rate of return on assets
       = Operating income percentage on sales x Total asset turnover

      b. By looking at the income statement relationships that affect the return on sales and the balance sheet relationships that affect total asset turnover, it is possible to determine the effect of changes in those income statement and balance sheet relationships on the firm's operational performance.

   2. **Financial performance** is dependent to a large degree on the firm's **capital structure**. This is the mix of debt and equity that composes the right-hand side of the balance sheet. This mix can have an effect on the asset composition of the firm, as well as on the degree of risk associated with the firm's capital balance.

a. Debt as a part of the capital structure has advantages, such as the deductibility of interest and the ability to finance assets without selling additional stock and diluting the return to the shareholders.

b. When the pretax return on assets (ROA) exceeds the cost of debt, the return on equity (ROE) will exceed the ROA. This is positive financial leverage. Conversely, if the ROA is less than the cost of debt, this will produce a return to the shareholders that is less than the ROA. This is negative financial leverage.

> See Exhibit 15-10 on page 712 of the text
> for an illustration of the effects of
> leverage or trading on the equity

c. Since interest is deductible for tax purposes the cost of debt, when compared on an after-tax basis, is lower than the cost of equity (i.e. in terms of dividend payments which are not tax deductible). This lower cost of debt, however, is offset at some point by the risk associated with "excessive" levels of debt.

F. **Earnings per share** is a widely used indicator of a company's performance, and is the only ratio required by GAAP to be displayed on the face of the income statement. Some companies have debt or equity that can be converted to common shares. If this conversion takes place, it is possible that it will dilute the common shareholders' earnings per share. In order to make shareholders aware of this potential dilution, GAAP requires companies to report fully diluted earnings per share, as well as basic earnings per share.

1. **Basic earnings per share** is the ratio of net income, less any preferred dividends, to the weighted average number of common shares outstanding during the period. Weighing for shares outstanding is based on the number of months the shares are outstanding during the period.

2. **Fully diluted earnings per share** must be calculated when a firm has securities outstanding that have the potential for conversion to common shares. Examples would include convertible preferred shares, stock options, warrants, and convertible bonds. This calculation is based on

the "what if converted" premise; meaning, if all potentially dilutive convertible securities outstanding were converted to common stock what would be the effect on earnings per share?

See an example of a weighted-average computation on page 716 of the text, and an example of the calculation of basic EPS and fully diluted EPS on page 717.

G. The bulk of financial statement analysis focuses on projecting future returns and estimating the future financial position of a firm in order to assist financial statement users in the decision making process. Items by-passing the income statement, special (unusual) items, extraordinary items, and discontinued operations usually have a one time effect on the firm. Analysts must recognize and adjust for this single period effect in their analysis.

1. **Items by-passing the income statement** are certain items, such as error corrections, prior period adjustments, retroactive changes in the application of accounting principles and foreign currency adjustments which do not appear on the income statement (see page 718 of the text for more detail). These items are generally excluded from the current year's ratio analysis, but should be taken into account in historical trend analysis in the year to which they relate.

2. **Special items** are revenue or expense items which are large enough or unusual enough to warrant separate disclosure. GAAP dictates their inclusion, as a separate line item, in the operations section of the income statement. This means that the items are disclosed *before tax* and so it is important to remember that any analysis that attempts to normalize income must adjust for the tax effects of the item.

2. **Extraordinary items** are unusual in nature, occur infrequently, and do not depend on management decisions. They are shown separately in the income statement, below income from operations, and are always shown net of tax.

3.   **Discontinued operations** involve the termination of a segment of the business. This segregation is necessary in order not to distort projections of future income from continuing operations. Results of operations for the discontinued segment, and any gains or losses on disposal, are reported *net of taxes* below after tax income from continuing operations.

See Exhibit 15-11 on page 721 of the text
for disclosure examples for extraordinary
items and discontinued operations

H.   **Efficient capital markets** fully reflect in the market price of a security all of the information available to the public. The role of accounting information in such a market would be to identify the different degrees of risk among the various stocks so that the investor can make the appropriate risk versus return decisions. Research indicates that the market discounts differing methods of reporting income in share price determination. The research also indicates that financial statement information is just one source of information used by the investor in assessing firm value.

I.   Many companies now operate in an international market. The degree of involvement may vary from international sales to operations of subsidiaries in a foreign country. This expansion of operations presents problems in accounting for transactions in foreign currencies, and in foreign-exchange conversion of foreign subsidiary's financial statements.

1.   Fluctuations in exchange rates can create gains or losses on unhedged foreign currency transactions. Transactions are initially recorded at the exchange rate in effect at the transaction date, however, the transaction may be settled at a different rate. This difference in exchange rates between the two dates (the transaction and settlement date) creates a foreign currency gain or loss on the financial statements.

2.   When consolidating international subsidiaries, GAAP requires that the sub's financial statements be converted differently depending on whether the subsidiary is considered to be **integrated** or **self-sustaining**. The conversion will require a **translation adjustment** to bring the balance sheet into balance. For more details see page 725 of the text.

PRACTICE TEST QUESTIONS AND SOLUTIONS

I   **True and false** - For each of the following statements, enter a T or an F in the space provided to indicate whether the statement is true or false.

_____   1.   Investors and creditors use only financial statement analysis to predict the amount of future expected returns.

_____   2.   Common size statements are useful in analyzing companies of different sizes.

_____   3.   The income statement effect of discontinued operations is reported as a part of continuing operations before income taxes.

_____   4.   An increase in the operating income percentage on sales would have a negative impact on the pretax operating return on total assets (ROA).

_____   5.   The current ratio is an indication of a firms ability to *quickly* meet its current obligations as they arise.

_____   6.   When a firm's return on equity exceeds its return on assets the firm has a debt component in its capital structure.

_____   7.   Extraordinary gains and losses are reported on the income statement, net of tax, as part of income from operations.

_____   8.   A firm having both convertible preferred shares and convertible bonds would not be required to show fully diluted earnings per share until one or both have been converted to common stock.

_____   9.   A decrease in inventory turnover due to excessive inventory build-up would have no effect on total asset turnover and pretax return on assets.

_____   10.   The dividend-payout ratio gives the reader an idea of a company's dividend policy.

Chapter 15

II   **Multiple choice** - For the following multiple choice questions, select the best answer and enter the identifying letter in the space provided.

_____   1.   The ratio that provides a measure of liquidity based on those assets that can quickly be turned into cash: cash, marketable securities and accounts receivable is the:

   a.   Average Collections Period Ratio
   b.   Current Ratio
   c.   Quick Ratio
   d.   Accounts Receivable Turnover Ratio

_____   2.   If a company had sales of $785,000, total assets of $292,712 and total operating expenses, excluding interest, of $741,825, what is the firm's return on assets?

   a.   14.75%
   b.   15.05%
   c.   14.25%
   d.   17.60%

_____   3.   In 19X2, Alpha Corp. had sales of $1,200,000, cost of goods sold of $780,000 and operating expenses of $360,000. Common shares outstanding for the whole period were 30,000. You noticed the firm had 500 convertible bonds outstanding with a conversion ratio of 10 shares of common stock for each bond received. If the bonds were converted, $5,000 in interest would be saved. What is the basic and fully diluted earnings per share? Ignore income taxes.

   a. $2.00, $2.00
   b. $2.30, $1.71
   c. $1.71, $2.00
   d. $2.00, $1.86

_____ 4. According to the comparative income statement, net income was $2,535,000 for 19X4, and $2,720,000 for 19X5. What was the percentage change in net income for 19X5?

    a.   7.59%
    b.   7.30%
    c.   4.80%
    d.   6.75%

_____ 5. McCann Pet Services had total current assets of $775,000, cash and marketable securities were $102,000, accounts receivable totalled $239,000 and current liabilities amounted to $310,000. What is the quick ratio?

    a.   .90
    b.   1.00
    c.   1.05
    d.   1.10

_____ 6. Schloeman Cleaning Supply Co. had credit sales of $3,200,000 in 19X4. The average number of days it took Schloeman to collect its receivables in 19X4 was 32 days. What was the average balance in accounts receivable? (Use 360 day year)

    a. $284,444
    b. $302,104
    c. $291,415
    d. $275,121

_____ 7. At present, Dirnbeck Furniture Mfg. has a current ratio of 3 to 1. Which of the following transactions will decrease the current ratio?

    a.   Replacement of an account payable by a 2 year note payable.
    b.   Payment of an outstanding account payable.
    c.   Purchase of inventory for cash.
    d.   Purchase of inventory on account.

Chapter 15

_____ 8. Company A has a total-debt-to-total-asset ratio of 50%. Company B carries no debt. Both companies have the same profit margin ratio and total asset turnover. Which company will have a higher return on shareholders' equity (ROE)?

    a. Company A
    b. Company B
    c. Neither
    d. Cannot answer with facts given.

_____ 9. At the beginning of the year, Tor Co. Ltd. had 100,000 common shares outstanding. On July 1, the company issued another 20,000 shares. Net income for the year ended December 31st was $ 1000,000. Basic earnings per share for the year are:

    a. $ 10 per share
    b. $ 8.33 per share
    c. $ 9.09 per share
    d. Unable to calculate from the information given

_____ 10. Billings Ltd. had net income for the year of $ 100,000 made up of a pretax operating income of $ 220,000 and an extraordinary loss, after tax of $ 32,000. Total assets had decreased over the year from $ 2,000,000 to $ 1,860,000. The company's pretax return on total assets is:

    a. 5.38%
    b. 5.18%
    c. 11.83%
    d. 11.40%

III   Problems

Problem 1:
A co-worker has come to you for help. He was given the following ratios and asked to fill in the blank spaces on the accompanying balance sheet and partial income statement. You are the office whiz, so have a go at it!

Cash	Accounts payable	$	75,000
Accounts receivable	Long-term debt		
Inventory	Common stock	$	200,000
Total current assets	Retained earnings		
Capital assets	Total liabilities		
Total assets	and equity	$	600,000
Sales	Cost of goods sold		

Total Debt to Total Asset ratio	50%
Quick ratio	.90
Total asset turnover	4x
Avg. collection period	9 days
Gross profit margin	40%
Current ratio	2.5

Problem 2:
Based on the income statement and balance sheet for McEntee Model Aircraft Sales which appear after Problem 3 on the next page, compute the component percentages for:

1. Cash
2. Cost of goods sold
3. Rent expense
4. Land
5. Shareholders' equity

Chapter 15

Problem 3:

Based on the income statement and balance sheet for McEntee Model Aircraft Sales compute:

1.   Working capital (current assets - current liabilities)
2.   Inventory turnover
3.   Total asset turnover
4.   Profit margin on sales
5.   Debt-to-equity ratio
6.   Basic earnings per share
7.   Pretax return on assets
8.   Return on shareholders' equity

McEntee Model Aircraft Sales
Income Statement
For the year ended December 31, 19X7

Sales		$ 5,250,000
Cost of goods sold		1,837,500
Gross margin		$ 3,412,500
Operating expenses:		
Payroll expense	$ 1,000,000	
Rent expense	400,000	
Depreciation expense	105,000	
Miscellaneous expense	999,167	2,504,167
Operating income		$ 908,333
Less interest expense		75,000
Net income before tax		$ 833,333
Less income tax expense (40%)		333,333
Net income		$ 500,000

McEntee Model Aircraft Sales
Balance sheet
December 31, 19X7

Assets

Current assets:		
Cash	$	65,000
Marketable securities		100,000
Accounts receivable		105,000
Inventory		320,000
Prepaid rent		40,000
Prepaid insurance		20,000
Total current assets	$	650,000
Non-current assets:		
Equipment	$	350,000
Less: accumulated depreciation		(125,000)
Plant		1,050,000
Less: accumulated depreciation		(370,000)
Land		310,000
Long-term investments		385,000
Total assets	$	2,250,000

Liabilities and Shareholders' Equity

Current liabilities:		
Accounts payable	$	70,000
Notes payable		45,000
Accrued taxes		105,000
Total current liabilities	$	220,000
Long-term mortgage	$	655,000
Shareholders' equity		
Common stock, $ 10 par; 100,000 shares authorized,		
10,000 issued and outstanding	$	100,000
Contributed surplus		410,000
Retained earnings		865,000
Total shareholders' equity	$	1,375,000
Total liabilities and shareholders' equity	$	2,250,000

Chapter 15

Problem 4:
The following data are taken from the annual reports of two companies in the same industry.

	ABC Ltd.	XYZ Ltd.
Sales	$ 8,000,000	$ 7,500,000
Operating expenses before interest and taxes	5,200,000	4,700,000
Interest expense	100,000	133,333
Income tax expense at 40%	1,080,000	1,066,667
Net income	$ 1,620,000	1,600,000
Average total assets during the year	$ 45,000,000	$ 40,000,000

Required:

a. Calculate the pretax operating return on total assets.

b. Disaggregate the ratio into its two components; operating income percentage on sales and total asset turnover.

c. Given the results of a. and b. which company shows the stronger performance.

> **For more practice analyzing financial statements, see Lotus Template files P15-28.wk1, P15-33.wk1, P15-38.wk1, P15-39.wk1 and P15-41.wk1.**

CHAPTER 15 ANSWERS AND SOLUTIONS

I   True and false

1. False   Financial statement analysis uses the statements to help predict future returns but other sources of information about future strategy, etc. are also valuable in assessing future returns.

2. True

3. False   Results of operations for the discontinued unit, and any gains or losses on disposal of the segment, are reported net of taxes below income from operations (and before extraordinary items) on the income statement.

4. False   Pretax return on assets can be determined by multiplying the operating income percentage on sales ratio by the total asset turnover. An increase in the operating income percentage on sales ratio would increase the pretax return on assets.

5. False   The quick ratio is a better indicator of the firm's ability to meet maturing obligations quickly without liquidating inventory.

6. True   This is an example of positive leverage.

7. False   Extraordinary gains and /or losses are reported, net of tax, after operating income.

8. False   The existence of convertible bonds and/or convertible stock would cause fully diluted earnings per share to be reported if they proved to be dilutive.

9. False   A decrease in the inventory turnover would have an adverse effect on both the total asset turnover and the pretax operating return on total assets.

10. True

II Multiple choice

1. C   The quick ratio is a good measure of the firms ability to meet maturing obligations through liquidation of marketable securities, account receivables, and cash.

2. A   Operating income / Avg. total assets = Return on assets
            $43,175 / $292,712 = <u>14.75%</u>

3. D $60,000 / 30,000 shares = $2 basic EPS
            $60,000 + 5,000 / 35,000 shares = $1.86 fully diluted EPS
            Remember, if the bonds are converted there would be no interest expense. The number of outstanding shares would increase by the number issued in the conversion.

4. B   <u>$2,720,000 - 2,535,000</u>   =   7.3%
                    $2,535,000

5. D   Quick ratio=cash+market.securities+accounts receivable/current liab.
                    <u>1.10</u> = $341,000 / $310,000

Chapter 15

6. A

$$ACP = \frac{\text{Avg. receivables}}{\text{Avg. daily sales}}$$

$$32 = \frac{\text{Avg. receivables}}{\$3,200,000 \,/\, 360} \qquad\qquad 32 = \frac{(x)}{\$8,888.89}$$

32 x $8,888.89 = $284,444 average receivables

7. D

When the ratio is greater than 1, an increase in both the numerator and the denominator of the same amount will cause the ratio to fall. (You can test the effect of the other transactions on the current ratio by making up numbers and adjusting it to reflect the transactions.)

8. D

There is insufficient information to answer this question. When a company carries debt as part of its capital structure and return on total assets is greater than the cost of the debt, then return on equity will be greater for the firm with debt in its capital structure. However, if a company carries debt and the return on total assets is less than the cost of the debt, then the return on equity will be greater for the company with no debt.

9. C

When shares are issued during the year, the weighted-average number of shares outstanding during the year must be calculated. In this case, the 20,000 shares were outstanding for one-half of the year and the 100,000 shares were outstanding for the entire year. This gives a weighted-average of 1/2(20,000) + 100,000 = 110,000 shares.

Basic EPS = Net income/Weighted-avg. shares outstanding
= $1,000,000/110,000 shares = $ 9.09 per share

10. D

Pretax return on assets = operating income/average total assets
Pretax return on assets = $ 220,000/[1/2($2,000,000 + 1,860,000)]
Pretax return on assets = 11.40%

III Problems

Problem 1:
(answers in bold)

Cash	**$ 7,500**	Accounts payable	$ 75,000
Accounts receivable	**60,000**	Long-term debt	**225,000**
Inventory	**120,000**		
Total current assets	**187,500**	Common stock	200,000
Capital assets	**412,500**	Retained earnings	**100,000**
Total assets	**600,000**	Total liab. and equity	600,000
Sales	**$2,400,000**	Cost of goods sold	**$1,440,000**

Total assets = total liabilities + shareholders' equity

Current ratio	= current assets/current liabilities
2.5	= current assets/ $ 75,000
current assets	= 2.5 x $ 75,000 = $ 187,500
Total debt to total asset ratio	= total liabilities/total equity
.50	= total liabilities/$ 600,000
total liabilities	= .50 x $ 600,000
total liabilities	= $ 300,000
Total liabilities	= current liabilities + non-current liabilities
$ 300,000	= $ 75,000 + long-term debt
long-term debt	= $ 300,000 - 75,000
	= $ 225,000
Retained earnings	= total liab. and equity - common stock - total liab.
	= $ 600,000 - 200,000 - 300,000
	= $ 100,000
Capital assets	= total assets - current assets
	= $ 600,000 - 187,500
	= $ 412,500

Chapter 15

Quick ratio	= (current assets - inventory)/current liabilities
.9	= ($187,500 - inventory)/$ 75,000
inventory	= $ 187,500 - (.9 x $75,000)
	= $ 187,500 - 67,500
	= $ 120,000

Total asset turnover	= sales/total assets
4	= sales/$ 600,000
sales	= 4 x $ 600,000
	= $ 2,400,000

Gross profit margin	= .40(sales)
	= .40($ 2,400,000)
	= $ 960,000

Cost of goods sold	= sales - gross profit
	= $ 2,400,000 - 960,000
	= $ 1,440,000

Average collection period	= avg. accounts rec./avg. days sales
9 days	= avg. accounts rec./ ($ 2,400,000/360 days)
avg. accounts receivable	= 9 days x $ 6,666.67 sales per day
avg. accounts receivable	= $ 60,000

Cash	= total current assets - accounts rec. - inventory
	= $ 187,500 - 60,000 - 120,000
	= $ 7,500

Problem 2:
Component percentage:
1. Cash = $65,000 / $2,250,000 = 2.88%
2. Cost of goods sold = $1,837,500 / 5,250,000 = 35%
3. Rent expense = $400,000 / $5,250,000 = 7.62%
4. Land = $310,000 / 2,250,000 = 13.78%
5. Shareholders' equity = $1,375,000 / $2,250,000 = 61.11%

Problem 3:
1. Working capital:
   Current assets - current liabilities = $650,000 - $220,000 =$430,000

2. Inventory turnover = Cost of goods sold / Average inventory
   5.74 = $1,837,500 / $320,000

3. Total asset turnover = Sales / Total assets
   2.33 = $5250,000 / $2,250,000

4. Profit margin on sales = Net income / Sales
   9.52% = $500,000 / $5,250,000

5. Debt-to-equity = Total liabilities / Shareholders' equity
   63.6% = $875,000 / $1,375,000

6. Basic EPS = Net income available to shareholders / avg. shares outstanding
   $50 = $500,000 / 10,000 shares

7. Pretax return on assets = Operating income before taxes / avg. total assets
   40.37% = $908,333 / $2,250,000

8. Return on shareholders' equity = Net income / Total shareholders' equity
   36.36% = $500,000 / $1,375,000

Problem 4:

a. Pretax operating return on total assets = pretax operating income/ avg. total assets
   ABC Ltd.
   = ($ 8,000,000 - 5,200,000)/ $ 45,000,000
   = $ 2,800,000/$ 45,000,000
   = 6.2%

   XYZ Ltd.
   = ($ 7,500,000 - 4,700,000)/$ 40,000,000
   = $ 2,800,000/$ 40,000,000
   = 7%

Chapter 15

b. Pretax operating return on total assets

> = operating income percentage on sales x total asset turnover

ABC Ltd.

> = ($ 2,800,000/$ 8,000,000) x ($ 8,000,000/$ 45,000,000)
>
> = .35 x .178
>
> = 6.2%

XYZ Ltd.

> = ($ 2,800,000/$ 7,500,000) x ($ 7,500,000/$ 40,000,000)
>
> = .373 x .1875
>
> = 7%

c. The results of a. and b. show that XYZ Ltd. has done better than ABC Ltd.. XYZ Ltd. has a higher pretax return on total assets as a result of both a higher operating income percentage on sales (.373 versus .35) and a higher total asset turnover (.1875 versus .178).

Chapter 16

Financial Statements: Conceptual Framework and Income Measurement

This chapter returns to the conceptual framework which underlies the practice of accounting. In a dynamic accounting and reporting environment, the conceptual framework is a cornerstone for accountants in the exercise of professional judgment. Developing an understanding of this framework equips us to deal with a future which will likely look very different from the status quo. This chapter also touches on some of the differences between Canadian accounting practices and those of other countries. Given the expanding global nature of business it is becoming increasingly important to understand how information is reported elsewhere. Finally, in an effort to highlight the implications of historical cost income measurement, and the advantages and disadvantages of alternate approaches, the chapter reviews four different ways of measuring income.

1. Describe the conceptual framework of accounting.
2. Identify qualities that make information valuable.
3. Present examples of accounting standards in other countries that differ from those in Canada.
4. Explain how identical companies can report different net incomes because of their choice of accounting methods.
5. Describe the major differences between financial capital and physical capital.
6. Explain and illustrate four different ways of measuring income: (a) historical cost/nominal dollars, (b) current cost/ nominal dollars, (c) historical cost/constant dollars,(d)current cost/constant dollars.

Chapter 16

REVIEW OF KEY CONCEPTS

A.   The purpose of the conceptual framework is to provide guidance to the users and preparers of accounting statements in terms of the general perspective or philosophy underlying specific accounting practices. It also provides a basis for future debates on the choice between alternate accounting policies.

1.   Exhibit 16-1 on page 745 of the text summarizes the conceptual framework of accounting. It is important to understand that although financial statements are often thought of as being general purpose in nature, the conceptual framework gives prominence to **investors** and **creditors**. The conceptual framework suggests that, above all, information should be **useful** to investors and creditors in their **decision making**.

      Investors and creditors require information that will aid them in making **resource allocation decisions**, in **predicting** a company's future **cash flows**, and in evaluating management in terms of fulfilling its **stewardship** role.

2.   One important **constraint** set out in the conceptual framework is that the **benefits** of providing information to financial statement users should **exceed the costs** of doing so. This suggests that in both disclosure and standard setting decisions it is necessary to evaluate the relevant costs and benefits. Costs include, but are not limited to, the costs of information preparation, and the cost to the firm from a competitive perspective of disclosing information which may be proprietary in nature. Benefits include improved resource allocation decisions on the part of the users of the statements. The assessment of costs and benefits is a judgemental process.

3.   **Materiality** is a second important constraint in the application of GAAP and the conceptual framework. This concept suggests that it is only necessary to account for and report information according to the terms of GAAP, if the information is significant or material in nature. Information that is immaterial in nature can be accounted for conveniently, which may not be in accordance with GAAP. For example, a company may expense a small capital asset acquisition, such as a calculator, rather than capitalizing and depreciating it over some future period. Whether the calculator is expensed or capitalized will not

affect a financial statement user's decision, and so the item is said to be immaterial and GAAP need not be applied.

4.   The conceptual framework suggests certain information attributes or **qualitative characteristics** that enhance the usefulness of accounting information to investors and creditors.

     a.   **Understandability** - information must be understandable by users with a reasonable knowledge of the nature of business and of accounting

     b.   **Relevance** - information that has predictive and feedback value and that is made available on a timely basis

     c.   **Reliability** - this involves the presentation of information which captures the economic substance of the transaction, is verifiable in nature (i.e. the information is objectively derived), and is neutral or free from bias. Information is neutral or free from bias if it is not consistently or systematically biased in one direction (e.g., income overstatement). Information that is consistently biased in one direction is likely to mislead financial statement users. In situations involving uncertainty, the conceptual framework suggests it is appropriate to be conservative in the valuation of net assets and in the estimation of net income.

     d.   **Comparability** - information that is prepared on a comparable basis both within a firm from period to period, and between firms, enhances the investors' and creditors' ability to use the statements for decision making purposes.

     e.   The conceptual framework recognizes that **trade-offs** are often necessary between the qualitative characteristics, especially between the relevance and reliability attributes. Professional judgement is required in developing the appropriate balance between the characteristics in a given reporting situation.

Before continuing, review Exhibit 16-3 on page 751 of the text.

Chapter 16

B.   The majority of accounting practices employed by countries throughout the
       world have many similarities, such as the use of accrual accounting, the use of
       the balance sheet and income statement, and the use of double-entry
       bookkeeping. Differences in government, culture, economic systems, and
       traditions contribute to different accounting practices in many countries.

       1.   The United Kingdom allows the use of either historical-cost, or current-
              cost accounting. LIFO is not employed for either financial statement or
              tax purposes, and purchased goodwill is charged against income
              immediately.

       2.   France is the leader in uniform accounting practices. Accounting
              records are considered legal control devices instead of as a source of
              information. LIFO is not allowed and companies are required to
              publish an environmental balance sheet reporting on employee benefits
              and conditions as well as on environmental matters. Companies are also
              required to publish comprehensive financial forecasts.

       3.   There is no difference in reporting between financial statements for
              outside use and statements for tax purposes in Germany. FIFO and
              LIFO are allowed but must correspond to the flow of goods.
              Depreciation schedules are dictated by the government and cash flow
              statements are not required.

       4.   Accounting in Japan is dominated by the central government and
              extensive cross-ownership exists between firms. Historical-cost
              accounting is prevalent in Japan and all practices are very conservative
              in nature.

       5.   It is probably not feasible to expect standardization in accounting
              practices among industrialized nations due to the many differences in
              the form of government and in the customs that currently exist.

C.   Income is determined on the basis of accrual accounting. Revenue is generally
       recognized when it is earned (i.e. goods are delivered or services are
       performed) and collectibility is reasonably certain. Expenses are matched to
       revenues. In order to present the economic substance of a transaction, GAAP
       provides accounting choices or accounting alternatives. The choice of
       alternative affects the amount and timing of revenue and expense recognition,
       and can have a significant effect on net income in any given accounting period.

1.   Revenue is generally recognized when it is earned and realized or realizable (i.e. collectible). However, there are additional circumstances when recognition is warranted without both elements being present.

     a.   Percentage-of-completion accounting allows recognition of revenue prior to all of the revenue being earned. This method is used, for example, when a company is involved in long-term construction projects which might span two or three years from commencement to completion. Under these circumstances, the percentage-of-completion method is considered a better measure of economic reality and performance than a revenue recognition method which only recognizes revenue upon completion of the project. The assessment of collectibility of revenue is especially important in the application of this method.

     b.   Recognition of revenue on instalment sales is allowable if collection is deemed to be relatively certain.

2.   Managers choose accounting alternatives on the basis of their financial reporting objectives. For example, managers may seek to maximize reported income (perhaps because of bonus arrangements), to minimize reported income (perhaps as a tax deferral tactic or in order to qualify for government assistance), or to smooth reported income (perhaps because the manager believes this will affect the market's risk assessment of the firm).

See Exhibit 16-4 on page 760 of the text for an illustration of the effect of alternate accounting policies on reported income.

D.   Companies are required to include a summary of their significant accounting policies as a part of the notes to the financial statements.

Chapter 16

Examine Exhibit 16-5 on page 762 of the text for excerpts from the accounting policies disclosure made by MacMillan Bloedel in their financial statements.

E.   In periods of rising prices a divergence develops between assets carried at historical cost and the current replacement value of those assets. In order to properly determine income for the period, invested capital must first be defined. The two theories commonly discussed are **financial capital maintenance** and **physical capital maintenance.**

1.   **Financial capital maintenance** maintains that income at the end of the period is that amount that could be paid to the shareholders and still maintain the original level of capital in the business.

2.   **Physical capital maintenance** maintains that income at the end of the period is that amount that could be paid to shareholders and still maintain the level of capital at current replacement cost.

See the example on page 765 of the text

F.   Accounting theorists and practitioners often argue about the best method of measuring income. Four methods are discussed in the text. They include: historical cost/nominal dollar, current cost/nominal dollar, historical cost/constant dollar, and current cost/constant dollar.

1.   **Nominal dollar** measurement represents the purchasing power of the dollar as it was reflected in the original transaction. In other words, the dollar is not restated for fluctuations that have occurred since the original transaction.

2.   **Constant dollar** measurements are achieved by restating nominal dollar values through the use of an index to approximate current purchasing power.

3. **Historical cost/nominal dollar** measures the value of assets according to traditional historical cost principles. Recognized income is the difference between the historical cost and the current revenue realized regardless of the current replacement cost of the asset transferred.

4. **Current cost/nominal dollar** measures income as the difference between realized revenue and the current replacement cost of the asset transferred. Proponents feel distributable income is only available after sufficient assets have been retained to provide for replacement of the transferred assets at current replacement cost. The focus is on income from continuing operations.

5. **Historical cost/constant dollar** applies general index numbers to the historical cost of an asset for income determination purposes. The purpose of the method is to provide a common basis for revenues and expenses in order to obtain a true measure of the resulting income.

6. **Current cost/constant dollar** use costs that have been restated to current replacement costs and then indexed using the general price index applied in the historical cost/constant dollar method. The purpose is to isolate constant dollar gains and losses.

Before going on to the questions and exercises, go back and review Exhibit 16-6 on page 767 of the text to reinforce your understanding of the four major methods of measuring income.

PRACTICE TEST QUESTIONS AND SOLUTIONS

I **True or False -** For each of the following statements, enter a T or an F in the space provided to indicate whether the statement is true or false.

_____ 1. Predictive value is a supporting characteristic of reliability.

_____ 2. The conceptual framework provides solutions to reporting problems faced by practising accountants.

_____ 3. Historical cost/constant dollar is the most popular approach to income measurement in Canada.

_____ 4. Advocates of physical capital maintenance feel that income should result from the difference between realized revenue and the current replacement cost of the assets transferred.

_____ 5. Nominal dollars are dollars that are not restated for fluctuations in the general purchasing power of the monetary unit.

_____ 6. Generally, indexes which are used in constant dollar accounting are general indexes.

_____ 7. The current-cost method stresses a separation between income from continuing operations and holding gains or losses.

_____ 8. The overriding criteria suggested in the conceptual framework for choosing reporting alternatives are cost/benefit and materiality.

_____ 9. Reliability is supported by verifiability, neutrality, and timeliness.

_____ 10. Because of the similarities in accounting systems, such as double-entry accounting and the use of a balance sheet and income statement, it is probable that early in the next century there will be a universal worldwide standardized set of accounting standards.

_____ 11. Income is an entity's increase in wealth during a period, that is, the amount that could be paid out to shareholders and still leave the company as well off as it was at the beginning of the period.

_____ 12. The concept of financial capital is supported by adherence to the historical cost principle.

_____ 13. Under the historical cost/constant dollar approach, no income appears until the asset is sold, and the intervening price fluctuations are ignored.

_____ 14. Financial statements are based on the concept of financial capital maintenance.

_____ 15. All of the qualitative criteria are equally important in all reporting situations.

II **Multiple Choice** - For the following multiple choice questions, select the best answer and enter the identifying letter in the space provided.

_____ 1. The method that applies a general price index number to historical costs is the:

    a. Historical cost/nominal dollar method.
    b. Historical cost/constant dollar method.
    c. Current cost/nominal dollar method.
    d. Current cost/constant dollar method.

_____ 2. The most popular approach to income measurement is commonly called the:

    a. Historical-cost method.
    b. Constant dollar method.
    c. Replacement cost method.
    d. Cost indexing method.

_____ 3. Oxley General Stores purchased 200 kerosene lamps for inventory at a unit cost of $15. One year later, 125 lamps were sold for $30 each. At the time of the sale, the per unit replacement cost of the lamp was $17. The general-price-level-index had increased 10%. Calculate the amount of income from continuing operations using the current cost/constant dollar method.

    a. $1,850.00
    b. $1,687.50
    c. $1,625.00
    d. $1,750.00

_____ 4. Refer to the facts in question 3 above, and calculate the amount of income using the historical cost/nominal dollar method.

    a. $1,850.00
    b. $1,875.00
    c. $1,750.00
    d. $1,687.50

_____ 5. Murphy Drugs purchased 300 bed pans for inventory at a cost of $10 each. One year, and much consternation later, Murphy sold 100 of the pans for $14 each. Current replacement costs were $13.25 each. The general-price-level-index had increased 10% during this period. Using the historical cost/constant dollar approach calculate the amount of income from continuing operations.

    a. $400
    b. $ 75
    c. $350
    d. $300

_____ 6. Been Country Crafts purchased 100 goose doorstops at a cost of $15 each. One year later Been was able to unload 75 of the critters for $40 each to a bus load of tourists from the city. Current replacement cost was $20 each. The general-price-level index had risen 5% during the period. Calculate the amount of income from continuing operations using the historical cost/ nominal dollar method.

    a. $1,500.00
    b. $1,818.75
    c. $1,575.50
    d. $1,875.00

_____ 7. Refer to the facts in question six above, and calculate the amount of the realized and unrealized holding gains under the current cost/nominal dollar approach.

    a. $375.00
    b. $500.00
    c. $425.00
    d. $318.75

_____ 8. Refer to the facts in question six above, and calculate the amount of the realized and unrealized holding gains under the current cost/nominal dollar approach.

    a. $375.00
    b. $500.00
    c. $425.00
    d. $318.75

_____ 9. Annapolis Sailboat Inc. was incorporated with $1,500,000 of capital in the form of cash and the entire amount was used to purchase inventory shortly after incorporation. The company had a very good year and sold all of the inventory for $4,000,000 one year later. Current cost of the inventory was $1,650,000 at the time of the sale. The general-price-level had increased 5% during the year. Under financial capital maintenance, income would be measured at:

    a. $2,200,000
    b. $2,500,000
    c. $2,350,000
    d. $1,750,000

_____ 10. Refer to the facts in problem nine above. Utilizing the physical capital maintenance approach income would be measured at:

    a. $2,200,000
    b. $2,500,000
    c. $2,350,000
    d. $1,750,000

Chapter 16

III   Problems

Problem 1:

Puleo Products was incorporated January 1, 19X1 at which point $80,000 in capital
stock was issued in exchange for cash. The cash was used to purchase 4,000 units of
inventory at $20 each. During the year Puleo sold 3,500 of the units for $34 each. At
the end of the year the replacement cost of the inventory was $23 per unit and the
general-price-level-index had increased 10% from the beginning of the period.
Compute the following amounts to be reported for each of the two methods indicated
below. Assume no other transactions and ignore taxes.

		Historical cost Nominal dollar	Current cost Nominal dollar
a.	Ending inventory	_____	_____
b.	Holding gain on units sold	_____	_____
c.	Holding gain on units unsold	_____	_____
d.	Income from continuing operations	_____	_____
e.	Retained earnings	_____	_____
f.	Paid-in-capital	_____	_____
g.	Total assets	_____	_____
h.	Total equity	_____	_____

Problem 2:

Refer to the facts in problem 1 and compute the following amounts to be reported for each of the two methods indicated below.

	Historical cost Constant dollar	Current cost Constant dollar
a. Ending inventory	_____	_____
b. Holding gain on units sold	_____	_____
c. Holding gain on units unsold	_____	_____
d. Income from continuing operations	_____	_____
e. Retained earnings	_____	_____
f. Paid-in-capital	_____	_____
g. Total assets	_____	_____
h. Total equity	_____	_____

Problem 3:

Jennifer is the owner of York River Mfg.. The company started business on January 1, 19X1. Company assets on January 1 included inventory purchased for $125,000, and equipment purchased for $250,000. York River uses no debt in its capital structure and has 1,000 shares of common stock outstanding. The equipment has a useful life of four years and a salvage value of $50,000. All of the inventory was sold during the year for $187,500, and replaced at year-end at a cost of $132,000. The company uses the periodic inventory method. Jennifer needs your help with the following.

Chapter 16

Required:

a. Compute operating income and earnings per share assuming the use of FIFO and straight-line depreciation.

b. Compute operating income and earnings per share assuming the use of LIFO and sum-of-the-years-digits depreciation.

c. Which of the two options would you suggest Jennifer use?

> **For additional practice computing income under the four alternative measures see Lotus Template file P16-39.wk1.**

CHAPTER 16 ANSWERS AND SOLUTIONS

I True and False

1. False — Information that helps users make decisions concerning the past, present, or future is considered relevant.
2. False — The conceptual framework provides a framework from which judgements may be made concerning reporting problems.
3. False — Accounting principles in Canada rely on the concept of historical cost/nominal dollar.
4. True
5. True
6. True
7. True
8. True
9. False — In order to be reliable information must be verifiable, neutral in nature, and have representational faithfulness (i.e. captures economic substance of the transaction).
10. False — As a result of the many different social, cultural, and political customs found throughout the world it is not likely a worldwide standardization of accounting practices will be forthcoming.
11. True
12. True

13. False   Intervening price fluctuations are ignored under the traditional historical cost/nominal dollar approach but not under the historical cost/constant dollar approach.

14. True

15. False   Trade-offs between the qualitative characteristics are required depending on the reporting objectives in any given situation.

II Multiple Choice

1. B.   The historical cost/constant dollar approach attempts to restate the original cost in terms of current purchasing power in order to arrive at an income measure that more closely reflects current dollar values.

2. A.   Historical cost/nominal dollar is the most popular approach in Canada and is a generally accepted accounting principle.

3. C.

Sales (125 x 30)	$	3,750
Cost of goods sold (125 x 17)		2,125
Income from continuing operations	$	1,625

4. B.

Sales (125 x 30)	$	3,750
Cost of goods sold (125 x 15)		1,875
Income from continuing operations	$	1,875

5. D.

Sales (100 x 14)	$	1,400
Cost of goods sold (10 x 110/100 x 100)		1,100
Income from continuing operations	$	300

6. D.

Sales (75 x 40)	$	3,000
Cost of goods sold (75 x 15)		1,125
Income from continuing operations	$	1,875

7. B.

Realized holding gains: (75 x {20-15})	$	375
Unrealized holding gains: (25 x {20-15})		125
Total	$	500

8. C.

Realized holding gains: (75 x {20 - 1.05[15]})	$	318.75
Unrealized holding gains: (25 x {20 - 1.05[15]})		106.25
Total	$	425.00

Chapter 16

9. B.   Remember, income based upon the concept of financial capital maintenance is measured after financial resources, in nominal dollars, are recovered (i.e. historical cost).

Sales	$	4,000,000
Cost of goods sold		1,500,000
Operating income	$	2,500,000

10. C.   Physical capital maintenance relies on valuations based on replacement costs. What is the current replacement cost of the assets transferred?

Sales	$	4,000,000
Cost of goods sold		1,650,000
Operating income	$	2,350,000

III Problems

Problem 1:

1.a.

Ending inventory, historical cost/nominal dollar:

(4,000 - 3,500) x $20 per unit = $10,000 ending inventory

Ending inventory, nominal dollar/current cost:

(4,000 - 3,500) x $23 per unit = $11,500 ending inventory

b.

Holding gains based on historical cost/nominal dollar do not exist.

Holding gains on units sold, current cost/nominal dollar:

(3,500 x {$23-20}) = $10,500 holding gains

c.

Holding gains based on historical cost/nominal dollar do not exist.

Holding gains on ending inventory, current cost/nominal dollar:

(500 x {$23-20}) = $ 1,500 holding gains

d. Income from continuing operations, historical cost/nominal dollar:

Sales	(3,500 x $34)	$119,000
Cost of goods sold	(3,500 x $20)	$ 70,000
Income from continuing operations		$ 49,000

Income from continuing operations, current cost/nominal dollar:

Sales	(3,500 x $34)	$119,000
Cost of goods sold	(3,500 x $23)	$ 80,500
Income from continuing operations		$ 38,500

e. Retained earnings, historical cost/nominal dollar:

Confined to income from operations $49,000

Retained earnings, current cost/nominal dollar:

Confined to income from operations $38,500

f. Paid-in capital is $ 80,000 for both alternatives.

g. Total assets:

	Historical cost/ nominal dollar	Current cost/ nominal dollar
Cash	$ 119,000	$ 119,000
Inventory	10,000	11,500
Total	$ 129,000	$ 130,500

h. Total equity:

	Historical cost/ nominal dollar	Current cost/ nominal dollar
Paid-in capital	$ 80,000	$ 80,000
Retained earnings	49,000	38,500
Holding gains:		
unsold inventory	n/a	1,500
sold inventory	n/a	10,500
Total equity	$ 129,000	$ 130,500

Chapter 16

Problem 2:

1.a.

Ending inventory, historical cost/constant dollar:

(4,000 - 3,500) x (**$20 x 1.10**) per unit = $11,000 ending inventory

Ending inventory, current cost/constant dollar:

(4,000 - 3,500) x **$23** per unit = $11,500 ending inventory

b.

Holding gains based on historical cost/constant dollar do not exist.

Holding gains on units sold, current cost/constant dollar:

(3,500 x {**$23-20[1.10]**}) = $3,500

c.

Holding gains based on historical cost/constant dollar do not exist.

Holding gains on ending inventory, current cost/constant dollar:

(500 x {**$23-20[1.10]**}) = $ 500

d.

Income from continuing operations, historical cost/constant dollar:

Sales	(3,500 x $34)	$119,000
Cost of goods sold	(3,500 x $20[1.10])	$ 77,000
Income from continuing operations		$ 42,000

Income from continuing operations, current cost/constant dollar:

Sales	(3,500 x $34)	$119,000
Cost of goods sold	(3,500 x $23)	$ 80,500
Income from continuing operations		$ 38,500

e. Retained earnings, historical cost/constant dollar:

Confined to income from operations $42,000

Retained earnings, current cost/constant dollar:

Confined to income from operations $38,500

f. Paid-in capital, under historical cost/constant dollar and current cost/constant dollar is the same:

$ 80,000 x 1.10 $88,000

g. Total assets:

	Historical cost/ constant dollar	Current cost/ constant dollar
Cash	$ 119,000	$ 119,000
Inventory	11,000	11,500
Total	$ 130,000	$ 130,500

h. Total equity:

	Historical cost/ constant dollar	Current cost/ constant dollar
Paid-in capital	$ 88,000	$ 88,000
Retained earnings	42,000	38,500
Holding gains:		
unsold inventory	n/a	500
sold inventory	n/a	3,500
Total equity	$ 130,000	$ 130,500

Chapter 16

Problem 3:

a. Operating income assuming the use of FIFO and straight-line depreciation:

Sales	$ 187,500
Cost of goods sold (FIFO)	125,000
Gross profit	$ 62,500
Less: depreciation expense*	50,000
Operating income	$ 12,500
Earnings per share**	$ 12.50

* Straight-line depreciation:

$$\frac{250,000 - 50,000}{4} = \$ 50,000$$

** Earnings per share ($12,500/1,000) = $12.50 per share

b. Operating income assuming use of LIFO and sum-of-the-years-digits depreciation:

Sales	$ 187,500
Cost of goods sold (LIFO)	132,000
Gross profit	$ 55,500
Less: depreciation expense*	80,000
Operating income	$ (24,500)
Earnings per share**	$ (24.50)

* Sum of the years digits depreciation
4/10 x (250,000 - 50,000) = $ 80,000

** Earnings per share ($24,500/1,000) = $24.50 per share **loss**

c. Jennifer, being the owner of a small growing business, probably needs these statements for a bank loan or to attract potential investors. Alternative A would probably be her best approach since it recognizes more income in the current period. Alternative B produces a loss. This example demonstrates the impact of alternate accounting policies on net income.